Praise for

VICTORY POINT

"Arguably the first ever foxhole perspective of the challenges, idiosyncrasies, and pecking-order class struggles between America's favorite modern-day warriors—the special operations growth industry—and America's historically favorite son—the 233-year-old United States Marine."

—Dalton Fury, *New York Times* bestselling author of *Kill Bin Laden*

"A valuable account of a grueling, ultimately successful campaign . . . critical insights into the challenges of fighting in the world's most rugged terrain, far from the media spotlight . . . The Marines in this book are blunt, tough, and valiant in the finest traditions of the Corps."

—Ralph Peters, military analyst and author of
Looking for Trouble: Adventures in a Broken World

VICTORY POINT

OPERATIONS RED WINGS AND
WHALERS—THE MARINE CORPS' BATTLE
FOR FREEDOM IN AFGHANISTAN

ED DARACK

BERKLEY CALIBER, NEW YORK

THE BERKLEY PUBLISHING GROUP
Published by the Penguin Group
Penguin Group (USA) Inc.
375 Hudson Street, New York, New York 10014, USA
Penguin Group (Canada), 90 Eglinton Avenue East, Suite 700, Toronto, Ontario M4P 2Y3, Canada
(a division of Pearson Penguin Canada Inc.)
Penguin Books Ltd., 80 Strand, London WC2R 0RL, England
Penguin Group Ireland, 25 St. Stephen's Green, Dublin 2, Ireland (a division of Penguin Books Ltd.)
Penguin Group (Australia), 250 Camberwell Road, Camberwell, Victoria 3124, Australia
(a division of Pearson Australia Group Pty. Ltd.)
Penguin Books India Pvt. Ltd., 11 Community Centre, Panchsheel Park, New Delhi—110 017, India
Penguin Group (NZ), 67 Apollo Drive, Rosedale, North Shore 0632, New Zealand
(a division of Pearson New Zealand Ltd.)
Penguin Books (South Africa) (Pty.) Ltd., 24 Sturdee Avenue, Rosebank, Johannesburg 2196,
South Africa

Penguin Books Ltd., Registered Offices: 80 Strand, London WC2R 0RL, England

The publisher does not have any control over and does not assume any responsibility for author or third-
party websites or their content.

www.victorypoint.info

PRINTING HISTORY
Berkley Caliber hardcover edition / April 2009
Berkley Caliber trade paperback edition / April 2010

Berkley Caliber trade paperback ISBN: 978-0-425-23259-0

The Library of Congress has catalogued the Berkley Caliber hardcover edition as follows:

Darack, Ed.
  Victory point : operations Red Wings and Whalers : the Marine Corps' battle for freedom in
Afghanistan / Ed Darack.
    p. cm.
  Includes index.
 ISBN 978-0-425-22619-3
  1. Operation Red Wings, 2005. 2. Operation Whalers, 2005. 3. Afghan War, 2001—Commando
operations. 4. Afghan War, 2001—Search and rescue operations. 5. United States. Marine Corps—
Afghanistan. 6. United States. Navy. SEALs. I. Title.

  DS371.4123.O66D37 2009
  958.104'7—dc22   2008047659

PRINTED IN THE UNITED STATES OF AMERICA

10 9 8 7 6 5 4 3 2

To the Marines of 2/3—and the entire Fleet.
Past, present, and future.

CONTENTS

Afghanistan. The name alone evokes visions of adventure and exploration in uncharted mountains, mystery and intrigue in a land traversed by history's crossroads, and above all, war in the breathless heights. A landlocked country, Afghanistan lies in a zone of cultural transition and geographic upheaval. From empty swaths of sun-beaten desert on its southwestern border with Iran, Afghanistan's landscape vaults into ice-hewn mountains in its northeast, encompassing a broad spectrum of climates and topographies between the two extremes.

Culturally, Afghanistan reveals itself to be a patchwork of humanity, a medley of tribes organized loosely within a variety of ethnic groups. Political boundaries are arbitrary to people in most areas of Afghanistan; what delineates regional boundaries here are ridgelines and valleys, with villages stitched together by meandering trails beaten into the sides of airy slopes.

And while most all of Afghanistan—both its people and landscapes—epitomizes the notion of ruggedness, the eastern Kunar province, that rarely visited and little-known pocket of the infamous Hindu Kush, can arguably claim the title as the most austere, the least tamed. The first bullets of the insurgency that would burgeon into the anti-Soviet resistance were fired here in the late seventies. Osama bin Laden was known to operate terrorist training camps in the Kunar and likely ordered the September 11, 2001, attacks against the United States in this province. And into the summer of 2005, the most fearsome of Islamic fundamentalist fighters operated in the Kunar.

At the core of this restive province stands a massif cloaked to the outside world by the very brutal landscape of which it is part, a mountain called Sawtalo Sar. The peak, one of the highest in this cloud-raked landscape, lies in the Pech River Valley region of the Kunar, just west of the frontier town of Asadabad. A number of valleys radiate from and around Sawtalo Sar, valleys such as the Korangal, the Shuryek, the Narang, and the Chowkay. Deeply recessed into the high landscape, the villages, pasturelands, and interconnecting ridges and zigzagging trails of these valleys would become the home of some of the most dedicated, well-trained, and fervent Islamic fighters remaining along the Afghan-Pakistan border—and, for that matter, the world.

As of the summer of 2005, the military forces of the United States had ventured little into the Korangal and Shuryek—and never into the upper reaches of the Chowkay. Regional Afghan political officers and even members of the Afghan military dared not enter these forbidding and terrifying places. Locals of these valleys—vehement and fierce adherents of their own brands of independence—have historically resisted outsiders' gestures, which they perceived as attempts to influence and control their isolated ways of life. However, bold and fervent Islamic groups including al-Qaeda, through payoffs and by manipulating loose familial and tribal ties, infiltrated these secretive aeries. With their observers perched high on the ridges of Sawtalo Sar and surrounding mountains—watching, always watching—the fighters ambushed convoys of humanitarian aid supplies, assassinated local Afghan police officers, and wreaked havoc on the local government, destroying hopes of a wholly unified Afghanistan through their acts of terrorism.

Then the United States Marine Corps arrived. The Marines—the go-anywhere, do-any-mission cadre of modest professionals who have proven time and again to be the most effective war-fighting machine in human history—would once again leave their mark, a mark of triumph, as they had done so many times before. The United States Marine Corps are a fully integrated land-sea-air expeditionary combat force—masters of light infantry maneuver and the "combined arms" assault—and their culture itself has powered individual Marine units as small as a four-man fire team to surmount even the most overwhelming of odds—in conflicts and battlegrounds of all types and climes, through-out their more than two-centuries-old history.

The success of the Marine Corps, in so many places, throughout so many slices of history, can be traced to the qualities at the very core of their ethos: adaptability, tenacity, and above all else, faithfulness—to their country, to their traditions, and to one another. As maniacally as the Japanese held their ground on Iwo Jima, Marines still raised the flag over Mount Suribachi. As overwhelming a force as the Chinese may have projected at Korea's Chosin Reservoir, the Marines still crushed their advance. And as deeply entrenched and fanatically emboldened as the radical Islamic forces surrounding two Marine Corps platoons in the Chowkay Valley may have been in August of 2005, those Marines still decimated their foe.

Victory Point chronicles Operation *Red Wings* and Operation *Whalers,* two Marine Corps missions that, in retrospect, represent not just a series of fierce battles, but a small war: a small war decidedly won by a battalion of Marines—the Second Battalion of the Third Marine Regiment.

Intent on thwarting the operations of a ruthless Islamic fundamentalist operator who had indirect ties to the highest echelons of regional and global extremist networks—including al-Qaeda and the remnants of the Taliban—the battalion struck out with their first large-scale mission soon after arriving in eastern Afghanistan: Operation *Red Wings*.

Employing Navy SEALs and a number of other non–Marine Corps assets, *Red Wings* spiraled into disaster just hours after a Naval Special Operations team inserted high on the slopes of Sawtalo Sar for the opening phase of the operation and fell prey to a horrific ambush. Virtually shut out of both the planning and execution of the rescue mission to save the ill-fated team because of Special Operations Command rules, the Marines stood on the sidelines, frustrated and helpless, as an Army Special Operations Chinook helicopter, loaded with eight Navy and eight Army Special Operations personnel, sped toward Sawtalo Sar, only to be shot down by an expertly placed rocket-propelled grenade—the impact of which killed all on board as the girthy Chinook fell onto the rugged mountain, exploding in a roiling fireball. The leader of the target cell, who called himself Mullah Ismail, but who was born Ahmad Shah, immediately claimed victory over the American "infidels." Islamic extremists throughout the globe hailed Shah, who was now responsible for the greatest one-day loss of United States Special Operations Forces personnel in the history of Special Operations Command—as well as the single greatest loss of American troops in the American war in Afghanistan.

Weeks later, after the dust had settled from *Red Wings* and the Marines had pored over intelligence reports and developed several blueprints for operations, the battalion unleashed Operation *Whalers;* this time, the ground component would consist only of Marines and attached Afghan National Army soldiers. Almost completely forgotten in the global war on terror, and virtually unrecognized by even Marine Corps historians, *Whalers* unfolded as a masterpiece of light infantry operations: indefatigable Marine grunts relentlessly executing a brilliant plan of action—a plan of action that would bring about the overwhelming defeat of Ahmad Shah's small army.

Victory Point details this amazing chapter of Marine Corps history—a history clouded by incomplete and inaccurate media reports and overshadowed by the special operations tragedies. The drama that unfolded in Afghanistan's Sawtalo Sar region in the summer of 2005 includes some of the most dramatic events in the history of warfare: the

U.S. Marine Corps, undeniably the military organization best suited for this merciless environment, ensnared and ultimately destroyed a tireless and deadly enemy who was quickly rising in power and prominence. In telling this story, *Victory Point* also sheds light on the Marine Corps ethos and their centuries-honed approach to fighting, on the incredible difficulties of waging a war in the Hindu Kush, and on the challenges of working in a "joint" environment, where Marines must rely on assets of other branches of the U.S. military. But most of all, this book chronicles Marines doing what Marines do best: winning the fight, and winning it their way.

The events of Operations *Red Wings* and *Whalers* represent some of the most harrowing in the history of modern warfare, exemplifying the very limits of human endurance, struggle, and the spirit of survival and triumph in one of the world's most fearsome environments. Despite the importance of these missions in the Global War on Terror, however, details of most aspects of *Red Wings* and *Whalers* remain shrouded in misreporting and rank nonreporting. With the exception of a few citations (most notably an article in the *Marine Corps Gazette* in December 2006), media reports have not even referenced Operation *Red Wings* as a Marine Corps operation, focusing on the tragic opening phase of the mission. Furthermore, virtually no media reports have even cited the name of the operation correctly. Named in honor of the Detroit *Red Wings* hockey team, I have seen and heard "Operation Redwing," "Operation Red Wing," and even "Operation Red Dawn" printed, televised, and broadcast. But this error is just the first in a long list of details incorrectly reported or omitted outright, a list that leaves the public record with just a few small brushstrokes of accuracy while the larger canvas remains mostly blank.

Operation *Whalers* (named for the Hartford/New England Whalers), which had the same objective as *Red Wings*, succeeded. But the details of the success went unreported—as well as overlooked by military historians. Another canvas left virtually blank.

Why the glaring oversights? While a number of reasons contribute to the void of accurate information, a lack of on-site reporters ranks at the top of this list. With the exception of a Marine Corps combat correspondent (Sergeant Robert Storm, one of the best), no photojournalists accompanied forces on the ground during *Red Wings* or *Whalers*. Instead, tidbits of information were fed to reporters far in the rear, at Bagram Airfield; these reports consisted of brief summaries—with few specific details. Erroneous, hearsay-inspired "accounts"—published by outlets spanning from blogs to major magazine and newspaper publications—bloomed to feed the public's hunger for information, creating a whirlwind of distorted facts and some blatant fiction.

I wrote this book in order to chronicle the amazing events in Afghanistan's Kunar province during the summer of 2005. While I am not, nor have I ever been, in the Marine Corps, I have written *Victory Point* from a Marine perspective. The Marine Corps planned and executed these operations (with the exception of those aspects tasked to the Naval Special Operations Forces personnel for *Red Wings*), and the Marines undertook the execution of them. I have gone to great lengths to gather information about and interview personnel of non-USMC units who proved vital in the support of these missions, including Army and U.S. Air Force aviation units. An amazing amount of effort and bravery went into these operations by non–Marine Corps units, particularly during the search and recovery phase of *Red Wings* as well as the Air Ambulance and close air support provided during Operation *Whalers*.

I would also like to make note on the spelling of Afghan placenames. The same location, cited on five different maps, will often be spelled five different ways. For example, what I cite as the Korangal

Valley, other writers and cartographers have referenced as the "Korengal Valley," "Karangal Valley," "Kiringal Valley," and even the "Giringal Valley." I chose to use spellings listed on recently published maps, published in English, but developed in Afghanistan. I also use both "standard" and metric measurements—each where most appropriate.

I should also give a quick overview of the genesis of my involvement and interest in this project. As a freelance writer/photographer, I sought to chronicle the training at a little-known Marine Corps base in the late winter of 2005, the Mountain Warfare Training Center, near Bridgeport, California. While at the MWTC, I spent time with the Marines of the Second Battalion of the Third Marine Regiment, who were training for deployment in, and would soon be departing for, Afghanistan. One evening after a training exercise at the base, I asked the battalion's executive officer, Major Rob Scott, and the operations officer, Major Tom Wood, if I could join the battalion in Afghanistan as an embedded writer/photographer. After consulting with the battalion commander, Lieutenant Colonel Andy MacMannis, Majors Scott and Wood informed me that I was welcome to come for as long as I wished.

And so, in late September of 2005, I journeyed to Kabul, Afghanistan, and after credentialing as a media embed, was sent to Camp Blessing, in the village of Nangalam in the country's eastern Kunar province. Over the course of my one-month embed (exceeding my officially allotted time of just ten days by nearly three weeks), I accompanied the Marines on a number of combat operations—inserting by helicopter, convoy, and by foot throughout the area, spending days in the field with Marines moving through all types of mountainous terrain, and listening to the incredibly candid stories of combat in the heights, often at night as we stood watch for Islamic fighters intent on attacking our positions.

The Marines with whom I spent time, from privates to the battalion commanders, provided me with insight not only into Operations *Red Wings* and *Whalers,* but into the incredible Marine Corps ethos. I am one of the very few lucky civilians to have learned about U.S. Marines not through books, movies, magazines, or newspaper articles, but through the only real way to learn about them—as well as about the incredible mountainous landscape in which they accomplished so much: in the field, during combat operations. This education was the toughest in my life, but I would have it no other way. My involvement with the Second Battalion of the Third Marine Regiment has allowed me to re-create these operations with the accuracy that the general public deserves, as well as to create a work the Marines of the battalion can point to as a record of their historic time in Afghanistan.

Ed Darack
Pickel Meadow, California

1

WELCOME TO AFGHANISTAN

Y'all mothafuckas better git ya gear on an' quit *bowl*-shittin'," Staff Sergeant Lee Crisp roared at his Marines as the rising sun began its daily pummeling of the rocky Afghan mountainscape. "Put y'all's gear on. Put it on! Put it on *now*!" the six-foot, two-inch, 225-pound platoon sergeant commanded, neck veins distending and sweat pouring from his forehead.

The Marines, members of Third Platoon, Fox Company (Fox-3) of the Second Battalion of the Third Marine Regiment (2/3) gazed solemnly at Crisp; having slept a total of just six hours in the last three days, they held out for every second of shut-eye they could grasp. Six hours of rest . . . *six hours* . . . three days into a foot mobile operation of unknown duration, bound for an undisclosed destination, moving through what they knew to be a cauldron of hardened Islamic extremist fighters. *Surrounding them?* Maybe. *How many?* Unknown. The Marines knew how well the enemy was able to melt into the truculent world through which Fox-3 was now venturing, that they had mastered the region's steep and treacherous terrain, that the extremists had the advantage of familiarity here. Most importantly, they knew of the bloodshed this very enemy had wreaked against a U.S. Navy special operations team and those attempting to rescue them only weeks before—just a few miles from Fox-3's current position. And no matter how well the Marines understood their situation, Crisp knew it even better, and seeing his grunts sprawled out on the bare earth, naked to him without their flak jackets and Kevlar helmets, enraged the staff sergeant to no end.

"Mothafuckas—you don't neva' know when shit's gonna happen!" Not even the most brazen of the Marines could feign sleep with Crisp looming over their sapped bodies. Inspired by the staff sergeant's abrasive motivational eloquence, the grunts pressed their hands into the gritty earth and reemerged into the brutality of the northeastern Afghan summer. "Put y'all's mothafuckin' gear on—NOW!"

Crisp's watch had just ticked past 9:20 A.M. local, on a date none of the Marines would ever forget: 14 August 2005. Before the sweep hand of the imposing staff sergeant's timepiece could tick through another full minute, Fox-3 would know well the enemy's vehemence, mastery of the terrain, and brazen war-fighting tactics . . .

By the time the grunts of Fox-3 took their rest under the penetrating glare of the staff sergeant that August morning, 2/3's Marines had lived, worked, and fought in the mountainous eastern Afghan provinces of Laghman, Nangarhar, and Kunar for over two full months. Before their arrival in-country, they'd trained hard for the rigors of mountain warfare. They'd diligently studied the cultures and customs of the people who eked out their livelihoods on the slopes and shoulders of these hidden peaks. And once in-country, 2/3's grunts had built and bulked their "Afghan mountain legs" through all types of projects and missions, often keeping on task for eighteen hours per day—for endless days on end. Their toils habituated them to the terrain, the climate, the ways of the locals, and the tactics of the enemy. They were now tougher, harder, and sharper than they ever could be back in the rear, regardless of training. But nothing could have prepared them for the ordeals they now faced. This was as real as it could get; for many, this was beyond real—something they never could have imagined they'd face. "Af-*fuckin'*-ghanistan," a lance corporal gasped as he rubbed his numb, bloody feet and pressed his body into a fading sliver of shade. "This is as far away from home as any of us can get."

"And we're about to go deeper into this shit," another in his fire team added.

Their training, acclimatization, and acquired knowledge aside, the grunts of Fox-3 that August morning could only describe the merciless swath of land on which they rested as a chunk of a faraway world, smashed onto the opposite side of the planet from their home at idyllic Kaneohe Bay, occupied by people of another time. Ironically, as the Marines pondered not what they knew of this part of Afghanistan, but how little they actually understood it, they not only stood at the bow of history's unfolding, they were forging that history.

Few locations puzzle and frustrate historians, geographers, war fighters—anyone with an interest in this crossroads of humanity—more than the mysterious tract of the planet we know as Afghanistan. The country's tortuous border circumscribes a complex aggregation of land best described as raw, austere, even forbidding and deadly. A part of either Central or South Asia (depending which geographer you consult), Afghanistan abuts land—and only land—on every point of the compass, with Iran defining its western border, Pakistan its southern and eastern boundaries, and the countries of Turkmenistan, Uzbekistan, Tajikistan, and even China hemming the landlocked country on its northern reaches.

As with most regions of the globe defined by extremes, understanding Afghanistan's multifaceted cultures and complex history requires learning about the land beneath the feet of those who created its history. A river striking through an otherwise parched countryside creates an agricultural corridor in which villages develop; a pass bisecting a redoubt of

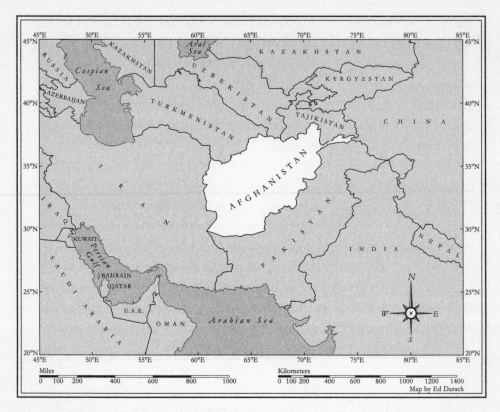

Afghanistan political map

high mountains defines a trade route; and of course, steep, frigid peaks block passage into and out of a province or even an entire neighboring country. While jagged mountains dominate Afghanistan's landscape, broad stretches of low, windswept desert define its extreme southern reaches, and the fertile plains of the Amu Darya River (formerly known as the Oxus River), Afghanistan's lowest point at 846 feet above sea level, mark the country's northern border with Turkmenistan and Uzbekistan.

But who can even mention or just think of *Afghanistan* without picturing soaring, seemingly unscalable mountains? More pointedly, who can muse about this region without envisioning that fabled arc of hidden peaks that rules the country's northeast, a place that has piqued the imaginations of countless would-be explorers and adventurers for centuries—the Hindu Kush? The northwestern extension of what geographers know as the Greater Himalayan Complex, the mountains of the Hindu Kush pierce the crystalline skies above Afghanistan's northeastern provinces and adjacent borderlands of Pakistan's Federally Administered Tribal Areas and Northwest Frontier Province, casting long, dark shadows onto the valleys over which they loom. Thrust miles above sea level through the same geologic processes as their world-famous cousins to the southeast, the Himalaya proper (capped by the 29,035-foot-high Mount Everest), the highest point of the Hindu Kush, the infamous Tirich Mir, lies just ten miles inside Pakistan's border from Afghanistan. Second in height to the 25,289-foot-high Tirich Mir, the mountain known as Noshaq lies squarely on the Afghanistan–Pakistan border, at 24,580-feet Afghanistan's highest point and the fifty-second loftiest spot of land on the planet. Although Noshaq stands as one of the world's highest peaks, the snow- and ice-plastered mountain, like most of the Hindu Kush, remains cloaked in obscurity. Climbing expeditions rarely tread Noshaq's cold slopes because of logistical difficulties in this extremely remote part of the world, not to mention the problems posed by the "leftovers" of years of warfare, most notably, Soviet land mines that pepper the landscape on the approach routes to the peak.

One hundred and twenty miles to the southwest of Noshaq, and over three vertical miles closer to sea level, the Marines of Fox-3 gazed at the pocket of the Hindu Kush that was theirs on the morning of 14 August 2005. Earthquakes shock the Hindu Kush, one of the planet's youngest and most geologically active ranges, more frequently than virtually any other belt of mountains on the planet, as the chunk of earth known as the Indo-Australian tectonic plate inexorably presses northward into the Eurasian plate, a process that gave birth to the crescent-shaped Himalayan chain and its western anchor, the Hindu Kush, and continues to push these mountains ever higher. Far into their objective, the grunts experienced the results of this geologic collision firsthand: jagged ridgelines, painfully steep gullies, immense boulders dotting the landscape, treacherously loose rock under every footstep, mountain faces scarred by innumerable slides and avalanches, and virtually no flat ground or even gentle slopes anywhere. A classic example of a young and fast-growing mountain range, the Hindu Kush resembles the temperament of a feral animal: brusque and savage.

Not to be outdone in severity by the rough-hewn land below, the sky overarching the Hindu Kush presents similarly ferocious elements. Afghanistan lies under a global subtropical belt of predominant high pressure, engendering clear, dry air, and hence arid land below. Fox-3 rested that morning at a latitude just south of that of Tehran, Iran, and just north of that of Baghdad, Iraq, on a roughly equal latitude to that of the Marine Corps base in California's Mojave Desert near the town of Twentynine Palms. Other deserts underlying this wide climatological band ringing the earth include the Sahara, Saudi Arabia's Rub 'al-Khali (the Empty Quarter), the Thar, and the Sonoran of North America, which lies to the east of the Mojave. The Hindu Kush's combination of high mountains and dry air has made for one of the least hospitable places in the world, with bitter-cold winters that see temperatures plunging below minus-fifteen degrees Fahrenheit, and summers where heat rockets to over one hundred and twenty, as Fox-3 would be experiencing just a few hours after their rest. The area's steep-walled valleys, like the Chowkay, with their large tracts of exposed rock, make life downright hellish for those venturing into these enclaves in the summer, as this rock re-radiates the sun's intense energy, turning these valleys into immense convection ovens. Between the extremes of the Hindu Kush's winter and summer months lie ephemeral spans of transition: spring lasts just a few weeks, witnessing crushing torrents of snowmelt during this annual stretch of rapid warming, and autumn brings precipitous drops in both daily highs and nighttime lows, as well as the arrival of snowfall. Yet another factor adding to the severity of 2/3's mountainous area of operation hails from the northern Indian Ocean, a thousand miles distant: moisture forced landward from the southwest summer monsoon. While the Hindu Kush is located on the far northwestern periphery of the monsoon's realm of influence, roving thunderheads frequently unleash torrents of pound-

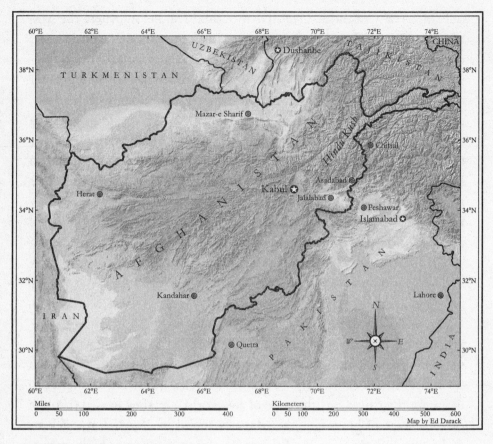

Shaded relief map of Afghanistan

ing rain onto its mountains and valleys during the summer, the range's high peaks often hiding the storms' approach. The ensuing cloudbursts loose roiling flash floods that snake down steeply incised gullies and rock-strewn streambeds, ultimately gushing into broad rivers. On their downward trajectories, flash floods in the Hindu Kush violently rout the coarse earth beneath them, plucking, and then driving toward low-ground, chunks of the landscape ranging in size from talcumlike silt to house-size boulders.

Extremes of land and sky aside, vegetation has managed not only to cling to the harsh slopes of the Hindu Kush, but to actually thrive—but only at certain altitudes. Over five thousand feet below where the Marines had begun their journey just hours before, nobody could mistake the environment as classic desert. But they'd now penetrated to an elevation of nearly eight thousand feet, a zone of thinner air and greener surroundings. Because precipitation typically increases with altitude, the upper Chowkay and other ridges and valleys of the Marines' area of operation bear witness to a broad spectrum of plant life, from swaths of grasses and ferns to low thorny shrubs, juniper trees, lush Himalayan deodar cedar, and soaring pines—vegetation both the Marines and their adversaries could, and did, use for cover, and that has been extensively harvested, through legitimate logging operations, but also for illegal transport into neighboring Pakistan.

In addition to woodcutting, the villagers who live in the Chowkay and surrounding valleys and mountainsides grow and harvest a variety of crops, including corn, wheat, rice, okra, spinach, onions, potatoes, and even opium, a crop traditionally used in the Hindu Kush as a cure-all, but also for profitable export. The locals also raise chickens and run goats and occasionally sheep throughout their mountainous home. On their trek up the Chowkay, the grunts marveled at the locals' ability to maintain their lives on "the edge of the world." As they passed through tiny enclaves of humanity, the Marines stared in disbelief at chickens and goats mulling around on the roofs of homes—homes built of rock straight out of mountain faces. From more than a hundred yards distant, a quick glance at these houses often deceives an onlooker into "seeing" them as just more large boulders clinging precipitously to the side of a harsh slope.

To raise their crops, the locals have excavated deeply cut terraces, the edges of which serve as on-ramps, off-ramps, and in some places, extensions to regional trail systems, the sole logistical network in the upper reaches of the area's valleys and ridgelines. With only one motorized vehicle per fifty people in the Kunar province (with most of these concentrated in the provincial capital of Asadabad), and with the terrain too steep in most places even for horses to negotiate, people simply walk, sometimes using donkeys for excess cargo.

During their Afghan tour, the Marines of 2/3 pushed high into the remote nooks of this otherworldly landscape, encountering people who had never before seen an outsider. Westerners often have trouble understanding the people of Afghanistan upon first researching this part of the globe, and the Marines proved no exception. But unlike most who study Afghanistan, the Marines would travel there, live there, melt in with the people there, and most importantly, help shape the future of Afghanistan.

So much of what we know of the place called Afghanistan—the region, the people, the history, the conflicts—comes wrapped in ambiguity, even confusion. To this day, many who live within the nation's borders not only refuse to acknowledge Afghanistan as a country, they don't even recognize the *concepts* of nation-states, discreet international borders, and national sovereignty.

Archaeologists have unearthed evidence suggesting that Afghanistan's human history stretches more than ten thousand years into the past. The suspected earliest denizens of the land that would become Afghanistan, the Ashvakas, lived in a region today known as the Afghan provinces of Nuristan and Kunar and adjacent lands of Pakistan. A Sanskrit word meaning "people of the horse," historians surmise that *Ashvaka* morphed into *Afghan*. Appending the suffix *stan,* which means "region of," yields *Afghanistan*: *realm of the people of the horse*.

But those early inhabitants lived just outside the intersection of routes of migration and conquest between central, southern, and western Asia. A number of different empires swallowed the land that would become Afghanistan over the years, but none of these conquerors ever firmly established any type of rule over the people in that part of the Hindu Kush that today is the Kunar province, where 2/3's Marines would conduct the majority of their combat operations during their tour.

In 330 BC, Alexander III of Macedonia, aka Alexander the Great, led his army into what would become Afghanistan during his infamous march toward the fertile Indo-Gangetic plains of India. While the military leader established outposts and conquered cities around the greater Hindu Kush (*Hindu Kush* roughly translates as "pass of India"), the fiercely

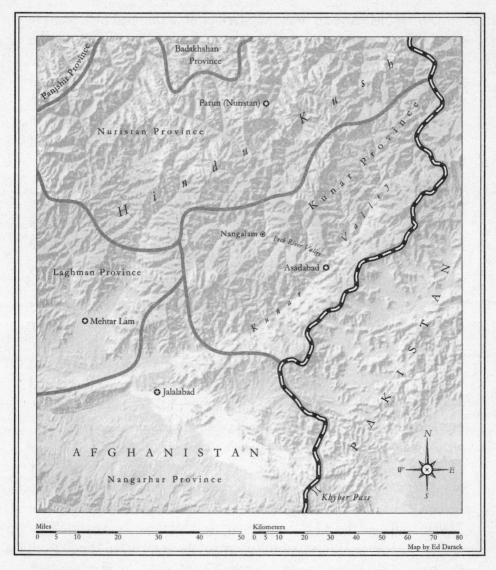

Shaded relief map of Afghanistan's eastern provinces

independent people of these mountainous hinterlands savaged his men—as did the Hindu Kush itself, with its cold temperatures and crushing winter snowfall. Alexander split his army in two upon returning to Kabul, sending one branch toward the Indus via the Kabul River, and personally leading the others up the Kunar Valley—passing the opening of the Chowkay Valley—and then crossing into what would become Pakistan at the Nawa Pass in 326 BC (many sources incorrectly state that Alexander passed through the Khyber Pass, forty miles to the south).

Invasions continued throughout the centuries following Alexander's foray, infusing religious and cultural ideologies from throughout Eurasia into the region, including Buddhism, as evidenced to this day by the numerous Buddhist artifacts and large statues that archaeologists continue to unearth. Despite such outside influences, however, the people of the hidden valleys in the region of the Chowkay, including the nearby Korangal, Shuryek, Narang, and the Pech River Valleys—all of which lay in the shadows of the enormous massif known as Sawtalo Sar— remained virtually untouched.

In roughly 650 AD, Arabs arrived, bringing with them a wholly new religious ideology: Islam. Fervent Muslim adherents spread their new faith throughout the region, often through forced conversion. But then an even more heavy-handed force descended upon this part of the world, Genghis Khan and his Mongol hordes, who decimated cities, wiped out entire regional populations, and left much of what would become Afghanistan devoid of humanity. And still, the hidden communities of the Hindu Kush continued as they had for thousands of years.

This isolation would, however, come to an end with the arrival of people from a place called Parsua, a mountainous region of Persia. This group migrated east, flooding into the valleys and onto the low ridges of the Hindu Kush. They were known as the Pashtun, a name that loosely translates as "people of the hills," derived from the place-name Parsua, and fierce independence and tight familial bonds defined their culture. During this influx, Islam again surged as a religion, specifically, the Sunni branch of Islam, as the Pashtuns adopted this ideology and helped to further its reach. Although they were traditionally divided along tribal and subtribal lines, both their language, Pashto, and their religion united the Pashtuns as a broad and far-reaching group. The Pashtuns, deft at military conquest and the annexation of others' land, soon dominated the region culturally and religiously.

As the Pashtuns pushed ever higher into the mountains of the Hindu Kush in the vicinity including the Chowkay, Korangal, Pech, and Shuryek valleys, the local inhabitants, who wished to have nothing to do with the outside world (the "outside world" being defined by the ridgelines surrounding their tiny villages), vehemently resisted their advances. The Pashtuns, however, overpowered the locals' defiance, forcing them to relocate to higher ground. These locals, who spoke dialects of a language related to Sanskrit called Pashai, also resisted the Pashtuns' attempts to quash their religious belief systems and adopt Islam. The Pashtuns felt the people of these valleys to be beneath them, referring to them as Kafirs (infidels); they termed their part of the Hindu Kush, modern-day Nuristan and adjacent lands of the Kunar province, Kafiristan, "place of the infidels." As the Pashtuns consolidated their power, however, they would continue to place ever-greater pressure on the Kafirs to accede to the ways of Sunni Islam.

Pashtun dominance took a quantum leap in 1747, when a man named Ahmad Shah Durrani, arguably the most renowned and celebrated in this people's history (many Afghans would later adopt the name Ahmad Shah as a sign of solidarity in spirit with the leader), paved the way for Afghanistan to become a nation-state by moving the center of authority of the Pashtuns from the Kandahar region to Kabul, enabling Pashtun monopolization of the Trans–Hindu Kush caravan trade route between India and Central Asia. From Kabul, where the region's center of governance remains to this day, Ahmad Shah began expanding his authority in all directions, slowly coalescing power. And yet the Pashai-speaking mountain people of Kafiristan still refused to accept not only the idea of centralized authority, but Islam as well. This struggle would continue for years, resulting in an unlikely outcome with far-reaching historical ramifications, especially for the Marines of 2/3.

During the 1800s through to the early 1900s, Afghanistan found itself once again squeezed between burgeoning foreign powers: England to its east in India, czarist Russia to its north in Turkistan, and the Persians to its west. Much has been made of the "Great Game," a term taken by English historians from a line in a British intelligence officer's letter to a colleague referring to British influence of Afghanistan, and it is true that the vast majority of aggressive "chess moves" of this period were British in origin. During the years of the Great Game, the Russians carried out some espionage missions and studied possible invasion routes into India (they ruled out passage through Afghanistan as they felt they could not maneuver artillery through the high, narrow passes of the Hindu Kush), but it was the British, initially for commercial reasons and then for geopolitical goals, who ventured repeatedly into Afghanistan. Three conflicts ensued between England and Afghanistan, culminating in the Treaty of Rawalpindi on August 19, 1919, granting independence to the hard-fighting and tenacious Afghans. While it was not until the early twentieth century that the British granted independence to the Afghans, they had all but given up on the region by the 1860s, as Russia's construction of a Central Asian railroad bypassing Afghanistan dashed England's hopes for monopolization of trade in the region, drastically reducing the strategic commercial importance of Afghanistan to Britain's East India Company.

Although the Brits ultimately retreated from Afghanistan, they did so only after leaving a number of historically significant marks on the country. One of the most notable, the drawing of the country's modern boundary, saw the English cunningly demarcate Afghanistan's border exclusively on slopes so that the surrounding territories, especially those to the east along the portion of the border known as the Durand Line, would have military units approaching Afghanistan from a superior position, firing down upon the Afghans during potential conflict. Visitors to the Khyber Pass are often stunned to find that the pass itself lies over five highway miles inside Pakistan and stands more than a thousand feet above Torkham, the point at which the main road connecting Pakistan and Afghanistan intersects the Afghan border. Historians also note that Afghanistan's leaf-shape outline was crafted not with the will or welfare of its people in mind, but with the buffering of the surrounding countries from one another as the primary criterion.

Possibly the most important and historically far-reaching consequence of the Great Game era, particularly for the Marines of 2/3, was the British installation of Abdur Rahman Khan as emir, or king, of Afghanistan in 1880. Rahman Khan, the "Iron Emir," took a fierce nationalistic stance, and sought the complete religious unification of the country. A Pashtun, he focused his ardor for Sunni Islamic conversion on the pagan "infidels" of the secretive ridges and valleys of Kafiristan. While the years since their arrival in the Hindu Kush had seen the Pashtuns chipping away at the lands and customs of the Kafir, intermingling blood and customs in many cases, Rahman Khan took a "convert or die" stance to the people who had yet to switch their religious allegiance to Sunni Islam.

And while some chose death through resistance, most acquiesced to conversion—but to varying degrees. In the past, many Afghans whom outsiders had converted quickly disavowed Islam as soon as those having effected their new religious adherence departed their villages. However, in the Pech River region, particularly in those villages of the upper reaches of the Korangal and the Chowkay valleys, some not only embraced Sunni Islam under Rahman Khan's press, but adopted its most extreme form. Calling themselves the Safis, meaning "the Pure Ones," the people of the Korangal, upper Chowkay, and segments of the surrounding valleys, while continuing to speak in dialects of the millennia-old Pashai language, would become the most conservative Muslims in all of Afghanistan, if not the world. Kafiristan had become Nuristan, literally "Land of Light"—meaning "Land of the Enlightened Ones."

Afghanistan, however, wasn't the only part of the globe where European colonial powers sought to influence lands dominated by Muslims. In North Africa, while the Great Game raged far to the east, a group of ultraconservative Muslims, inspired by burgeoning anticolonialist sentiments, conceived the Salafiyya movement. Members of this group, who saw themselves as strict adherents to the Salafi, which means "following the forefathers of Islam," would many decades later radically alter the course of human history, igniting the Global War on Terror through their extremist acts. Often incorrectly referred to as Wahhabism (in reality a small offshoot of the Salafiyya movement, Wahhabism emerged through the interpretations of the Salafi by Muhammad ibn Abd al-Wahhab in the eighteenth century on the Arabian peninsula), Salafis would become increasingly powerful, widespread, and ever more extreme throughout the twentieth century, establishing madrassas throughout the Middle East as well as in Pakistan for the teaching of ultraconservative, ferociously anti-Western interpretations of Islam.

In addition to learning about the Pashtuns and their culture, practicing conversational Afghan phrases (in both Pashto and Dari, both official languages of Afghanistan, although Pashto predominates the area where the Marines would deploy), and studying the nuances of Sunni Islam, the Marines of 2/3 focused much of their predeployment studies on a period of the country's history particularly relevant to their forthcoming tour, the Soviet-Afghan War. While the latter was triggered by and fought for starkly different reasons than that of the American invasion of Afghanistan in 2001, the Marines would glean both tactical and cultural insight by researching individual battles of the period. But while most studies of the Soviets in Afghanistan discuss the war during the 1980s, the Soviet "invasion" actually began many decades prior to the Christmas Eve 1979 insertion of Spetsnaz special operations teams in the country, the event marking the war's official commencement.

The Soviet-Afghan relationship actually began a few months prior to Afghanistan's transition from British protectorate status to independent statehood, when Lenin issued a March 27, 1919, message to the Afghan king stating: "The establishment of permanent diplomatic relations between the two great peoples opens up an extensive possibility of mutual assistance against any encroachment on the side of foreign predators on other people's freedom and other people's wealth." A number of economic-assistance and trade agreements followed, and by the 1930s, the two countries had established a strong bond. But in the post–World War II years, the Soviet Union grew increasingly aggressive, its leaders' eyes scanning all corners of the globe, from Cuba, to Africa, to Southeast Asia, in the hope of expanding its empire.

In 1955, Nikita Khruschev traveled to Afghanistan and signed a ten-year extension to the Soviet-Afghan treaty of neutrality and nonaggression, first ratified in 1931. But this signing was more than a mere extension of an old agreement; it marked the beginning of an era of Soviet investment in construction, education, and military expansion. During the following decades, the Soviets built numerous roads and highways—the vital Salang Tunnel giving an all-weather connection between the north and south of Afghanistan—high-rise living quarters, a massive state farm outside of Jalalabad, and the enormous Bagram Airfield, among many other projects. The Communists also brought to Afghanistan a full spectrum of military equipment, from AK-47 rifles to T-series tanks, armored troop carriers, Mig-17 jets, and MI-8/17 "Hip" multirole helicopters, which they instructed the Afghans to both fly and maintain. Interestingly, Afghanistan also established limited ties with the United States in the 1950s; the U.S. military even undertook some training exercises with the Afghans over a number of years, but never transferred large stocks of weapons to them as the Soviets had done. When the Soviets inevitably crossed paths with the Americans during their respective military training missions, they reportedly cooperated with each other, albeit quietly.

Of course, along with their financial, educational, and military aid, the Soviets brought their Communist ideology and propagandizing tools, too, and in 1973, Afghanistan took yet another hairpin turn on its historical pathway when Mohammad Sarder Daoud seized control of the government from King Zahir Shah (who was Daoud's cousin) during a July 17 coup d'état, ending decades of lackluster and corrupt monarchical rule. Daoud installed himself as the country's first president and declared Afghanistan a republic. Having gained power with the help of the subversive, pro-Marxist People's Democratic Party of Afghanistan (PDPA), members of which expected big political payoffs once he took authority, he shocked the party when he ordered a crackdown on the group as soon as he assumed power.

Daoud immediately instituted massive social and political change in Afghanistan, but his attempts failed miserably and most of the country spiraled into turmoil. Then the PDPA returned, with a vengeful blood-lust, killing Daoud and most of his family on April 27, 1978. The country was declared the Democratic Republic of Afghanistan, led by Nur Muhammad Taraqi, the secretary general of the now-hard-line-Communist PDPA. Taraqi announced the institution of an array of liberal economic and social changes, key among these the replacing of laws founded on Islamic tradition with those based on Marxism, forcing men to cut their beards, and a push to introduce girls into the education system.

But the people, particularly those of the distant Hindu Kush, immediately resisted what they felt to be a monumental threat to their traditions and way of life. While most simply disobeyed the new laws, others became agitated, particularly those in areas that held the most conservative of Islamic beliefs. And then on June 22, 1978, the first shots of a conflict that would ultimately explode into the Soviet-Afghan War rang out—in Nangalam, at the western end of the Pech River Valley, just a few miles from the Chowkay and the Korangal valleys, fired by the descendants of the infidels-turned-Muslim purists, the Safi. The Communist government immediately responded with tanks, artillery, and aerial bombing. As the residents fled into the surrounding hills and valleys, the Communists attacked Nangalam's mosques, burned Korans, then poured gasoline on the villagers' homes and burned them. The government troops found a widow and her child who hadn't fled into the hills with the other villagers, and doused them with gas, burned them alive, and threw their charred bodies onto one of the village's main intersections. The story of Nangalam spread throughout the valleys of the region like the gas-fueled fires themselves, sparking further unrest, only to be put down with similar brutality. In October of that year, however, men of the village of Kamdesh, north of Nangalam in the heart of Nuristan, attacked a government outpost and obliterated it. And that uprising wasn't put down. The war against the new government was on, between the Soviet-backed Communist government and those who saw themselves as the warriors of Islam, literally, "those who struggle": the infamous mujahideen.

The Soviets poured millions of dollars' worth of military and infrastructure aid into Afghanistan throughout 1978; they also sent countless advisers to help the Taraqi regime quell the fast-growing revolt against the new government. Despite the Soviets' increasingly aggressive posture in Afghanistan, the United States seemed to barely wince at the radical move to hard-line Communist rule. In 1978, the United States sent an ambassador to the new regime, a U.S. Marine veteran of World War II named Adolph "Spike" Dubs, one of the nation's leading experts on the Soviet Union at the time (whom the KGB wrongly considered a spy). In February of 1979, however, Islamic militants kidnapped him, sequestering Dubs in a room in the Kabul Hotel. Government security forces, under the close advising of a Soviet KGB agent, dismissed the wishes of U.S. State Department officials for a peaceful resolution, and opened fire on the room, killing Dubs—a grim portent of the shortsighted tactical mind-set the Soviets would embrace throughout Afghanistan in the years to come. While the United States had been granting Afghanistan a small amount of foreign aid at the time, Dubs would have been the key to an expansion of this assistance. With his death, however, U.S. aid—at least overtly—withered to nothing. But other American funds, of the covert sort, would begin arriving in just a few months.

The blooming insurgency against Afghanistan's Communist puppet government in 1979 consisted of a few disorganized, loose-knit bands of Islamic fighters scattered throughout the Hindu Kush and other parts of Afghanistan. In March of 1979, the people of Herat, in western Afghanistan, revolted against the government's reforms, storming a prison and liberating political prisoners. Then they rounded up and killed fifty Soviet advisers and their families—decapitating them and placing their heads atop sticks surrounding the town. Days later, Taraqi's retaliation began—from the sky—as five-hundred-pound bombs destroyed much of the city, killing an estimated five thousand people. Soon thereafter, an entire division of Afghan soldiers based in Herat renounced their allegiance to the new government and joined the mujahideen.

Taraqi's government once again put down an uprising in Nangalam in the summer of 1979, using both land and airpower, razing much of the beautiful enclave—again. Whatever animosity the Safis who dwelled in the lower valleys may have held toward their onetime aggressors, the Pashtuns, was at least temporarily put aside now that they had a common enemy, the "Red Kafir." After the brutal strikes by the Taraqi government forces against Nangalam and other villages—indiscriminate raids that killed men, women, children, dogs, and other animals—refugees, including the fighting-age males who now considered themselves mujahideen, began to migrate into Pakistan. Pakistan took them in and would continue to welcome the now-homeless Afghans through the coming years, a relationship vital for the eventual outcome of the war. But while Pakistan served as a critical ally at the time, its aid was offered less for humanitarian reasons than as a political maneuver.

Pakistan, which had won its independent statehood through partition from British India in 1947, has maintained a tenuous relationship with Afghanistan for decades. While those unfamiliar with the region might believe that the two countries have enjoyed close, almost familial ties (if for no other reason than they share Islam as a national religion and *stan* as the last syllable in their names), Pakistan aligned itself strategically on the other side of the table from Afghanistan's global commitments—with the United States—while the Soviets embraced Afghanistan. Few can forget the shoot-down of American Francis Gary Powers's USAF/CIA U2 spy plane over the Soviet Union—or Khrushev's ominous PR move of drawing a red circle on a map around the city from which Powers launched his craft: Peshawar, Pakistan.

Afghan-Pakistani relations have been marked by tension ever since Pakistan emerged as an independent state. In 1955, hostilities over their shared border culminated in Pakistan closing its trade route with the Afghans, threatening to harm Afghanistan's fragile economy—an act Pakistan would repeat through the years. But then the Soviets intervened and provided an alternative logistical plan, which furthered the bond between the Afghans and the Soviets. The Durand Line was also a source of conflict between the two countries. The Durand Line effectively split in two a region known to the Pashtuns as Pashtunistan, and many Afghans to this day refuse to acknowledge it, crossing unchecked over the invisible line just as people in the southwestern United States pass from Utah to Colorado. Afghans, during the drawing of their borders, sought to have included as part of their country those areas now known as the Northwest Frontier province and the Federally Administered Tribal Areas of Pakistan; although this effort was to end in failure, the Pakistani government, in a wink-and-nod style compromise, pretty much keeps out of many of these regions, allowing the people to govern themselves.

The greatest single element shaping Pakistan's strategic planning and positioning through the years, however, lies to its east: India. Pakistan and India have fought three bloody wars throughout the years, and as India developed close ties with the Soviet Union in the decades following World War II, Pakistan felt increasingly squeezed by inimical flanking powers, particularly in the late 1970s with the aggressive Soviet influx into Afghanistan. Furthermore, many historians believe that Pakistan has long considered Afghanistan to be a buffer zone, providing "strategic depth" into which Pakistan can retreat, regroup, and realign its forces in the event that India overruns its eastern border. In the late 1970s, Pakistani president Zia-ul-Haq envisioned a continuous Islamic union, stretching from Pakistan, through Afghanistan, to Iran. As the Soviet-backed campaign against the mujahideen exploded in magnitude and viciousness, Zia felt that providing support to the resistance was not only necessary, but that Pakistan's very survival hinged on supporting it. But he'd have to do this covertly, as a direct war with the Soviet Union—which India could easily join on Pakistan's eastern front—would virtually assure Pakistan's demise.

Still reeling over the U.S. military pullout from the Vietnam War, in which the Soviet Union was globally regarded as the behind-the-scenes victor over the United States, many officials within U.S. national security circles began to pay ever-closer attention to the Soviet's involvement in Afghanistan in the late 1970s. The United States had been monitoring the steady inflow of financial, human, and military resources over the years, and when the Communist Taraqi government engaged the mujahideen in "hot" military campaigns, many in these circles smelled blood—of a thousand little insurgent cuts. Chief among these U.S. strategists was President Carter's national security adviser Zbigniew Brzezin-ski, who believed that if the United States jumped in early enough, the Soviets could be pressed to move from shadowy military enablers to front-line fighters—and hence, front-line casualties. He formulated what would become the strategically vital Operation *Cyclone*. Put into motion with Carter's signature on July 3, 1979, a little more than a year after the first shots rang out in Nangalam, the operation initially authorized millions of dollars' worth of aid to be secretly funneled to the anti-Communist guerrillas. The project, which would remain top secret for years—unknown even by U.S. congressmen and senators at the time—would mark the beginning of a near decade's worth of covert military aid to the mujahideen that would ultimately total billions of dollars. But again, like President Zia's wishes to keep Pakistan officially uninvolved, the United States would have to execute the plan not just delicately, but with the utmost secrecy. And that would involve dealing with Pakistan—again, not official state-to-state cooperation, but through members of the CIA working with one of the most effective yet feared intelligence organizations in the world, Pakistan's ISI.

A controversial, shadowy organization within Pakistan's military, the ISI (Inter-Services Intelligence), maintains as its official role the defense of Pakistan's interests through the gathering and analysis of intelligence both inside Pakistan and in neighboring countries. In reality, however, the ISI, particularly after Zia resurrected the organization (it had withered in power under Zia's predecessor, Zulfiqar Ali Bhutto), would fight Pakistan's "shadow wars," keep tabs on internal media, and attempt to influence political machinations within Pakistan and even India—and, of course, carry out its official duties of gathering information. Many in Pakistan, even those in their military, however, feared the ISI, as they operated virtually autonomously, with utmost anonymity, and wielded almost unlimited power. They were the ideal conduit through which the United States could secretly effect misery on the Communists.

In September of 1979, Hafizullah Amin, an American-educated rabid Communist whom Moscow eyed suspiciously as harboring anti-Soviet sentiment, assumed the presidency of Afghanistan after forces loyal to him murdered President Taraqi. But the situation throughout the nation continued to collapse at an alarming rate. Amin had tens of thousands of political prisoners executed, and began to drive hundreds, ultimately millions, of Afghans out of their homes into refugee camps. The Afghan-on-Afghan fighting crushed morale in the army, engendering mass desertion—and those deserters quickly joined with those fighting the growing, albeit disorganized jihad. In October of 1979, the mujahideen of the valleys surrounding Sawtalo Sar took up arms once again—outside of Nangalam, in the Chowkay, the Korangal, and throughout the Kunar Valley including the city of Asadabad (also known to locals as Chagha Serai). From that point onward, they pledged to never lay down their arms until the Red Kafirs had been obliterated.

Just a few months later, "the most serious threat to peace since the Second World War"—as stated by President Jimmy Carter—began with the raid by Soviet Spetsnaz special operations forces, who quickly took Kabul, killing Amin, and installed Babrak Karmal as the country's third president. The world's outraged eyes focused on the Soviets, now pouring into the seemingly helpless country from the north in armored personnel carriers, tanks, and heavy trucks, as destitute men, women, and children, carrying the barest of their possessions, marched into Pakistan. Brzezinski, ever the anti-Communist hawk, looked upon the situation with delight, writing in a memo to Carter: "We now have the opportunity of giving to the USSR *its* Vietnam War."

The Afghan Bureau of the ISI now assumed the critical role of enabling a coordinated insurgency against the Soviets. As the Soviet Bear lumbered throughout Afghanistan indiscriminately swatting at the small groups of mujahideen with tanks, helicopters, artillery, and machine-gun rounds, the bureau worked feverishly to coalesce the seven main "parties" of mujahideen, each with thousands of fighters, into a unified force. The party leaders, who based themselves just a few miles from the Afghan border in Peshawar, Pakistan, while single-minded in their determination to destroy or drive the Red Infidel from their homeland, nevertheless held deep-seated animosities for one another. Of the seven parties, three held moderate beliefs, and four were led by die-hard extremists. Chief among the most radical, Gulbadin Hekmatyar, the youngest and most aggressive of the leaders, founded Hezb-e Islami Gulbadin (HIG) in 1975 in Pakistan after spending two years in a Kabul prison for murder (of a fellow PDPA member). With his establishment of the HIG in Pakistan, Hekmatyar gained a wide range of ties in the country, leading the ISI to believe that he was "their guy" more than any of the other seven leaders. And while on paper all seven would be treated equally, HIG fell perfectly into President Zia's strategic outlook for influence of Afghanistan for Pakistan's needs.

The methods by which the Soviets engaged the Afghan populace and the mujahideen would provide the Marines of 2/3 great examples— of how *not* to fight a conflict. The storied Soviet warrior of World War II who selflessly and valiantly defended the motherland against Nazi assault was nowhere to be found in Afghanistan. Mostly conscripts, the Red soldiers in Afghanistan lived in squalor, could barely aim their rifles, wanted nothing more than to go home, and many became addicted to hashish. They also arrived with old, clunky equipment, ill suited for war in the mountains: tanks and heavy transport vehicles incapable of negotiating narrow, twisting mountain roads armed with guns that could elevate to just thirty degrees, leaving high-perched mujahideen well out of the range of potential fire. While the Soviet paratroopers and the Spetsnaz performed better, too few were deployed to Afghanistan to make much of a difference in the long run. During their studies of the war, however, the Marines found the most important lesson learned to be the aggressor's apparent outlook on winning: the Soviets seemed to believe that they could just arrive in Afghanistan and reinforce the Afghan Communist army, who would do the majority of the work of quelling the insurrection. Most Afghan soldiers defected and joined the mujahideen, however, forcing the poorly trained and equipped Soviets onto the front-line fight. But they would be fighting a counterinsurgency, a complicated—at times ultrafrustrating—type of warfare requiring heavy, heavy, *heavy* interaction with the locals to engender working relationships that enable the rebuilding of a nation and the flushing out of the enemy. Instead, the Soviets just bombed much of the country into oblivion. What they didn't bomb, they shot, and what they didn't shoot, they shelled with artillery, and what they didn't shell with artillery, they rocketed. And so on and so forth. The Soviets committed the most gruesome and widespread acts of inhumanity since World War II. Genghis Khan would have been proud—and jealous—of the Communists' modern, efficient weapons.

Meanwhile, the Afghan Bureau of the ISI inhaled money from the United States throughout the 1980s, acquiring arms, food, and supplies from countries around the globe, and training the mujahideen in camps along the border. Not wanting to tip off the Soviets that outside forces had been aiding the fighters, the ISI didn't procure fancy, state-of-the-art gear, but run-of-the-mill weaponry: AK-47s, rocket-propelled grenades, light machine guns, grenades, recoilless rifles, mortars, Chinese 107mm and 120mm rockets, and other basic light infantry implements. As well, they kept representatives of the CIA and other American agencies strictly separated from the mujahideen themselves, ostensibly to maintain the illusion that the insurgency was self-supported, but in reality to maintain complete control of which parties received the money and how these funds were used.

But America wasn't alone in its desire to repulse the Soviets. The Saudi Arabian government matched the United States in funding during the 1980s; the Brits, too, chipped in, as did Kuwait and some other Arab states. Of course, every nation sought to influence the war for different reasons—Pakistan to maintain "strategic depth," the United States to beat down the Communist Soviets, and the Saudis in their desire both to free their fellow Muslims from the Communists and to spread their official state religion, that of the Salafi school of Sunni Islam.

By the mid-1980s, that part of the Hindu Kush to which 2/3 would deploy two decades later became a tempest of clashing external interests. While the Soviets had retreated from most of the area after 1980, having pushed into the Chowkay (out of which the residents quickly and handily blasted them), Saudi Arabians, dressed as local Pashtuns, meandered down the Kunar Valley with suitcases stuffed with tens of thousands of dollars—money to be handed out to help build mosques and madrassas that would teach their brand of Islam. Other Arabs, unaffiliated with the Saudi government, showed up, too. Based out of Peshawar, these "Afghan Arabs" represented the most radical of all the Islamists in the world, even more so than the followers of Hekmatyar. Their beliefs were guided by the teachings of the "Muslim Brotherhood," an organization founded in Cairo, Egypt, in the 1920s, and based on the teachings of the Salafiyya movement, and some in the jihad movement saw them as arrogant, hateful—even toxic. The Afghan Arabs had come not so much to help free the Afghan people or to stand with them in Muslim solidarity on the front lines, but out of a burning hatred of the European Infidel, and included among their ranks the son of a wealthy Saudi businessman the world would come to know all too well: Osama bin Laden.

Fueled by money from the United States and Saudi Arabia, and armed with high-resolution and time-relevant satellite imagery and other intelligence from the CIA—as well as, later in the war, the much-hyped Stinger missile, which leveled psychological "what if" blows to Soviet pilots more than actual aircraft downings—the mujahideen froze the Soviet's war effort into a virtual stalemate. True, the Soviets had control of the cities and major highways, but they rarely dared emerge from behind their encampments' perimeters or step from their armored vehicles. The Soviets, having surmised that the ISI was responsible for training and equipping the mujahideen, struck back at Pakistan, not with bombs or rockets, but with Afghans themselves—chased out through the intentional attacks on civilian targets for the sole purpose of causing a humanitarian and economic crisis by inundating Pakistan with masses of refugees, many of whom arrived maimed by one or more of the millions of land mines the Communists had scattered throughout the Hindu Kush. Newly elected Mikhail Gorbachev, under intense and growing pressure from within as well as from countries throughout the globe, realized that he had no choice but to pull his troops out of Afghanistan. The Soviet Bear had been brought to its knees by the mujahideens' 'thousand little cuts.'

The last of the Soviet troops crossed the Amu Darya River on February 15, 1989. The shock waves of the war that saw over 13,500 Soviet deaths and tens of thousands of wounded would contribute to the downfall of the Communist state a few years later, and with that, the war in Afghanistan landed a far more crushing blow against the USSR than the Vietnam conflict ever could have on the United States.

In addition to over 40 million land mines—many disguised as toys to attract children—the Communists had left in their wake somewhere between 500,000 and 1 million dead, 1.5 million maimed and injured, 5.5 million refugees chased into Pakistan and Iran, over 2 million internally displaced, arsenic- and mercury-tainted water wells (one of their preferred tactics to render countless villages uninhabitable), and a virtually impotent puppet government now headed by a man named Mohammad Najibullah, who would see the demise of his power and lose his life in just a few years.

Afghanistan would descend once again into chaos in the years after the Soviet withdrawal, as the seven mujahideen parties and various ethnic groups moved from warring against the Red Kafir to attacking one another, further destroying an already crippled, destitute country. From Pakistan's standpoint, Afghanistan no longer stood as a base of a foreign threat, and they had their "strategic depth" once again; both Pakistan and Saudi Arabia would continue to provide limited amounts of foreign aid, but not enough to rebuild a nation. The United States, however, pulled its support from the fighters completely, not so much because they had achieved the desired end state of a demoralized Soviet withdrawal, but because U.S. leaders had learned that a disproportionate allotment of American money had been funneled by the ISI to Gulbadin Hekmatyar, whom they regarded as a potentially severe threat to the United States—possibly another Ayatollah Khomeini—should he ever gain national power. Hekmatyar, who spurned the Reagan administration by refusing an invitation to the White House in 1985 to celebrate the mujahideen freedom fighters, openly decried the Americans as infidels—although he was more than happy to accept ISI-routed American funds. The warlord would go on to kill untold scores of civilians in the power struggle that ensued after the Soviet withdrawal, and then continue to vex American interests into the next millennium.

America seemed to have forgotten about Afghanistan by 1990; the internal conflicts of the country would reduce the crushed state to ashes in just a few years. But out of those ashes would rise yet another threat to the United States, one that would require not secretive international maneuverings, but direct action by American forces.

2

THE BATTALION

While the Fourth of July stands as the most hallowed date on the historical calendar of the United States, for many Americans the less conspicuous date of 10 November ranks in the same echelon. Some actually consider this autumn day to be the most important of the year, eclipsing birthdays, religious holidays, even wedding anniversaries, as on 10 November 1775, at Philadelphia's Tun Tavern, Captain Samuel Nicholas, under decree of the Second Continental Congress, established what would arguably become the most venerated, the most feared by America's enemies yet beloved by its citizenry and allies, the most tireless, brave, and selfless, and the most daring yet professional family of war fighters in history: the United States Marine Corps.

Captain Nicholas, the Marine Corps' first Commandant, who would designate the Tun Tavern as the Continental Marines' headquarters and recruitment center (Nicholas appointed the Tavern's owner, Robert Mullan, to undertake the recruiting operation), quickly stood up two battalions of Marines, who quenched their thirsts with the Tavern's beer and feasted at the adjacent eatery, Peggy Mullan's Red Hot Beef Steak Club at Tun Tavern. Not four months after their fateful birth, the Continental Marines entered battle for the first time, immediately establishing what would become an enduring tradition of fortitude and decisive victory at the Battle of Nassau, where Captain Nicholas and 230 of his Marines (accompanied by twenty Continental Navy sailors) stormed onto the shores of the Island of Nassau and captured the British stronghold of Fort Montague. Then, on 3 March 1776, these "soldiers of the sea" took all of the island, seizing a large cache of British cannons, mortars, and rifles—later to be used against their one-time owners.

In the centuries that would follow that christening expedition to the Bahamas, the U.S. Marine Corps would indelibly burn into historical records as well as the psyches of millions—if not *billions*—chronicles of virtually unimaginable travails pitting spirit, skill, courage, and camaraderie against malevolent adversity and often overwhelming odds throughout the globe, in all climes, from scorched desert, to dripping jungle, to piercingly cold alpine heights. Throughout their history—a history that began almost eight months before the very birth of the nation their ranks would shed so much blood to foster and pledge to defend to the last—the United States Marine Corps has produced victories not just exemplary, but iconic of the wars in which they fought.

In the First Barbary War of the early 1800s, the Marines would prove that they could succeed in combat for their country not only on the home front, but as a world-class expeditionary force capable of defending American interests anywhere on the planet. Ultimately arising out of a failed diplomatic attempt to maintain security of American merchant shipping through payoffs to pirates of the "Barbary States" (the modern African nations of Libya, Tunisia, Algeria, and Morocco), the then-fledgling U.S. government dispatched a small group of Navy frigates—crewed by sailors and defended onboard by U.S. Marines—to the Mediterranean to protect American vessels from the marauders. Over the course of the following years, the U.S. Navy would fight a series of engagements in the region that resulted in mixed outcomes. The relative stalemate would end, however, in the spring of 1805 at the Battle of Derne, when U.S. Marine First Lieutenant Presley O'Bannon led five hundred of his men, accompanied by local mercenaries (whom he and his Marines helped train), six hundred miles from Alexandria, Egypt, across the scorching Sahara Desert over the course of forty-five days, to storm the heavily defended Derne outpost—Tripoli's primary defensive rampart—as U.S. Navy ships supported their ground efforts by pounding the fortress with heavy gunfire. Once captured, O'Bannon personally raised the American flag above Derne, marking the first time in U.S. history that the American flag flew above foreign soil.

The Battle of Derne would become one of the most popularly enduring in all of the Marine Corps' history, being referenced in the second line of the famous "U.S. Marines' Hymn," reading "To the shores of Tripoli." The well-known Marine Corps officer sword, which would become the weapon issued for more years than any other in the U.S. military, also hails from this battle.

O'Bannon and his Marines' training of and fighting alongside local forces marked the beginning of what would become a long-standing Marine Corps approach to waging war against America's enemies—an approach that would yield immense dividends in theaters throughout the world in the decades to follow. Of course, 2/3 would continue to carry this tradition forward in Afghanistan's Hindu Kush during their deployment over two centuries in the wake of O'Bannon and his mens' work with indigenous fighters in the North African desert.

Counterinsurgency, or as the Marines often call the mission type, "COIN," requires troops to work closely with local populations—proving their intention to aid and not to conquer and gaining a population's trust and allegiance—to root out terrorists, insurgents, even rank criminals, securing and stabilizing a region to lay the foundation for rebuilding towns, villages, and basic infrastructure like water wells and smooth, all-season roads. Successful counterinsurgency campaigns engender economic development, improved education and healthcare institutions, capable and honest security agencies, and inspire the rise of democratic regional and national governments out of the ashes of oppression—goals 2/3 would steadfastly pursue during their deployment to Afghanistan in 2005. A counterinsurgency fight, while often "going kinetic" for short periods of time, will typically have Marines sending food, fuel, generators, bandages, and clean water "downrange" far more often than 5.56 mm and 7.62 mm rounds. Due to the expeditionary capability of the Marine Corps to go anywhere on the planet within just days or even hours to support American interests—from merging into global wars to interdicting small village-to-village skirmishes—the Marine Corps has engaged in countless tiny, yet significant, COIN fights around the world throughout its history, not to mention its undertaking of an array of non-combat humanitarian aid and assistance missions. Tactically far removed from the renowned amphibious assaults of distant beaches or the over-land charges into walls of hardened enemy troops, Marines would weave the subtle concepts and practices of the counterinsurgency fight—like simply determining friend from adversary on a dusty third-world alleyway—deep into their doctrinal fabric through their decades of combat.

Some of the most significant U.S. Marine Corps COIN campaigns occurred early in the twentieth century, in the Dominican Republic, Nicaragua, Panama, Honduras, and Haiti, in what would become known as the "Banana Wars," a name derived from American agricultural interests (foremost the United Fruit Company) having benefitted from the outcomes of these interventions against destabilizing insurgencies. For the Marines (and other service branches that would establish units to engage in counterinsurgency operations in years following the Banana Wars), one of the most significant outcomes of this era would be the codification of their unique style of fighting small guerrilla armies and bands of insurgents into book form: the *Small Wars Manual*. First published in 1935, the *Small Wars Manual* covered a wide range of diverse topics including tactics, psychology, supply plans, the occupation of towns, armed native organizations, light artillery, and animal transportation, among a series of other topics. The counterinsurgency precepts outlined in the *Small*

Wars Manual, combined with the U.S. Marine Corps institution pioneered by O'Bannon of working closely with local fighters aligned with American interests, founded the conceptual warfighting framework on which 2/3 would build its success in Afghanistan. In the words of Major Rob Scott, 2/3's executive officer during his address to the battalion's officer corps while training for their Afghan deployment, "Gentlemen, the *Small Wars Manual* will be our Bible in this fight."

Despite the achievements of the U.S. Marine Corps over the course of more than two centuries in places like the remote Pacific, Europe, Vietnam, the Caribbean, North Africa, Central America, and beyond, most American civilians (and even many in other branches of the U.S. military) don't know what a U.S. Marine really *is*, or *how* Marines achieve their stunning victories. Stated simply, Marines are *naval infantry*—ship-borne troops historically moved throughout the globe by naval vessels, then delivered to terrestrial hot zones by amphibious landing craft. A force of highly trained and disciplined "soldiers of the sea" who emerge from crashing surf to charge into the fight, Marines have also been historically tasked with boarding other vessels and maintaining security on their own ships.

Marines have traditionally not only fought alone in battlefields and confrontations unsuitable for larger and hence less nimble armies, but side by side with conventional soldiers in a joint task force in conflicts where their fighting proved not just an augmentation of combat power, but a synergistic "force multiplier." Much smaller than the U.S. Army, the Marine Corps can mobilize at the bark of an order for deployments of all types and sizes, and having been born and raised with their naval brethren (the Second Continental Congress established the Continental Navy less than one month prior to the birth of the Marine Corps), Marines historically have been able to deploy anywhere in the world, granted some proximity to a coastline. On ship, Marines aren't just passengers, they are every bit as integral to a Navy flotilla as the sailors who command the craft, maintain those crafts' engines, and navigate the flotilla through the high seas. And while Marines share slices of doctrine, tactics, and terminology and even some cultural foundations with both the Army and Navy, and although they administratively fall under the Department of the Navy, the U.S. Marine Corps represents a unique and distinct force with ever-evolving capabilities irreproducible by others, casting them as the tip-of-the-spear embodiment of the concept of global force projection.

Although their numbers measure just a fraction of those of the Army, Marines are almost always the "first to fight," vehemently charging into combat against America's enemies. As well, Marines represent the United States' "911 force," whom the president can send downrange for up to sixty days without a formal congressional declaration of war for "such other duties as the President may direct," as outlined in the National Security Act of 1947. Resourceful, quick, and staunch in meeting any challenge regardless of type or scale, United States Marines stand alone in the world of war fighters not only in their history of battlefield conquest, but in their broadly diverse and adaptable mission spectrum, their expeditionary bloodline, and their centuries-honed ethos.

Truly understood by only the Marines themselves, the deep-rooted USMC ethos—their *way*—can best be described as a nucleus of values built of heritage, patriotism, discipline, competitiveness, and above all else, boundless fidelity—to their country and to all of its citizenry, to one another, and to the legacy of the Marine Corps. Their ethos allows them to push onward in a seemingly hopeless fight against an enemy of much greater size and firepower, ultimately not just to survive, but to stand atop a battlefield as victors, as they did in Belleau Wood. And in Khe Sanh. And in Iwo Jima. Marines become Marines not in order to fight; Marines become Marines to win, and to win decisively—for their country. Marines understand the concepts of surrender and defeat, but only as they apply to those against whom they fight. Never to themselves. They know America as the greatest country in the history of mankind, and to deprive the current or any succeeding generation of the opportunities America avails to its citizens, by allowing inimical forces any influence whatsoever over their nation, would be tantamount to shoving one's own mother into a gutter.

Marines view themselves not as an institution of military power, but as a force of and for the citizenry of the United States of America. They hold the concepts of a civilian-commanded military, individual liberty, and national sovereignty as their most sacred. Just as Marines prize freedom for their own country's citizenry, they despise tyranny abroad. They are infamously selfless, to one another on the battlefield as well as "parochially," with other service branches in a joint environment, and of course, to their nation. Marines feel their greatest honor derives from sacrifice—sacrifice for their country as a whole as well as for individual citizens, be those citizens teachers, doctors, truck drivers, or businesspeople geographically and emotionally separated from the nation's current fight, as well as those who would wait at an airport for Marines to return from a long and gut-wrenching combat tour and then spit in their faces and screech "monster!" The ethos that incites Marines to fight ever harder in the world's bloodiest battles also engenders restraint, both in less clearly defined combat zones of a counterinsurgency nature and back home—and anywhere in between, at all times.

As an institution, the Marine Corps marches forward in a continual state of flux. Always conscious of their perceived relevancy in a world of changing political and military landscapes and fickle domestic mindsets, Marines constantly strive to maintain and modify their readiness for overcoming the world's current and future threats by improving their doctrine, their weapon systems, and themselves—as both war fighters and citizens. Fiercely competitive, not only on the world's battlefields, but back home with other services (and often one another), Marines continually strive for the highest training and competency standards in the Department of Defense. They value stringent physical fitness levels, mandating institutionally as well as on a Marine-to-Marine basis what many non-Marines consider not just tough, but harsh training standards. Ever fearful of even the slightest whispers of "unification"—i.e., the death of the Marine Corps (attempts at which have been made more than a dozen times during their history)—Marines ceaselessly push themselves to prove not only their relevancy, but their necessity. They pride themselves on their potency while always maintaining a culture of resourcefulness and frugality—doing "more with less"—ever innovative and willing to improvise. Marines feel that they exist not only because they are needed, but because America wants a U.S. Marine Corps. Harshly self-critical—almost to a fault—they live to adapt, to change, to never lie static, and always be not just ready, but ultraprepared and outfitted to defeat any threat America may face.

In the earliest days of the Continental Navy and Marine Corps, Marine and Navy commanders were tasked with carrying the will of the nation to destinations where they would fight incommunicado from their higher commanders, instilling out of necessity not only a lineage of independence, but a confidence in action to bolster that independence, as well as an ever-heightened sense of loyalty. While Marine commanders far from home have altered specific mission plans countless times during military expeditions—unknown to their superiors back in the United States until their return—Marines act solely for the success of the operation. Regardless of where on the planet a problem has arisen, U.S. presidents have always been able to maintain the highest levels of confidence in a mission's success upon commanding: "Send in the Marines."

Although historically a ship-based force, the U.S. Marine Corps of today can best be described as a compact and adaptable mobile military. Not just a small army with a proportionally sized supporting air force wrapped into and backed up by the world's most powerful navy, the Marine Corps distinguishes itself through its synergy, an ethos-charged synergy of elements diverse in capabilities, but unified in mind-set—a mind-set ever evolving but always revolving about one component: Marine infantry. And those Marine infantry today can deploy by sea— on large ships, thunderous hovercraft, inside brusquely armed amphibious assault vehicles, or strapped to high-speed landing craft; by air—from ship-based helicopters, around the world on Marine Corps C-130J Hercules, even by parachute; and overland—in rumbling convoys of "7-Ton" troop carriers, speeding across a desert in a line of Humvees, tucked inside amphibious armored personnel carriers, light armored vehicles, or M1A1 Abrams tanks. With so many ways to move about the planet, the modern Marine Corps can simultaneously sustain numerous small- and medium-size campaigns while continuing to support large-theater efforts—throughout the entire globe.

Masters of light infantry maneuver warfare at all scales, the Marine Corps has at its disposal a full spectrum of weapons systems—60 mm and 81 mm mortars, vehicle-mounted TOW missiles, handheld SMAW and AT4 rocket launchers, 155 mm howitzers, and M1A1 Abrams tanks, to name a few. Marine infantry must learn to fire and maintain with utmost precision such weapons as the tried-and-true "Ma Deuce" M2 .50-caliber machine gun, the MK19 40 mm automatic grenade launcher, the man-portable and devastating M240 light machine gun, and the M249 SAW (squad automatic weapon), which, chambered in 5.56 mm, is lightweight but lethal in the hands of a Marine.

In the skies above grunts on the move, USMC aviation ranks second to none in laying waste to enemies in close proximity to Marine infantry—a mission known as close air support. Utilizing both helicopter (rotary wing) assets that today include the AH-1W Super Cobra and the UH-1N Iroquois "Huey" and tactical air or TACAIR platforms—fixed-wing F/A-18 Hornets, both the single-seat and two-place versions, and the legendary AV-8B Harrier, one of the world's most unique and versatile aircraft, capable of vertical/short takeoffs and landings, Marine aviators have time and again annihilated enemy positions in support of their on-the-ground brethren with gun runs, bombing strikes, guided missiles, and screaming volleys of rockets. Marine aviation of another sort, the troop transport and cargo, or assault support "lift birds," always plays a vital role in any campaign, inserting and extracting troops, resupplying grunts with food, water, fuel, ammunition, and packages from home during extended-duration operations, and "sling loading" large weapon systems like the 155 mm howitzer from ships at sea deep into a developing or ongoing fight.

Of the myriad weapon systems in the modern U.S. Marine Corps arsenal, one stands out above all others: the M16 service rifle. The M16, which grunts have used since the Vietnam War, while extremely versatile and capable, holds its distinction not for its rate of fire, or for its durability, or for its accuracy. The M16 service rifle maintains its salient position not for what it is or what it can do, but because of who holds it, the most important component of the Marine Corps, the storied enlisted infantry Marine.

A U.S. Marine is "born and raised"—*made*—at one of two Marine Corps recruit depots, MCRD San Diego, California or MCRD Parris Island, South Carolina. Recruits arrive at night by bus, the prospective Marines having said their good-byes to their families and friends in towns and cities throughout the country just hours earlier. Modern recruits sign on to serve their country not out of desperation or lack of opportunity, as some movies and news media outlets portray, but out of the desire to fulfill a commitment to their country—ever-charged by the attacks of September 11, 2001, and the ongoing threats posed to America by terrorists throughout the world—as well to experience not just a challenge but a life defined by the rewards of overcoming what others might consider insurmountable obstacles, time and again. They come to the Marine Corps to continue a family tradition, having been raised on stories told by their Marine Corps fathers, grandfathers, or great-grandfathers. Or they come after learning about the historic exploits of the Marines in books, magazines, or even movies. Some even come after viewing USMC television advertisements, always noting that unlike those of other services, Marine Corps recruit commercials don't offer free education, civilian job training, or money to entice enlistment; Marine Corps advertisements offer nothing but the opportunity to call oneself a United States Marine. The bus doors slam open and a drill instructor climbs aboard, and lives begin anew.

Throughout its history, the Marine Corps has waxed and waned in numbers of battalions, wartime necessity and peacetime contraction pushing and pulling its head count through the years. The Second World War saw the greatest number of Marine Corps battalions, the newly minted units having played pivotal roles in the Pacific Theater victory. And while many of those battalions raised for the war effort would see their end come just months after the armistice—as most of the Marines brought in during the war returned to civilian life—a few would continue to defend American interests long after the 2 September 1945

Japanese surrender. The Second Battalion of the Third Marine Regiment was one such battalion.

Initially activated on 1 May 1942 as the Third Training Battalion at New River, North Carolina, outbound recruits from MCRD Parris Island quickly bolstered the unit to fighting strength, and on 17 June 1942, the Second Battalion of the Third Marine Regiment was officially born. Marines of 2/3 would enter combat for the first time on 1 November 1943 as some of the first troops ashore for the opening phase of the Bougainville Campaign, an effort on and around the South Pacific Ocean's Bougainville Island, an operation that would last through August of 1945. The Marines of 2/3 fought continuously for a month on Bougainville, hacking through tangled, dripping jungle as they charged after Imperial Japanese soldiers. They then moved to Guadalcanal to train for an assault on Guam, a battle that they would remember as their most significant contribution to America's World War II victory.

Temporarily decommissioned shortly after the end of the war, the Second Battalion of the Third Marine Regiment was reactivated in 1951 to bolster troop strength in support of the Korean conflict, but the battalion wouldn't see action until Vietnam, when in April of 1965, Marines of 2/3 roared into the fight against the North Vietnamese during operations in the Da Nang region. The battalion's grunts rotated through tours in the Southeast Asian conflict until the autumn of 1969, having overrun the NVA in a number of fierce engagements, including the infamous Hills Fights, where, with Marines of 3/3, they seized the tactically vital Hill 861. After finishing operations in the A Shau Valley and Khe Sanh region in October of 1969, 2/3's grunts would leave Vietnam—and the battalion wouldn't put rounds downrange at an enemy again for more than thirty-five years.

The Island Warriors—2/3's nickname referencing the location of their home station (since the early summer of 1971) of Marine Corps Base Hawaii at Oahu's Kaneohe Bay—would enter an active combat zone again as a battalion during their deployment in support of Operation Enduring Freedom VI, about four and a half years after the initial 2001 U.S. invasion of Afghanistan. Led at the time by Lieutenant Colonel Andrew MacMannis, the Marines of 2/3 learned in 2004 that they would journey to the eastern Afghan provinces of Laghman, Nangarhar, and Kunar in the late spring of 2005 and continue the fight that their sister battalion—the Third Battalion of the Third Marine Regiment—would be waging from the fall of 2004 until 2/3's arrival seven months later. The battalion, composed of seasoned war fighters as well as fresh-faced "boot" Marines, undertook a vigorous long-term training package to fully ready themselves for combat in the mountains of the three provinces, including drills at their home base and a live-fire exercise at the Puhakuloa Training Area on Hawaii's Big Island. Their predeployment workup would culminate, however, at two bases in California, the Marine Air Ground Combat Center at Twentynine Palms and a base that would prove critical for acclimatizing 2/3's Marines to the rigors of mountain combat, the Marine Corps Mountain Warfare Training Center, located in a remote nook of California's eastern Sierra Nevada Mountains with an adjunct training area in the mountains outside of Hawthorne, Nevada.

Marines often zealously proclaim that they "take the fight to the enemy" like no other military service branch—of *any* country. Capable of sending self-sufficient combat units to any location on the globe, the U.S. Marine Corps codified the very essence of their expeditionary warfare tactics into a doctrinal approach known to all Marines by five letters: *MAGTF*—an acronym for Marine Air-Ground Task Force, the rubric defining the modern USMC war-fighting construct that integrates all of their elements of combat power—from aircraft, to heavy artillery, to mortars, to logistical support, to tanks, *everything*—around Marine infantry.

Explained simply, a MAGTF (pronounced Mag-Taff) defines how Marines fight in their "organic" state: synergistically "force-multiplied" by Marine aviators above (usually very close above), heavy artillery batteries in the rear, tanks flanking them, and a host of other elements in direct support, a battalion—or larger unit—of infantry Marines can thunder onto an enemy position with devastating power. The physical embodiments of the MAGTF concept come in three primary forms, each based on infantry unit size: the Marine Expeditionary Unit, or MEU; the Marine Expeditionary Brigade, or MEB; and the MEF, the Marine Expeditionary Force. The largest of the three, the MEF typically has at least a division—and sometimes more—of Marines composing the infantry component. The MEB has as its infantry core a regiment (three battalions) of Marines, and the MEU is built around a single battalion. MAGTFs, each of which is made of four elements, a Command Element, a Logistics Combat Element, an Aviation Combat Element, and of course, the Ground Combat Element (the grunts themselves) can, however, be stood up in other sizes, too, for a variety of purposes.

The utilitarian elegance and explosive potency of a MAGTF derives from the smooth integration of all its components as well as its straightforward leadership structure—one commander runs the entire show. Military theorists speak of a variety of tenets vital to waging a successful military campaign, and the two most important about which they speak, write, and ponder are intimately related to each other: unity of effort and unity of command. When the commander of a Marine Expeditionary Unit (a full colonel), says "go," everyone "rogers up" and does just that: they *go*—the grunts, the heavy lift helicopters, the TACAIR and rotary-wing close-air-support components—everyone; the Marines of an MEU (or any other MAFTF) work together as a well-oiled and devastatingly effective machine, all unified in mission orientation and goals, and each resolute in his specific task, bonded throughout by their infantry-centric, ethos-driven mind-set. Dissent, unsolicited or irrelevant input, and compromise simply don't exist in the Marine Corps command structure, and while a commander works closely with and seeks the ideas of his senior leadership during the planning phases of an operation, upon execution, the Marines of the task force act in symphonic harmony under the sole directorship of the boss.

As the Marines of 2/3 pushed through the weeks of training at Twentynine Palms and their Afghan deployment loomed ever closer on the horizon, the battalion emerged as a motivated, fully capable unit. The ever-thoughtful Lieutenant Colonel MacMannis worked closely with the battalion's executive officer, the hawklike Major Rob Scott, to ensure a smooth transition from training to the Afghan fight, mulling over a broad spectrum of details from travel to ammo, to how to disperse the battalion once in-country. Working closely with Scott and MacMannis, Major Tom Wood, the battalion's brusque and tirelessly ultracommitted operations officer, further refined his already crack tactical skills through planning, replanning, and then observing—eagle-eyed—the performance of the Marines on the ground in the training area.

And as 2/3 trained, 3/3 carried on the Afghan fight—feeding information (invaluable for 2/3's preparation for the fight) back to the Island Warriors in the form of classified after-action reports, which 2/3's intelligence officer, the brilliant Captain Scott Westerfield, inhaled, poring over every minute detail of the documents. Having developed a solid overall picture of the area of operation to which 2/3 would soon deploy, Westerfield quickly began to take interest in a number of the area's Islamic extremist terrorist and insurgent cells and their respective leaders; and while not particularly conspicuous on the surface of the pool of information, ripples of one insurgent leader kept nudging his attention more than any other . . .

The training at Twentynine Palms would reach a feverish pitch throughout the four-week training cycle at the Combat Center. Every one of the 820 Marines of the battalion—from administrators, to supply officers, to the all-important logisticians, the vital Navy Corpsmen (medical specialists attached to Marine units), and of course the grunts themselves—worked day and night amid the tan, chiseled mountains and sweeping plains of the Mojave Desert training base. They undertook a diverse series of regimens that included culture, convoy operations, intelligence gathering, and advanced weapons training. While much of the work to be done on the ground in Afghanistan would be COIN in nature, 2/3's leadership knew that the fight would undoubtedly go heavily kinetic, especially after the spring thaw that would allow the enemy easier movement throughout the peaks and passes of the Hindu Kush. And the way to best prepare the grunts for a dynamic, harsh fight, was not just to provide specialized training, but to immerse them in the heart and soul of modern USMC ground combat—to give them live-fire, combined-arms MAGTF immersion.

Located deep within the confines of the Combat Center, a broad sweep of rolling desert known as the Delta Corridor stands as a training theater for the "bread and butter" of the Marine Corps' hard kinetic fight: the combined-arms assault. In a training exercise called the Mobile Assault Course, 2/3's infantry would maneuver onto a set of "notional" targets in the Delta Corridor, fully supported by integrated Marine Corps aviation assets, artillery fire, mortars, and Abrams tanks. Mounted on large 7-Ton trucks like they'd have in Afghanistan, the Marines (a company at a time) would speed toward the distant target as U.S. Marine F/A-18 Hornets and AV-8B Harriers roared high overhead, M1A1 Abrams tanks tore across the desert on their flanks, AH-1W Super Cobra and UH-1N "Huey" gunships skimmed above the area's rocky crags, and an "arty" battery of six M198 155 mm howitzers shimmered under the rising sun far in the rear, awaiting a "call for fire."

Carefully monitored by the "Coyotes" of the base's Tactical Training Exercise Control Group, who oversee, coordinate, and augment training, a small group of the battalion's Marines known as the FiST, or Fire Support Team, positioned themselves on a small rocky outcrop about a mile distant from the target complex. Composed of a team leader, a forward air controller, an artillery forward observer, 81 mm mortar observer, and their respective radio operators, the FiST represents the "eyes" of the attack. Located a few hundred yards below the FiST, Marines of the "nerve center" of the combined arms assault—the Fire Support Coordination Center (FSCC)—would "deconflict fires" as the assault progressed. The concept behind the combined-arms attack—throwing a massive volume of coordinated "fires" onto a target as an infantry unit maneuvers onto that target—requires an extraordinary level of detail and tactical acumen to work the medley of platforms of air and ground elements into an integrated assault package. With so many muzzles about to flash, bombs about to drop, and arty rounds about to go downrange, the FSCC must carefully plan all aspects of the attack, including "deconfliction," by vertical and horizontal offsets for aircraft so as not to cause a collision with a mortar or artillery round, deconfliction by time (shutting down mortars just before an aircraft drives in for an attack run), and of course, they must manage the battlefield to absolutely mitigate the chance of any friendly-fire "blue-on-blue" incidents.

About a half mile from the FiST—hidden within a cleft of two large boulders—a five-man scout/sniper team kept close watch on the target area, adding to the overall SA (situational awareness) for all elements of the attack. In actual combat, the snipers would scan for any enemy attempting to egress from or carry in more supplies to the target, and if confirmed by higher to proceed, they would interdict them—either directly through the finely rifled barrel of an M40A3, or through a call for fire from artillery, mortars, or even from an aerial platform. With all elements in place and in "good comms" with one another, the range goes hot, and the spectacle of a U.S. Marine Corps assault unfurls in a dusty, explosive drama.

With the Coyotes having developed a practice scenario where an enemy has both well-entrenched fighting positions and a small antiaircraft defense system, the Marines of the Fire Support Coordination Center begin the attack with both 155 mm howitzers and 81 mm mortars to suppress those air defenses, allowing the helicopters and jets to roll in unencumbered by a ground threat. Because both the arty battery and the 81 mm mortarmen lie in positions where they cannot see the target directly, their forward observers within the FiST act as their "eyes on." These supporting fires are called indirect fire assets (because their users cannot typically see the target directly), and the Marine Corps maintains a strict doctrinal approach to utilizing them—including attack aviation assets, which are also considered indirect assets—where the FiST and the FSCC maintain tight control of them while they are in direct support of infantry.

Peering at a hulk that the Coyotes have identified as an antiaircraft missile battery through a high-power binocular system, the arty FO calls for a single round of high explosive—"HE"—to go downrange. Ten miles in the rear, the gun team plugs in the coordinates the FO has passed them, and the M198 tube belches a thundering fireball, loosing a hundred-pound projectile downrange. Seconds later, the round sails past the FiST, and with a bright yellow flash, sends a fountain of desert into the air—about thirty meters from the target. Then the 81 mm mortar team, directed by their FO, barrages another antiaircraft piece; the forward observers for each call back to their respective teams over secure radio networks with "fire adjustments." After a few more cycles, both the arty and 81 mm mortar rounds hit dead on—the Coyotes make the call that the threat has been neutralized. Now it's TACAIR's turn. Two F/A-18s, call sign Smoke-21 and Smoke-11, have been holding at a point about ten miles to the west. The arty FO calls for two final rounds to be fired—illumination rounds. The "illums" burst directly over the target area, each releasing a parachute-slowed chunk of burning phosphorus, marking the "back door" of the suppression package, and laying the welcome mat for the jets at their front door of the assault.

As the infantry speed toward the target—still miles away—the illum rounds slowly drift down toward the target buildings—the forward air controller, or FAC, who goes by the radio call sign Venom-11, gets Smoke-21's eyes on the target using the burning illum rounds as reference. With both the FAC and the pilot looking at the same piece of ground, the controller passes a nine-line brief—a list of essential information for a close-air-support attack—and then once Smoke-21 confirms he has received the information correctly, Venom utters the phrase all USMC aviators crave hearing, "Smoke-21, you're *cleared-hot*." In this case, Venom has cleared-hot Smoke-21 to drop six five-hundred-pound MK82 "dumb" bombs. Out of the southwest, Smoke-21 dives toward the target—and at around two thousand feet, pulls the roaring aircraft's nose up and releases all six. Seconds later, the target erupts in a wall of fire the length of a football field. The Marines of the FiST cheer as the concussive *whump-whump-whump* echoes throughout the range, and then hustle to work Smoke-11 into the attack—just as the FSCC reports that two AV-8B Harriers are inbound. Four strafing runs and two bomb drops later, the TACAIR components return to base just as the infantry approach the target and prepare to dismount, and the Abrams tanks—considered a direct maneuver element augmenting the infantry and thus not requiring a forward observer—send red-hot 120 mm sabot rounds into the target at thousands of feet per second with deadly accuracy. The 81 mm mortars restart their barrage, then the arty FO calls for a smoke screen to obscure any "enemy" from getting their eyes on the grunts. More 155 mm rounds sail past, followed by a wall of thick white smoke rising from the shells' points of impact, visibly barricading the target zone. Marine combat engineers, riding in a massive Hercules tank, prepare to clear a notional minefield with one of the Marines' favorite tools of the warfighting trade, the M58 Mine Clearing Line Charge, or MICLIC. Towed behind the Hercules, once armed, the Marine engineers "button up" the tank, ensuring the hatches of the beast are secured, then let the MICLIC rip. The hiss of a rocket motor directs everyone's attention to a long "rope" unfurling over the minefield—the rope, 350 feet in length, is made of Composition-4 high explosive; five pounds per foot, for a total of 1,750 pounds. The line of C-4 flops on the ground, then detonates, blasting the Hercules with a concussive shock wave and sending a mushroom cloud of pulverized desert about a thousand feet into the air. In an actual minefield, any explosives would have been obliterated.

With the minefield cleared, the 81 mm mortars shut down as the Marines dismount and prepare to overrun the target complex as AH-1W and UH-1N attack helicopters emerge from a bank of drifting smoke. With the Abrams tanks continuing to light up individual targets with their turret-mounted .50-caliber machine guns, the Cobra and Huey gunships make pass after cleared-hot pass, slamming the target area with rockets and guns—even an air-launched TOW missile from the Cobra. With the supported Marines now approaching the "danger close" zone of the gunships' attacks, the birds are called off, and the Marines themselves put rounds downrange onto specific targets with their M16s, SAWs, and M240s. With "boots on deck," the grunts secure the area—something no bomb, rocket, or missile can do, regardless of its level of technology or how many slam into a target. In an actual combat scenario, double-rotored CH-46E Sea Knight "Phrog" helicopters would

soon be hitting the deck, either to extract the grunts or to add reinforce-
ments, as massive CH-53E Super Stallion helicopters pluck the artillery
pieces—one per helicopter—from the desert, either to carry back to a
ship or to move to another part of the fight.

With the combined-arms training complete, 2/3 traveled four hundred miles north to the Mountain Warfare Training Center, their last—
and arguably most important—predeployment destination before heading
to Afghanistan. Initially established in 1951 in the wake of the Frozen
Chosin campaign to train Marines for cold-weather combat and survival,
the Mountain Warfare Training Center today is one of the most important in the Department of Defense because of the ongoing war in Afghanistan. While at the MWTC, the Marines of 2/3 undertook training in
cold-weather survival, mountain mobility, steep-earth climbing, high-
angle sniper training, even mule packing—and like their combat training
at Twentynine Palms, their mountain workup had them immersed in the
harsh realities of their environment and tasks. At an adjunct training area
in the mountains outside of Hawthorne, Nevada—peaks that bear stark
physiographic and meteorological resemblance to those of eastern
Afghanistan—the Marines of the battalion learned firsthand just how
difficult moving from one mountainous point to another—even just a
kilometer distant—can be, burdened with heavy body armor and under
the press of a multiday combat load. Navy Corpsmen kept busy with
hypothermia victims at night and heat-exhaustion and dehydration during the day, not to mention twisted and sprained ankles.

The final exercise at the center had Marines undertake a five-day
field operation that culminated in their meeting with "village elders"
played by local role-players in a mock Afghan village erected by MWTC
personnel. Instructed by Marines of the training center who had recent
Afghan experience under their belts, the role-players gave many in the
battalion their first direct taste of the subtleties and frustrations of
counterinsurgency work in an austere land. Marines struggled to communicate with the "elders" using their issued language cards and Dari
and Pashto phrases they'd already memorized. Then they struggled
even harder to get simple answers to what they felt to be the most basic

of questions. "How many people live here?" "Where is the nearest village beyond this one?" Stymied throughout all their attempts, the Marines quickly realized that gaining the trust of the locals—a cornerstone of the COIN fight—would be far easier said than done.

As the Marines of the battalion finished their training and looked ahead to the real deal, Rob Scott, Tom Wood, and Scott Westerfield pondered the months ahead and the list of hurdles the battalion would face. They'd undoubtedly be difficult times, not just because of the brutal terrain and deadly enemy, but also for the challenges posed to them by rolling into a combat command structure where they would not be fighting as a component of a MAGTF, but as part of a "combined joint task force." The Marines' MAGTF/combined-arms training had them prepared for the most complex and dynamic of combat situations, but while in Afghanistan, they wouldn't have access to Marine aviation assets or to Marine artillery—and they'd be answering to the Army as their higher. They'd be fighting in an area where a slew of other services' units—American, Afghan, and European—would be undertaking missions as well. Further complicating matters, MacMannis would be leaving Afghanistan after just one month as part of a scheduled change of command where he'd pass the battalion to Lieutenant Colonel Jim Donnellan, who would be literally thrust not just into the Afghan fight (without having trained with 2/3), but into the position of commanding Marines already deep in the throes of war.

2/3's first combat deployment since Vietnam would be far more complex and gut-wrenchingly difficult than any in the battalion could imagine. But the dividends yielded from their work would be far greater than any of them could have dreamed.

3

SYNERGY OF
SUCCESS

As 2/3 battled notional enemies on training grounds in Hawaii, Nevada, and California, 3/3 fought a multifaceted counterinsurgency campaign deep in the Hindu Kush that yielded strengthened regional stability and a beaten-down enemy, forging a broad operational pathway for 2/3's upcoming deployment. Commanded by Lieutenant Colonel Norman Cooling—who would subsequently lead his battalion in yet another successful COIN fight in Iraq's Al Anbar province just nine months after returning from Afghanistan—3/3 stormed after Islamic extremists throughout the hinterlands of eastern Afghanistan and built networks of long-term security and trust between the isolated region's people and the nascent Afghan government, one of the cardinal objectives of Operation Enduring Freedom.

3/3's victories didn't come easy, though. The battalion had been assigned an area of operation roughly the size of South Carolina that consisted of six contiguous provinces: Laghman, Nangarhar, Khowst,

Paktia, Logar, and Kunar. And they'd arrived just in time to face the brunt of one of the harshest winters in those provinces' recent history, with temperatures crashing below minus-twenty degrees Fahrenheit at high-altitude locations like Gardez and crushing snowfall that icy gales caused to drift to more than ten feet in depth in some places. Yet the battalion, fully prepared for the conditions as a result of their focused and rigorous predeployment training at Twentynine Palms and the Mountain Warfare Training Center, kept a hard-charging operational pace, always maintaining at least one platoon of Marines outside the wire at each of 3/3's forward operating bases at all times, as well as kicking off one battalion-scale operation per month. And while the Marines of 3/3 consistently attained their mission goals throughout their deployment, they achieved them not by working within their MAGTF structure, but as a component of a larger "joint task force," an environment built of multiple command layers where other U.S. military units could operate simultaneously in 3/3's area—some of them with entirely different command rules than those to which 3/3 adhered.

While the concept of unifying all components of a military campaign under one distinct commander has been one the USMC has embraced and forged doctrine around since the birth of the Marine Corps, a codified framework for all U.S. services working with one another—*jointly*—emerged only recently with the Goldwater-Nichols Department of Defense Reorganization Act of 1986. Prior to the Goldwater-Nichols Act, military command flowed from the upper echelon of each service branch—the Army, the Navy, the Air Force, and the Marine Corps—down to the individual unit level of a respective branch for operations. But interservice rivalries, often ego-driven and funding-oriented, sometimes led to virtual paralysis at the operational level, ultimately yielding tactical inefficacy and sometimes injury and even death. The act, which keeps the responsibility for training and equipping personnel of each branch in the hands of the service chiefs, established geographically defined "unified combatant commands" (Central Command, European Command, Southern Command, etc.), each composed of personnel from all of the armed services. In this construct, a Marine unit may work for an Army commander or an Air Force unit may work for a Marine Corps commander within a combatant command. The act also removed direct war-fighting authority from the Joint Chiefs of Staff, to mitigate the chances of feuding among the individual services over command authority of a campaign or region. The Joint Chiefs of Staff serve as strategic advisers to the president, while the unified combatant commanders execute command and control for specific operations. In the case of Operation Enduring Freedom, when 3/3 arrived, command flowed directly from the president, through the secretary of defense, to Central Command (CENTCOM), to the Afghan theater-wide umbrella command: Combined Forces Command-Afghanistan (CFC-A), which was chiefed by U.S. Army Lieutenant General David Barno. Authority flowed to 3/3 from CFC-A through Combined Joint Task Force 76, a U.S. Army–led coalition responsible for not all—but virtually all—military operations in Afghanistan. The Twenty-fifth Infantry Division, commanded by Major General Eric Olson, formed the core of CJTF-76. The command path to 3/3 then channeled through Combined Task Force Thunder, commanded by U.S. Army Colonel Gary Cheek of the 25th Infantry Division—Cooling's direct boss while in-country. Task Force Thunder controlled military operations in Afghanistan's eastern reaches: fourteen contiguous provinces known as Regional Command East (RC-East), including, of course, the six provinces assigned to 3/3, which were designated as "Tactical Area of Responsibility Trinity," but also referenced simply as Area of Operation Trinity, or AO Trinity.

While limited in terms of supporting assets, including aviation and logistics, and although his battalion was spread thinly across six provinces, Cooling and his staff succeeded in maximizing his Marines' capabilities in the difficult COIN fight, in great measure due to the relationship Cooling forged with Colonel Cheek. Both are war fighters down to their bone marrow, and Cheek understood how Marines fight—in the COIN realm as well as in the hard kinetic fight. Cheek also understood the Marine Corps' elegantly unfettered command structure and the powerful synergy of the MAGTF, not to mention the famous USMC ethos. Furthermore, while each hailed from different service branches, the two shared one very, *very* important thread: each understood the critical importance of gaining and maintaining the support of the indigenous population as a conduit to gaining the intelligence needed to root out insurgents. They recognized that, although kinetic operations were necessary to destroy terrorists and insurgent leaders, those operations would be self-defeating if they were conducted indiscriminately, without regard for their impact on the average Afghan citizen. However, while RC-East fell under the command of Cheek's Task Force Thunder, special operations forces—*non*-conventional units—also undertook missions in the same geographic area. However, not only did they not fall under Cheek's or Cooling's commands, special operations forces—"SOF"—could conduct missions without apprising either commander of mission details. In fact, SOF units, whose priority mission was counterterrorism and not counterinsurgency and whose preferred method was the direct-action raid, could actually initiate operations anywhere in the AO without informing either Cooling or Cheek that they would be there at all. This difference in priorities and approach posed an immense challenge not only to unity of command, but to the greater, theater-wide unity of effort.

Military units trained for highly specialized, focused applications such as deep reconnaissance, targeted kill-capture missions, and sabotage (among many other nonconventional roles) trace their roots into the furthest recesses of warfare's history. Throughout time, a combatant's "main effort" has often required specialized augmentation forces to help pivot the odds of a campaign's success toward that combatant's favor. Modern U.S. military units trained for special purposes first saw action in World War II; the U.S. Army Rangers and the U.S. Navy's Underwater Demolition Teams played vital roles in the greater war effort's ultimate victory. Initially established in 1952 as part of the U.S. Army's Psychological Warfare Division, the fabled Green Berets, aka Special Forces (the name Special Forces, which refers solely to the Army's Green Berets, is often incorrectly used as a substitute for the broader general term *special operations forces*) worked closely with Vietnamese fighters aligned with U.S. interests to aid America in the Vietnam War effort, with the ultimate goal of those native forces becoming completely self-sustaining. Green Berets, working in small units, embodied the concept of "economy of force" as they stood up fully capable South Vietnamese military units, obviating the need for larger infusions of conventional U.S. military forces. But the nonconventional mission of greatest consequence for modern U.S. special operations units—with massive ramifications for conventional forces as well—didn't culminate in victory, but fiery disaster.

Having transformed Iran into a "populist theocratic republic" after ousting the pro-U.S. Shah Mohammed Reza Pahlavi, a cadre of fundamentalist Shiite Muslim clerics headed by Ayatollah Ruhollah Khomeini fomented a mob of restive youths into attacking American interests in their country in late 1979. Angry that U.S. President Carter allowed the exiled shah to be treated for his advanced lymphatic cancer at a clinic in New York City, the mob—who called themselves the Imam's Disciples—stormed the U.S. embassy and the Iranian Foreign Ministry in Tehran in early November of 1979, taking sixty-six American workers hostage—and refused their handover until the shah returned to Iran to face a trial. In early April of 1980, after months of feckless diplomatic negotiation attempts, the Pentagon put a small, newly formed counterterrorism unit on alert, the First Special Forces Operational Detachment-Delta, led by U.S. Army Colonel Charles Beckwith, who developed the unit from a concept to an operational force. The soldiers of what would come to be popularly known as "Delta Force" prepared to embark on a complex hostage-extraction mission they'd been rehearsing and rerehearsing for months, Operation *Eagle Claw*.

As the last wedge of twilight succumbed to pitch darkness above the Middle Eastern country of Oman on 24 April 1980, six U.S. Air Force C-130 Hercules cargo aircraft roared into the sky off the island of Masirah. The aircraft carried 132 personnel (Beckwith and his force, Army Rangers, and support crew), food, water, weapons, and huge rubber bladders filled with jet fuel. Shortly after the Hercules took to the sky, eight U.S. Navy RH-53D Sea Stallion helicopters lifted off the deck of the nuclear-powered carrier USS *Nimitz* in the Gulf of Oman. Both the Hercules and the Sea Stallion groups were destined for a secret rendezvous/refueling point in Iran's Dasht-e-Kavir Desert code-named Desert One.

But equipment malfunctions exacerbated by a type of atmospheric phenomenon known as a *haboob,* where fine, talcumlike dust rises thousands of feet above the desert, led Beckwith to abort the mission, as these failures rendered three of the original eight helicopters mission-incapable. Upon maneuvering his Sea Stallion to return to the *Nimitz* after refueling at Desert One, one of the helicopter pilots became disoriented in a plume of rotor-wash-blasted sand and dust, and careened into an idling C-130, killing eight servicemen as the two aircraft erupted in flames. The unsuccessful mission, which Beckwith had hoped would be one of the most spectacular in the history of combat, instantly vaulted to the fore of the world's greatest military disasters.

During the ensuing investigation—as America viewed images of the thinning, blindfolded hostages on their televisions—a number of factors emerged that, in aggregate, seem to have portended doom for the operation long before the aircraft launched into the Middle Eastern night. Chief among these factors was that while all four branches of the military were involved, there was virtually no integration either for training or for command chains—straining, if not breaking, the bond of unity of effort and unity of command that was absolutely vital for the mission's success. Miscommunication throughout the entire mission also played a role in defeat: while meteorologists tasked with helping plan the mission were fully aware of the possibility of *haboobs*—they are common in the region in the spring, forming as a result of updrafts from lines of thunderstorms—they were not allowed to warn either the C-130 pilots or the helicopter pilots, who were shocked and mystified to come across (and barrel through) two of the strange, dark, and disorienting "curtains" during the mission. And no central combat operations center—a node vital for maintaining command and control throughout a mission—was designated for the mission itself, leaving the helicopter pilots unaware of the operation's status as they tried to locate Beckwith while on the ground at Desert One. Furthermore, the

Navy RH-53Ds hadn't been thoroughly checked for maintenance issues before being handed over to the U.S. Marine Corps pilots who would fly them. From a wide-field perspective, the investigators could see that each piece of the greater "operational machine," while individually capable, wasn't integrated so that the machine could function—at all.

While the Goldwater-Nichols Act radically changed the organization of the Defense Department's conventional forces, Congress—reeling from the Operation *Eagle Claw* disaster and a SOF-conventional-forces communications-equipment integration debacle during Operation *Urgent Fury* in Grenada in 1983—added a provision to the Goldwater-Nichols Act that would, for the first time, codify a framework for all U.S. nonconventional units. And so, on 13 April 1987, President Reagan signed into law the Nunn-Cohen Amendment to the Goldwater-Nichols Act. Three days later, the Department of Defense activated the United States Special Operations Command. USSOCOM, a body that many consider to be the fifth branch of the military, was born.

A wide variety of specialized units fall under the authority of Special Operations Command, from special operations weather teams—who help other SOCOM units plan, prepare, and augment missions—to Air Force Combat Controllers, to Green Berets, to Navy SEALs, and a multitude of others. Prior to the Goldwater-Nichols Act and the establishment of USSOCOM, nonconventional units often felt themselves cast as the "redheaded stepchildren" of a particular service, having to plead for training and operations funds while their conventional-service counterparts enjoyed a relative bounty of military procurement. With the Nunn-Cohen Amendment, SOF units receive their own, distinct funds for equipment and training as well as for actual operations. The amendment also calls for individual SOF units to train with one another—Army Green Berets with Navy SEAL teams with Air Force Combat Controllers, etc. While Beckwith's soldiers had thoroughly rehearsed their portion of Operation *Eagle Claw,* had they been working under a command like SOCOM, in addition to the other benefits afforded by such an organization, all of the mission's elements would have been able to train and rehearse together, likely preventing the disastrous outcome at Desert One.

The capabilities that Special Operations Command units bring to a fight span a broad range of mission types, from foreign internal defense, or FID, which the Green Berets mastered in Vietnam with their work with local fighters, to direct-action "hard hit" teams, to counterterrorism groups, and many, many more. All four conventional branches of the U.S. military provide personnel for SOCOM units (the Marine Corps was the last to join SOCOM with their MARSOC units), and once with a SOCOM unit, troops fall under an entirely new command structure. And unlike the Army, Air Force, Navy, and the Marine Corps, SOCOM not only controls training and equipping of individual units, by doctrine they also control units operationally (although they can be temporarily tasked to fall under the command of a division-level conventional command, such as Combined Joint Task Force 76), creating an environment where SOF units and conventional forces can either work in a synergistic union or render each other's efforts counterproductive.

Because of the nature of the fight in the earliest days of Operation Enduring Freedom—where the first and foremost goal was the toppling of the Taliban regime—Secretary of Defense Donald Rumsfeld felt that Special Operations Command units, particularly the Army's Special Forces with their global orientation and years of foreign internal defense work and capability to topple an "asymmetric" and elusive enemy, best fit the bill to lead the charge. Hence his ultimate designation of SOCOM as the main effort of the war, meaning that SOF units would be supported by conventional forces (Operation Enduring Freedom marked the first time in American military history when SOF had been tasked as the lead, *supported* element in a large-scale campaign). But special operations forces are just that—*special,* units extremely capable at highly focused mission spectra. After the incredible work that the SOF teams completed in early OEF—linking up with the Northern Alliance, going far, far downrange virtually unsupported, ground-directing precision interdiction strikes from F-15s, B-52s, B-1s, and other platforms, and facing side by side with their Northern Alliance allies often overwhelming forces of Taliban—the fight evolved into one of stabilization and nation building, which requires long-term conventional-force commitment versus short-term get-in-get-out roles that SOF teams often perform. And as the conflict would reveal, this long-term military commitment would be one of a counterinsurgency nature, necessitating that American forces work closely with locals to pull the rug of support out from under terrorists and other destabilizing elements in addition to kinetically engaging those inimical groups.

During 3/3's predeployment workup, Cooling studied not only the enemy and their tactics, but the complex command structure in which he and his battalion would fight. With an eye for ensuring that the toils of his Marines would have lasting effects on the overall mission, the battalion commander and his staff focused on the myriad SOF command lines driving into AO Trinity, forming not a single chain of command, but one best described as a complex web of invisible strands. The SOF teams used most frequently would be those tasked directly by Major General Olson, the commander of CJTF-76, through a unit called Combined Joint Special Operations Task Force-Afghanistan, or CJSOTF-A. The ground units under the command of CJSOTF-A were mostly Special Forces, broken into groups called Operational Detachments, either company-size Operational Detachment Bravos (ODBs), or the smaller, team-size Operational Detachment Alphas (ODAs). The ODAs and ODBs primarily worked FID missions with an emphasis on border security along a corridor called Joint Special Operations Area (JSOA) "Oklahoma," which ran along the frontier with Pakistan and "on top of" the eastern edge of AO Trinity. But other teams could be sent in by levels even higher than CJSOTF-A—directly from a SOF command working in concert with CENTCOM (a unit called SOC-CENT). Additionally, SOCOM itself could insert teams, ordering units to hit the ground in Afghanistan from SOCOM's command center at MacDill Air Force Base in Tampa, Florida. And beyond that, supposedly, are the so-called Tier-1 SOF teams, whom the president or the secretary of defense can activate directly, for those missions deemed to be of the highest national priority (such as acting on time-critical intelligence indicating the location of Osama bin Laden).

Cooling and his staff, upon studying the after-action reports of the Third Battalion of the Sixth Marine regiment (whom 3/3 was replacing in their November 2004 Afghan deployment) as well as their on-the-ground experience once in-country, realized that one of their greatest operational hurdles would be maintaining an ever-productive relationship with locals in areas where SOF conducted direct-action raids. The Marines of 3/3 worked day and night to establish and strengthen ties with the Afghan people as soon as they hit the ground in AO Trinity, developing strong bonds over weeks and months that led to multisource human intelligence. This "HUMINT" led to scores of weapons-cache discoveries and the identification of enemy hideouts. Just as important—*more* important in the minds of many—3/3's COIN campaign fostered bonds of trust and friendship between the Marines and the locals, helping to legitimize the national government in the minds of Afghans living in some of the farthest recesses of the Hindu Kush.

But a one-hour direct-action raid by a SOF team that captured or killed the wrong—i.e. *innocent*—target and left piles of smoldering collateral damage in the form of dead livestock and destroyed homes would undermine—even destroy—the benefits of months of 3/3's work with locals. Cooling noted during his research that some of the SOF hits relied on what he and his staff considered to be questionable intel gleaned not from numerous counterbalanced and cross-referenced sources (as Cooling mandated before his Marines conducted any kinetic operation), but from single individuals, whom some SOF teams "ran" through monetary payouts and used repeatedly without cross-checking their statements. Furthermore, these units weren't required to share intel with either Cooling or Cheek preoperation, often assuming the posture that their missions were of such a degree of importance and specialty that disclosing their information with a conventional unit might compromise them—as they felt that conventional forces couldn't maintain operational security to a high enough degree to be entrusted with such intel. And by USSOCOM doctrine, these teams didn't have to share intel anyway—even if a compelling reason surfaced, such as the need to compare their information with that of the Marines for accuracy to ensure that an intended target really was who they thought he was, and not an innocent noncombatant—allowing the individual who should have been the target to slip into the night as he heard the raid going down a few houses down from his location. Cooling knew that relying on single-element or even a small number of HUMINT sources risks a unit being led astray by the personal grudges a source may harbor against another villager, or just plain financial greed.

While the vast majority of the SOF units operating in RC-East worked with exceptional professionalism, Cooling knew that at any moment—and without notice—a misdirected hard-hit raid might go down and ruin weeks or even months of COIN work of untold value. But he also knew of the doctrinal brick wall he and his staff faced: SO-COM could have units undertake missions whenever they wanted, wherever they wanted, and however they wanted, with or without informing 3/3 or Task Force Thunder; and in theory, even without informing CFC-A Command, which ran the entire Afghan Theater. Frustrated by the nonintegration of SOF with conventional forces, and by the extreme difficulty—sometimes impossibility due to unannounced operations—of simply deconflicting a conventional unit's plans with those of SOF units, Cooling and his staff brainstormed avenues to partially integrate and to fully deconflict operations so that both his battalion and any SOF team undertaking simultaneous missions in a given area not only wouldn't interdict each other, but would actually aid each other, fostering a synergy of mutual effort. Cooling viewed SOF teams as uniquely capable and ultraspecialized but absolutely vital entities in the larger war-fighting machine—much like an AH-1W Super Cobra, an artillery battery, or a Marine scout/sniper team, any of which he could directly control as part of a MAGTF. But by doctrine he couldn't control a SOF team—directly. So the hard-charging Texan, who'd graduated near the top of his class at the U.S. Naval Academy, worked with his staff to create his own way to utilize special operations forces—for the benefit not of just his battalion or those SOF teams with which 3/3 would work, but for the entire war effort in AO Trinity.

Cooling, however, didn't want to control the SOF units; he just wanted to ensure that his battalion's COIN efforts wouldn't be under-mined. So he and his operations officer, Major Drew Priddy (also a Naval Academy graduate), developed their own operational model, not one where missions would be planned to "employ" SOF under 3/3's command, or for special operations teams to take the lead over the bat-talion's Marines, but one where SOF and 3/3 would work as equal players for the benefit of the overall operation—each, in essence, would work for the operation. The two most salient issues Cooling and Priddy faced in developing operations of this novel style were command and control, and intel—called C2I. The two officers wanted to be able to craft missions that adhered fully with the concept of unity of effort, and as much as possible with unity of command, and also to share intelli-gence with SOF teams in order to determine which targets had the highest probability of being actual "bad guys" and which ones might have been incorrectly identified. But while the concept seemed to them to be an effective work-around to the situation in AO Trinity, they'd have to get "buy-in" from the teams themselves as well as the nod from Major General Olson. So Cooling went to Colonel Cheek and then to CJTF-76 headquarters at Bagram Airfield, and Priddy arranged face-to-face meetings with members of the ODAs and ODBs, Navy SEALs, and a group of Army Rangers—Task Force Red—at 3/3's headquarters at Jalalabad Airfield.

Priddy received warm responses from Special Forces and the Navy SEALs, who fell under the command of CJSOTF-A. Task Force Red also found the new operational model agreeable, but the Rangers worked directly for SOCOM and had no official area of operation—they went anywhere SOCOM directed them, so working with them on such missions would prove more difficult. Cooling had success as well—with Cheek, a vociferous advocate for Cooling and Priddy's plan, and with Major General Olson, who immediately embraced the model. The ops began . . . sharp, well-vetted intel rolled in, 3/3 and SOF units weeded out bad guys, and the Marines' COIN campaign flourished. The battalion primarily worked with Special Forces and Navy SEALs, who found the model to work as a powerful "force multiplier," enabling them to achieve far more than they could have achieved if working alone. Cooling and Priddy had effectively adapted the essence of a MAGTF and applied it to build a conventional-forces-SOF team. During the planning stages of each operation, SOF and 3/3 would pore over each other's intel, develop a general "scheme of maneuver," and then execute. Because they'd incorporated SOF into their operations, Cooling and Priddy elevated the saliency of their missions, grabbing the attention of Olson, which paid the dividend of gaining 3/3 access to scarce aviation assets, essentially placing the *A* back into the "MAGTF" the Marines emulated in-country. So in addition to balancing SOF intel with theirs to ensure that the direct-action raids were limited, contained, and mitigated collateral damage, the battalion gained additional resources to which they would not otherwise have had access, helping them to operate more or less as a MAGTF.

Typically, SOF would undertake the first phases of an operation as 3/3 supported them by cordoning off a village while a direct-action team took down a target. Once SOF's part of the mission was complete, they'd "exfil" (typically by helicopter), and 3/3's Marines would conduct a Medical Capabilities mission (a MEDCAP), where medical supplies and health care would be doled out; during one operation, 3/3 aided over five hundred villagers in a remote part of AO Trinity with everything from simple bandages to inoculations, to casting broken limbs, to enabling locals to better care for themselves by stocking basic medicinal aids and information on how to use those aids. The Marines would then continue to maintain security in a region and undertake various humanitarian assistance missions, typically handing out school and other supplies. 3/3's operations typically spanned a week or more in duration, with the "kinetic" portion lasting just the first few hours.

Myriad noncombat-oriented agencies formed integral components in 3/3's greater COIN efforts in Afghanistan. Chief among these were the PRTs, or Provincial Reconstruction Teams. Tasked with digging clean wells, building roads, schools, and mosques, and helping to maintain other vital infrastructure in the tiny villages throughout AO Trinity, 3/3 employed the PRTs as one of their most effective and long-term

COIN "weapons." During an operation, Marines would list the needs of a village, pass that information to one of the PRTs, and within weeks, the lives of the villagers would improve. 3/3's leadership would also meet regularly with other agencies, both of the Afghan and U.S. governments, and nongovernmental organizations like the Red Cross and others associated with United Nations relief workers and U.S. AID.

The Cooling-Priddy operational model reached its zenith of success in early February of 2005 with Operation *Spurs*. Named in honor of the San Antonio Spurs basketball team (3/3 used sports-team names—primarily Texas basketball teams—for their major operations during their deployment), *Spurs* had Marines of India and Lima companies driving into the heart of the vicious Korangal Valley. Inserting by day via U.S. Army CH-47s, the grunts cordoned off target zones while U.S. Navy SEALs captured a number of known and suspected Islamic fundamentalist combatants. The operation culminated in a number of meetings with village elders (called *shura* meetings), and then a MED-CAP. 3/3 Marines maintained a presence in the Korangal for weeks after *Spurs*, continuing to pressure one particular individual who had proved to be cunningly elusive both to 3/3 and to the SOF teams who were there before 3/3's arrival in Afghanistan. This individual was a man named Najmudeen.

A known militant who based his efforts out of the Korangal Valley, Najmudeen held the distinction of having his name on a list of the most wanted Islamic extremist fighters not just in AO Trinity, or in RC-East, but in all of Afghanistan. SOF had been trying for over eighteen months to catch him through a number of failed direct-action operations. Cooling and Priddy soon reasoned that the best way to take him was not through quick hard-hit raids, but through a consistent campaign of pressure, forcing him over time to come forward. SOF commanders scoffed at this plan; they believed that Najmudeen could only be killed or captured, and that the militant would never surrender or pledge allegiance to the new government of Afghanistan. But in early April, CJ-SOTF-A Command jaws hit the floor when they learned the news that near the town of Nangalam, deep in the Pech River Valley, Najmudeen met Captain Jim Sweeney, India Company commander, halfway across a bridge, stating to Jim, "Welcome, my friend." The battalion's continuous platoon-level presence in the Korangal Valley over the course of three harsh winter months—an uncomfortably austere, drawn-out, and downright unglamorous mission (particularly when compared to SOF direct-action raids)—had forced Najmudeen to live in a series of small caves, where he fell gravely ill and lost all options but surrender. Weeks of subsequent debriefing yielded reams of actionable intelligence from the former militant, intel vital for future operations—including those 2/3 would undertake within a matter of weeks.

In late March, after 3/3's operational ingenuity had led to success and subsequent COIN progress, members of 2/3's predeployment site survey arrived, including Colonel MacMannis, Tom Wood, and Scott Westerfield. As Westerfield dug into the intelligence-gathering side of things and Wood worked with Priddy to gain a full understanding of the way 3/3 developed joint operations with SOF, MacMannis realized that while there would be a change of battalions, the operational tempo must remain consistent. As soon as 2/3's main element arrived in early June, they would prepare to launch a battalion-size operation against the greatest remaining threat in the region. And Scott Westerfield would spend the following months identifying that threat.

3/3 had achieved success not just through operational ingenuity, but through consistency—keeping the pressure on the bad guys even through the dead of winter. Because it was now primarily a COIN fight, MacMannis felt it was far better to continue to coerce the enemy out of the hills and onto the government of Afghanistan's side than to take them on kinetically. But with the spring thaw coming, the enemy was undoubtedly going to force the Marines to put rounds downrange, and with the operational model set forth by 3/3, the Island Warriors would have a full spectrum of opportunities open to them to win the fight.

4

INTO THE
HINDU KUSH

Marking the final stretch of their Afghan tour with yet two more successful battalion-level operations in the wake of *Spurs,* 3/3 maintained its vigorous tempo straight through to the bitter end of their OEF deployment. But while the battalion's pace and outlook remained rock solid, the command structure under which the Marines of 3/3 stood in Afghanistan changed just weeks before 2/3 rolled in to replace them—and changed in a way that would dramatically affect the operational construct that Cooling and Priddy had developed and that 2/3 looked to adopt. New commanders replaced not one or two, but all three levels of command above 3/3 in Afghanistan, with Lieutenant General Karl Eikenberry taking the reins of CFC-A from David Barno, Major General Jason Kamiya taking over CJTF-76 from Olson, and just two weeks before 3/3 officially handed over authority to 2/3, Colonel Patrick Donahue of the 82nd Airborne (known in-country as Task Force Devil) assuming command of RC-East from Gary Cheek.

And while Donahue and his staff would ensure a smooth transition for 2/3, working to provide all types of support from intel, to aviation, to artillery for the Marines for both their COIN campaign as well as kinetic ops, Major General Kamiya, after assuming command of CJTF-76 in mid-March, seemed to favor an operational balance weighed less heavily on the counterinsurgency fight and more on aggressive counterterror missions. Further influencing the way 3/3 (and soon thereafter 2/3) would be able to plan and undertake operations, a new CJSOTF-A commander took over—one who sought strict adherence to USSOCOM doctrine—doctrine stating that SOF teams could operate with complete independence of conventional forces—and never "for" them (or their operations)—although SOF could be supported by conventional units. And while Olson had praised the operational model in which 3/3 and SOF worked together—and the SOF units themselves found the arrangement to work excellently for them—Kamiya seemed to agree with the new CJSOTF-A commander. Furthermore, and of equal significance, Kamiya sought a greater focus on the Tora Bora region (roughly seventy miles to the southwest of the Pech and Korangal Valley areas), where he felt that forces under his control should pursue direct-action counterterror campaigns, necessitating that 3/3 Marines reduce their presence in the Korangal in order to push into the Tora Boras—at the likely cost of allowing extremist forces to more aggressively move into and around the important corner of the Hindu Kush, virtually assuring a retrogression of the stability 3/3 had worked so hard to achieve in that area.

In mid-March, 3/3 kicked off Operation *Mavericks,* which the battalion planned and executed as an analogue of *Spurs.* Utilizing Navy SEALs, the Marines focused on villages in northern Laghman province, destroying an extensive al-Qaeda cave network, capturing eighteen suspected insurgents and terrorists, and undertaking extensive humanitarian relief efforts to help locals during a spate of devastating floods. *Mavericks* once again proved that operations planned with careful, detailed SOF-conventional-forces integration could yield outcomes often greater than the sum of the participating units' capabilities. Operation *Celtics* followed in May, its latter phases focusing Marines on the Tora

Bora region—as Kamiya had ordered. But no targets could be found—and no confirmed target list had been passed to 3/3 from their higher command levels. Meanwhile, enemy activity in the Korangal Valley steadily burgeoned as the Marines reduced their presence there to support *Celtics* and winter gave way to summer.

And while 3/3 continued their run of successes throughout the spring of 2005—killing, capturing, and forcing the surrender of numerous insurgent leaders and their henchmen—other, lower-level operators who aspired to regional and global Islamic extremist notoriety sought to fill the voids. Mortar, rocket, and IED attacks (most inaccurate and ineffective, but menacing nonetheless) grew in frequency in the spring throughout the Pech Valley region, undertaken by a few of what intel revealed to be small-time operators based out of the Korangal Valley area. Having been apprised by 3/3's intel officer of a series of target individuals through both HUMINT and signals intelligence (SIGINT), Drew Priddy set out to develop another operation of the *Spurs* model in which 3/3 would work with Navy SOF to capture or kill the insurgents responsible for the recent "spring thaw" attacks and henceforth work to further stabilize the Korangal, the hypocenter of insurgent and terrorist activity in the Kunar province.

In developing the mission's foundation, Priddy contacted Navy SOF (NAVSOF), known in RC-East as Task Force Blue, aka the SEALs and their direct, organic support—in this case members of SEAL Team 10 and their attached units. With the successes 3/3 had attained by working with NAVSOF in *Spurs* and *Mavericks* in mind, Priddy felt confident that he and TF Blue's chief planner could formulate an op that would clear the Korangal of the identified targets and stabilize the region with Marine presence, interdicting other budding extremist elements from establishing new toeholds there. Priddy's Task Force Blue equivalent, Lieutenant Commander Erik Kristensen—who hadn't yet worked with Priddy but who coincidentally graduated with him in the same Naval Academy class in 1995—seized the opportunity to work with 3/3, and he and Priddy, communicating by phone and secure e-mail, immediately began to build a 'shell' of an operation that at that point

had the tentative working name of *Stars*, after the Dallas Stars professional hockey team. The two planned *Stars* in the same vein as *Spurs*
and *Mavericks*: share intel, vet a specific target list, kick off with NAV-
SOF "shaping" the objective through reconnaissance and surveillance;
then, as Marines conduct a wide cordon of the area of interest, a SEAL
direct-action team takes down those targets that NAVSOF has positively identified in the first phase of the mission. NAVSOF then exfils,
and Marines continue "presence operations," undertaking humanitarian assistance and MEDCAP missions.

On 14 May, 2/3's advanced echelon (ADVON) arrived in Afghanistan; one hundred strong, the ADVON preceded the arrival of the battalion's main element by just a few weeks. And as the newly on-deck
Marines jumped into the faraway world of eastern Afghanistan, Cooling, MacMannis, and Donahue agreed that having Marines of 2/3 par-
ticipate in *Stars* would help transition them from training to real-world
combat operations in one clean sweep—and keep with MacMannis'
desire to maintain a consistent op tempo for the region during the turnover period. Furthermore, the Marines knew that during the spring
thaw, fresh fighters would begin flowing into the region from Pakistan
through the porous border, necessitating an even more vigilant presence. They would unleash *Stars* in early June of 2005, just as the main
element of 2/3 would begin rolling into Afghanistan.

But in late May, the ongoing intel feed that drove the *Stars* concept
and defined its specifics fell off the map—just disappeared. "The ISR [in-
telligence, surveillance, and reconnaissance] in the Korangal is just un-
matched, just amazing," Drew Priddy told Tom Wood shortly after
Wood's arrival. "As soon as a single Marine enters the valley—or even
passes by its mouth—every bad guy knows what's going on, all the way
up to the highest reaches of the Korangal. And then they just scatter, just
vanish, probably back into Pakistan—and the intel hits die." Tom quickly
grasped the operational situation in the region once he was in-country,
being thoroughly briefed by Priddy on the most effective methods of developing missions. *Stars* was out as a formal operation, but the quick-
thinking and determined operations officer resolved to formulate a new

mission—2/3's first battalion-level op—that would use the *Stars* shell as a foundation. The battalion just needed specific intel on the whos, the wheres, and the whens to snap the plan into shape and merge the Marines of 2/3 into the fluid, uninterrupted op cycle Cooling and 3/3 had established and that MacMannis looked to have 2/3 seamlessly maintain.

That job fell squarely on Westerfield's shoulders. Having absorbed the intel that 3/3 had been feeding him in the months prior to 2/3's arrival, the boyishly enthusiastic intel officer knew that determining even the most basic targeting attribute—the *who*—had proven to be more complex than any that the United States had ever faced. The enemy throughout Afghanistan—in particular in the Pech, Korangal, and surrounding valleys—couldn't be defined in monolithic terms like the Nazis, or the Imperial Japanese, or even Saddam Hussein's forces. Westerfield knew the enemy of the region not as broad-based and cohesive, but as an amorphous patchwork of "bad guys"—leftover Taliban, Taliban aspirants, al-Qaeda foreign fighters, a multitude of flavors of independent Islamic extremists (primarily foreign, but some domestic), and even some semiorganized criminals. All, however, shared two common threads: pursuit of regional instability for their own gain, and extremist Islamic beliefs—beliefs, Westerfield understood, that the bad guys could use to manipulate the deeply pious local populace in such places as the Korangal, coercing villagers to join their ranks, or at the very least, provide a base of support for their insurgent and terrorist efforts. But to know this enemy required that Westerfield not just glean everything relevant from classified intel reports, but *see* that intel through the lens of Afghanistan's history, in particular, through those historical elements most relevant to 2/3's fight: the Soviet-Afghan War and its aftermath, which shaped contemporary Afghanistan and the enemy that American forces would face head-on during the invasion of 2001 and subsequent years.

Destitute, depopulated in many places—crushed throughout—Afghanistan could hardly be called a country by the time the last Soviet military convoy rumbled across the Amu Darya. The greatest losers of the war, of course, weren't the Soviets, but the Afghan people, many of whom weren't even living in Afghanistan anymore, but in squalid refugee camps in Pakistan and Iran. Afghanistan's mosaic of humanity had been shattered, not just by the inhumane Soviets, but after the war by those factions that had beaten the Russian Bear into retreat. Evermore-extreme waves of influence ebbed, flowed, and sometimes crashed upon the region as the country spiraled into civil war—and Westerfield knew that these external forces influenced the Kunar perhaps more than any other part of Afghanistan, because of the province's location along the Pakistani border near Peshawar—an influence that sustained the insurgent stronghold of the Korangal and surrounding valleys that the Marines faced.

The ISI had waged a masterpiece of a shadow war in the 1980s, coordinating the seven mujahideen parties to achieve the strategic short-term aims of Pakistan, the Saudi Arabian government, and the United States without allowing restive party leaders and their power-hungry commanders on the ground to tear at one another's throat (not too much, at least). But as tight a lasso as the ISI held around the mujahideen, the Pakistanis didn't command a total monopoly on the anti-Soviet efforts in Afghanistan. "Freelancers," hailing primarily from Saudi Arabia, but also from Kuwait and other Arab states, set up shop in Peshawar, looking to influence the region through an array of mechanisms, from recruiting mujahideen aspirants and training them to fight the Red Bear, to funding hard-line Salafist madrassas. Well financed, either by their families or by benefactors in their home countries, those at the helms of these groups commanded small numbers of foot soldiers, many of whom had been prisoners in places like Egypt and Saudi Arabia and were conveniently released early to fight (and die) for the jihad in Afghanistan—a place about which many of these ex-prisoners and general miscreants knew nothing, even its location on a world map. Afghan Arab leaders easily manipulated those of the lower ranks, who were often impoverished and uneducated (save for their extremist indoctrination), emotionally leveraging their ignorance—a standard and very effective practice for terror and insurgent ringleaders.

The most notable of these Peshawar-based "Afghan Arab" groups, the Maktab al-Khidmat al Mujahidin al-Arab, or MAK (frequently referenced as the Afghan Services Bureau), had been spawned by the teachings of the Salafist Muslim Brotherhood. Two personalities who would rise to the forefront of global extremist infamy would join MAK, which was founded by a Palestinian Islamic theorist named Abdullah Azzam: Ayman al-Zawahiri and Osama bin Laden. But MAK played only a relatively minor role in the Soviet-Afghan War; they trained just a handful of fighters and built a few cave networks and small medical centers. It was their financing (with bin Laden's money) of logistical efforts for mujahideen inside Afghanistan that proved to be their greatest contribution to the Soviet defeat. After the November 1989 car bomb murder of Azzam in Peshawar, bin Laden and Zawahiri guided the MAK to hyperextremist—*apocalyptic*—levels as the leaders of the secretive organization the world would come to know as al-Qaeda, "the Base," a name that has been traced to the final line of the group's seminal treatise, penned by Azzam in 1987.

With the goal of securing hard-line Salafist ideological allegiance in return for their aid, other Arab groups supported the critical logistical efforts for mujahideen in Afghanistan. While money and supplies poured into the ISI from the U.S. and Saudi governments, the transport of weapons, food, fuel, and other supplies to the mujahideen from the Pakistani border presented the ISI with monumental—and prohibitively expensive—hurdles, often exhausting their monthly expenditures. Wealthy Arab supporters of the jihad bolstered the effort, with aid given not to the ISI to funnel to the fighters, but to the party bosses in Peshawar and sometimes directly to their commanders in Afghanistan to pay for mule and horse trains to carry the vital cargo of munitions and other supplies down the final, critical logistical pathways. The majority of this help, however, went to the two most fundamentalist parties, those of Gulbadin Hekmatyar (HIG) and Mohammad Khalis's Hezb-e-Islami-Khalis (HIK). Because HIK, which took the lion's share of this funding, dominated the organized resistance movement in the Kunar and Pech River Valley regions for most of the war, this area experienced a strong inflow of extremist Salafist ideology.

Wealthy Arabs also financed the development and maintenance of strict fundamentalist madrassas in and around Peshawar. Chief among these in importance for the Kunar province were the so-called Panjpiri madrassas of the town of Panjpir in the Swabi district of Pakistan's Northwest Frontier Province. The Panjpiri madrassas, principally the infamous Darul Quran Panjpir Madrassa, disseminated the hardest line of Salafist ideology. And they had many, many fresh faces to whom to preach: Swabi held claim to one of Pakistan's largest Afghan refugee camps; many who fled the Kunar province, particularly after indiscriminate Soviet carpet-bombing campaigns throughout the Kunar and Pech valleys in the mid-eighties, came to this camp, then returned to the Kunar after the war. Refugee camps throughout Afghanistan would prove vital components to the jihad against the Soviets, for the nurturing and recruitment of new mujahideen, as well as for providing safe havens for the fighters' families while the mujahideen battled the Communists.

Hekmatyar, too, would influence eastern Afghanistan's refugees, encouraging them to join HIG and his associated Lashkar-e Isar (Army of Sacrifice), not just by co-opting those in any of the hundreds of established refugee camps, but by creating his own. Just over one hundred road miles from Asadabad, the earthen-walled Shamshatoo Refugee Camp, about twelve miles southeast of Peshawar, would turn out thousands of fundamentalist fighters since the Pakistani government gave "Engineer Hekmatyar" the dusty swath of earth in 1979. With mosques, madrassas, medical facilities—even its own newspaper—the Shamshatoo camp, according to U.S. intel officers, was an important insurgent and terrorist base of operation for fighters moving into and out of eastern Afghanistan well into 2005.

In the early 1980s, the Arab influence pushed even farther into Afghanistan, spreading north of Kunar into Nuristan, through a man named Mawlawi Afzal, the Panjpiri-educated leader of Dawlat-I Inqilabi-yi Islamiyi Nuristan (Islamic Revolutionary State of Nuristan), a party that may have also influenced the people of the Korangal, Pech, and Kunar valleys. Another disciple of the Panjpiri madrassas, Jamil al-Rahman, broke away from Hekmatayar's HIG in 1985 and formed yet another ultrafundamentalist Salafist group, the Jama'at-e Da'wa, in the heart of the Kunar. Attracting both money and fighters directly from Saudi Arabia and Kuwait, this party achieved, by some accounts, greater power in the Kunar than even HIK during some stretches of the Soviet-Afghan War.

Vicious factional warring and withering disunity defined Afghanistan after the departure of the Soviet military; party leaders' and individual commanders' lustful quest for glory and regional dominance trumped any proclivity they may have held for peaceful Islamic unity. While no true victors emerged from the innumerable clashes during this period, the Afghan people, now virtually overlooked by the rest of the world, maintained their status of mass victimization at the hands of brutal war. Those who returned to Afghanistan from the refugee camps found razed villages, tainted water sources, and faced the dismal prospects of an ineffective central government in Kabul (often under siege), incapable of reining in the venal warlords who ravaged much of the country. But in the mid-nineties, a virtually invisible and stunningly unlikely factor would effect the reshaping of the country once again; Afghanistan would experience yet another tumultuous change.

Accounting for roughly 65 percent of its gross domestic product, cotton—and the textiles produced from the crop—is *the* most important of Pakistan's domestically produced commodities. In 1993 and 1994, however, swarms of tiny white flies descended upon the prime cotton-growing areas in the Sindh and Punjab provinces, carrying with them the microscopic baggage of the leaf curl virus. Production plunged by over a third from its 1992 peak during the ensuing plague. With an economic crisis exploding before her eyes, Prime Minister Benazir Bhutto dispatched her husband, Asif Zardari, to the Central Asian republic of Turkmenistan to broker a deal to buy raw cotton to bridge Pakistan's supply gap. The deal was finalized in short order, but the commodity had to be transported—through the warlord-plagued, anfractuous Afghan province of Herat, where bandits associated with Hekmatyar's HIG hijacked the first of the convoys. Pakistan, once again viewing Afghanistan through the conceptual lens of "strategic depth," realized that they needed a convoy protection force, and they needed that force immediately.

Pakistani officials sought to enlist the help of a former mujahideen fighter and student of the writings of Abdullah Azzam, an ethnic Pashtun named Mohammad Omar—*Mullah* Mohammad Omar, who had made recent overtures to the Pakistani government to grant him aid in building a national-level Afghan party that he claimed would quell all intra-Afghan fighting (easing the draining refugee problem in Pakistan by allowing the Afghans to move back to their homes). His fervor for strict national control of the populace and his location along the transit corridor between Turkmenistan and Pakistan cast the one-eyed Omar as the perfect candidate around which to build a force that would ensure the safe passage of the vital cotton crop. The Bhutto regime and the ISI supported him with arms, money, training, and most importantly, the procurement of personnel: *talibs* (students) of extremist Pakistani madrassas. These students weren't intellectual aspirants, however; they were disaffected, hopeless, and angry youths drawn into viciously anti-Western institutes of indoctrination that preached violence against any of those who strayed from their extremist ideologies—even other Muslims. But . . . they excelled at keeping the highway open for road trains of Pakistani cotton lorries; Pakistan got its cotton and Mullah Omar got his army of "students." In the wake of swarms of diminutive flies, the Taliban burgeoned into a regional force of reckoning.

Harshly enforcing the most draconian interpretations of Islamic law, the ruthless Taliban, many of whom claimed that they had organized to fight the rampant brutality of warlords against civilians, themselves raped women, children, and even men, plundered villages, and placed a vise grip on Afghan society. Pakistan, once again exerting influence over Afghanistan, continued to fund and aid the Taliban through much of the nineties, drawing on the execrable group and their hangers-on as they needed. Of course, just as they denied aiding the mujahideen in the 1980s, the Pakistanis staunchly maintained that they had no connection to the Taliban in the 1990s. In 1996, another base of funding and support for the Taliban arrived, this time on a large private jet landing at the dusty town of Jalalabad: Osama bin Laden and his extensive entourage. Exchanging money for protection (very large sums of the money he'd inherited from his father's construction conglomerate), the Saudi Arabian nihilist had grown increasingly bold and determined in his new brand of shadowy international terror, financing a number of terrorist training camps in eastern Afghanistan including many in the Kunar province, where he, by some reports, gained familial ties through marriage—and where by some accounts, he ordered the 9/11 attacks.

While effective against other internal armed factions and warlords, the Taliban didn't stand a chance against the U.S. forces who invaded Afghanistan as a swift response to the terrorist attacks of September 11, 2001. Within weeks, U.S. forces and their indigenous Afghan allies crushed the Taliban, decimating the group even faster than they had risen under Pakistan's nurture. And while bands of fighters aligned with the ideals of Mullah Omar would reassemble and call themselves Taliban, the movement was for the most part completely decimated by December of 2001, as most of their leadership and many of their underlings had been killed or captured and their bases of support had vanished.

The decades of violent, wrenching upheaval had left an intricate and perplexing "enemyscape" throughout the Kunar province. On two large marker boards in his office at 2/3's Combat Operations Center (COC) at Jalalabad Airfield, Scott Westerfield listed the broad mishmash of extremist groups that the Marines of 2/3 would face: al-Qaeda terrorists from Pakistan, Saudi Arabia, Yemen, western China, Egypt, Chechnya, and beyond; surviving and aspiring "Taliban" fighters; members of HIG and other Islamist groups based along the border region; and local timber smugglers and small-time criminal gangs occasionally aiding and abetting the extremists out of opportunism as fighters-for-hire. In all, *twenty-two distinct* groups, collectively termed anticoalition militia, or ACM (*coalition* referencing the union of Afghan forces and those of the United States and European and other nations), threatened stability throughout the Kunar and 2/3's greater three-province area of operation. Further complicating the intel picture, information revealed that individual fighters and cell leaders might hold allegiances with not just one, but a multitude of extremist camps. To Westerfield, the "enemy" presented an enigma cloaked in the shadows of the Hindu Kush, and he resolved to unmask the most salient and dangerous of these cells.

2/3, known in-country as Task Force Koa (after a Hawaiian god of war), would work with a wide range of indigenous combatants and local support, many of whom had fought not just the Soviets, but the Taliban and other extremist groups. While some former Afghan mujahideen joined forces with contemporary extremist groups, a far greater number would align themselves with the new Afghan government. Known as "combined" operations (as opposed to "joint," where different units of American forces work with one another), 2/3, like 3/3 before them, would conduct a number of missions side by side with Afghan National Army soldiers, Afghan National Police officers, Afghan Border Security agents, and the highly skilled and little-known Afghan Security Forces (ASF) personnel. The Marines would have Pashto interpreters attached to their units as well, whose intimate familiarity with local customs and supply chains would prove vital to 2/3 by identifying friend from known or potential foe—a key advantage in their fight against the mysterious enemy. Westerfield knew that he'd have to lean hard on these sources, but furthermore, he'd have to carefully integrate information streams derived from them with others at his disposal, learning along the way to determine trustworthy information from "noise."

Long before Westerfield would include in-country intel gleaned by 2/3 in his workflow, the intel officer had been vexed by one particular individual whose name he'd seen on numerous classified reports. Westerfield didn't know where he was from, or what organizations he'd been aligned or was now aligned with. He didn't even know if he'd planned or taken part in any large insurgent operations—almost certainly he hadn't, just some small ambushes. Faceless to Westerfield, the insurgent could easily be overlooked, seeming, at that point in early June of 2005, to be just a two-bit operator. But what tugged at Westerfield's attention wasn't what this small-timer had done, or what the intel officer thought he was capable of doing, but what Westerfield surmised the insurgent aspired to be.

"Why go after old real estate?" he asked Tom Wood during an intel briefing one early June afternoon. "We already know who the HVTs and MVTs [High and Medium Value Targets] are. And more importantly, they know that we know who they are. I'm sure of it. We need to identify the hungry ones, the ones at the bottom who want to claw their way up to fill any real or perceived insurgent power vacuums. They're the guys who'll cause us the biggest problems. They'll do anything. *He'll* do anything." Westerfield used an "investment" metaphor to define his strategy. "We should buy low. Get in at the bottom before he has a chance of proving himself of medium or high value," he said with a sarcastic grin, vowing to uncover everything about the target—a target about which he, at that time, knew little. But that little included the target's name: Ahmad Shah. While 2/3 would have some of the world's most advanced SIGINT and imagery intel (IMINT) made available to them by Task Force Devil, Westerfield knew that the only way to glean positive, actionable intelligence on Shah would be through time-tested, boots-on-the-ground HUMINT work. He needed a solid lead . . .

The 720 Marines and their attachments of 2/3's main element began departing Hawaii on the first of June 2005, leaving behind the breezy, cloud-dotted summer skies of Oahu and the friends and family who had come to see them roar away on chartered jumbo jets bound for the other side of the globe. Days later, they launched into Afghanistan on Air Force C-17s and C-130s from Ganci (Manus) Air Base in the northern lowlands of Kyrgyzstan, en route to Bagram Air Base, just north of Kabul. From Bagram, the battalion dispersed throughout their Maryland-size, three-province area of operation as the Marines of 3/3 prepared to come home. With battalion headquarters located at Jalalabad Airfield (JAF) in Nangarhar province, all but one platoon of Echo Company established themselves at Camp Wright in the Kunar's provincial capital of Asadabad; Fox Company went to Laghman province's Mehtar Lam forward operating base; and Battalion Command based Golf Company just down the road from their JAF COC at the Jalalabad Provincial Reconstruction Team base (J-Bad PRT). Based on Cooling's advice, MacMannis had Weapons Company train and deploy as a standard infantry company; known in-country as Whiskey Company, they co-located with Headquarters and Services Company at the Battalion COC at Jalalabad Airfield. And placed far in the hinterlands of the Kunar's Hindu Kush, at the head of the Pech Valley at the storied village of Nangalam, First Platoon of Echo Company (Echo-1) took up residence at what the battalion would come to know as the "edge of the empire," a lonely, frequently rocketed and mortared outpost at the end of a long, rutted dirt road, a firebase named Camp Blessing.

The Marines of Camp Blessing would prove vital to the successes of the battalion's forthcoming operations, in a number of ways. The first of 2/3's Marines arrived at Blessing in mid-May as part of the ADVON: Second Lieutenant Patrick Kinser—Echo-1's platoon commander—and his radio operator, Lance Corporal Corey Diss. Just hours after arriving at the outpost, Kinser and Diss embarked on their first combat operation in Afghanistan, a patrol with Marines of 3/3 led by Second Lieutenant Rick Posselt, a close personal friend of Kinser's from the Basic School as well as Infantry Officers' Course. Kinser immediately felt at home in the austere terrain, having trained as a mountain leader at the Mountain Warfare Training Center and having proven time and again to have a never-ending reserve of stamina on the grueling training grounds in the mountains of California and western Nevada during the battalion's predeployment workup.

The patrol, composed of 3/3 Marines, ASF, and Kinser and Diss, pushed outside of Blessing's wire at dawn on 20 May and traveled through the dusty streets of Nangalam, past houses of stone and mud and across donkey-plowed fields. Breathing the pure, dense air of a Hindu Kush morning, Kinser felt that he'd stepped into his true element as he made eye contact with the locals he knew only from books, magazine articles, and lectures prior to arriving at this enclave "forgotten by time." As the patrol pushed down the deeply incised Pech Valley, the roar of the Pech River gave Kinser an intuitive understanding of the raw natural power of the magnificent landscape, inspiring in the young lieutenant an insatiable appetite to press farther into the cavernous valleys and onto the chiseled peaks and ridges that surrounded him.

The Marines and ASF wasted no time during their patrol, covering eight klicks (kilometers) in just a few hours under the rising sun—a sun that warmed the landscape in a way that Kinser had never experienced before, showering the terrain with crisp yet enervating heat. "Wow, sir, you ever seen any place like this?" Diss asked Kinser during one of the patrol's few rests.

"Hell no," the tall, chiseled-featured, and guttural-voiced lieutenant who resembled a young Clint Eastwood replied as he shot glances at the scene before them—an abandoned home, a solitary tree clinging to a vertical rock face, a boulder the size of a school bus perched at the edge of an overhanging cliff. "And you, Diss?" he asked his RO with a half-cocked grin.

"Well, sir . . ." The lanky lance corporal scanned around and thought for a second. "I'm from the middle of the San Luis Valley in southern Colorado. We got high peaks *all* around us there, sir, some of them over fourteen thousand feet. It's a huge, beautiful valley, sir. Really different than any other place in Colorado. Cool in the summer, cold like Alaska in the winter. But, sir, nothing—I mean *nothing*—like this. Both places have mountains, but this place—it's like—it's like *Mars* or something, sir."

The patrol pushed past a steep, triangular incline of shattered rock that doglegged in front of the opening of a shadowed valley. "Korangal," Posselt announced, motioning with a nod. Lieutenant Kinser stopped in his tracks, firmly gripping his M16A4 at his side, and stared into the throat of what he had come to know as one of the most deadly corners of the War on Terror.

"Korangal." The lieutenant nodded and shot a quick glance to Diss, who was equally taken by the ominous sight. "Hope to spend some time up there," Kinser remarked with an almost lustful grin. The patrol broke off the Pech three klicks farther east of the Korangal's opening, at the village of Matin, where the group entered the Shuryek Valley. The terrain now steeper and the trails narrower, Kinser bounded up the west side of the valley, his swelling enthusiasm for the terrain far overwhelming any burning in his leg muscles. Diss, as he would do throughout the entire deployment, kept up with him.

"Glad I was born and raised at seven thousand feet in Colorado, sir. Not sure I could keep up if I was born in Florida or something." *Crack!* "Wha? . . ."

"Contact!" Posselt bellowed. *Crack!*

"Single shots. Sniper fire," Kinser calmly surmised as he raised his M16 from behind the cover of a large boulder and scanned the vaulting terrain with his ACOG (Advanced Combat Optical Gunsight, a sight that projects a bright view of the subject with clear ranging tick marks projected in red, mounted to most of the battalion's M16s). "Ever been shot at before, Diss?" he asked. Diss shook his head. "Me neither. Not sure I like it too much, but I'm really gonna love shootin' back as soon as we find these fuckers."

"There it is, that small house up there!" Posselt yelled.

"Got it." Kinser located the house, built of and surrounded by stones, naturally camouflaging it. "Can't see anyone up there, though."

"ASF caught a glimpse. They're hiding in there," Posselt stated. "We'll direct-lay some 60s."

"That'll let 'em know we got their position," Kinser said, beginning to laugh.

The first 60mm mortar, fired by direct laying, where the mortar-men hand-elevates the tube (with the bottom of the launcher placed on the ground with no base plate), landed just short of the building. *Whump!* The explosion echoed throughout the valley. The second shot hit dead-on.

"Hey, Diss. We're officially in the war now. Congratulations," the lieutenant proudly announced as he stood atop the rock Diss crouched behind, scanning the area.

"Thanks, SIR!"

The patrol closed on the house and discovered two men, huddling inside—and one Chinese rip-off version of a Soviet Dragunov 7.62mm sniper rifle. Just hours after moving into their new home, twenty-four-year-old Second Lieutenant Patrick Edward Kinser of Jonesville, Virginia, and nineteen-year-old Lance Corporal Corey Diss of Center,

Colorado, became the first Marines of 2/3 deployed as a battalion to directly engage an enemy in over thirty-five years.

"I think I'm gonna like it here in the Hindu Kush," Kinser said with a big grin.

"I'm just gonna make sure to keep the radios working, sir," Diss replied.

As Scott Westerfield delved into the work of unmasking Shah and other targets on his list in early June, Tom Wood set about developing a plan to eliminate those targets. He contacted Erik Kristensen, and the two worked up a model based on *Stars* to restabilize and bolster security in the Korangal Valley area that used NAVSOF for the first two phases of the mission. But while the SEALs of Team 10 and their associated SEAL Delivery Vehicle Team (SDVT—SEALs who would tactically support Team 10) were eager to join with 2/3 for the mission, the new CJSOTF-A commander put a halt to the notion. No longer would the Marines be able to assume de facto tactical control of their entire missions through intel sharing and detailed planning of each phase of an operation that would then have SEALs and Marines working side-by-side "for the op," and not for one another. Rather, the mission would be required to adhere to a "supported/supporting" flip-flop command and control structure: NAVSOF would assume command of the operation for the opening phases (with Marines supporting them—*on the Marines' own operation*); once the SEALs and SDVT personnel departed, the Marines would take control and theoretically be "supported" by SOF, but supported only in that they would have access to certain special operations assets that typically wouldn't be deployed in service of conventional forces.

The order blindsided Wood; he viewed the construct as a blatant and unbelievable smack in the face of the basic command and control rules to which his institutional Marine Corps DNA governed him to adhere. The order—founded on USSOCOM doctrine (and issued through that doctrine's strict interpretation)—roared down the pike directly from CJSOTF-A, and 2/3 would have to live with it. But the op had to proceed. SIGINT and HUMINT hits trickled in; nothing ground-breaking, but Westerfield was steadfastly working hard with his Marines to zero in on Shah; more importantly, the intel officer and his chief, Staff Sergeant Chuck Atherton, were developing a feel for the target's movements, enabling Wood to sketch a general plan of attack against the insurgents and terrorists, allowing the Marines to further the stabilization work that 3/3 had begun, but that had been disrupted.

Wood—who first became a Marine as an enlisted grunt before working through a university degree to become an infantry officer—redoubled his efforts and hatched a plan that would use conventional forces exclusively: Marines would hit the ground from the very beginning of the op, with later phases merging local Afghan National Army soldiers into the mission. Like the initial *Stars* model (the concept of which had already been approved by Colonel Donahue by early June), a small reconnaissance and surveillance team would monitor the target cell's suspected area of interest from a clandestine location, shaping the op through their continuous feed of information about the target area. Once the team positively identified the target(s), the main force would insert by helicopter—at night for maximum surprise—both cordoning the area and, with the help of the reconnaissance and surveillance team, taking down the cell. Later phases would have Marines maintaining security and presence by undertaking humanitarian and MEDCAP work.

For the opening phases of the op, Tom looked to use Ronin, one of four scout/sniper teams that composed the Battalion's Scout/Sniper Platoon (part of Headquarters and Services Company). Ronin was led by thirty-three-year-old Sergeant Keith Eggers, an unassuming Californian who had not only completed both the grueling summer and winter Mountain Leader Courses at the Mountain Warfare Training Center (courses with student attrition rates upward of 50 percent in which select Marines train to lead units through mountainous and cold-weather environments), but had been a mountain leader instructor at the base during the nineties, making him ideally suited for the Kunar's terrain. Almost superhumanly athletic, Keith regularly carried over 120 pounds of gear—including encrypted radios, MREs and water, an M4 carbine, an M9 9 mm sidearm, a rangefinder and scope, and the M40A3 7.62 mm bolt-action USMC sniper rifle—throughout the Hindu Kush, leading his team for miles at a time, often covering thousands of feet of altitude gain in single movements. Tom's plan would have Eggers lead a team of six (a standard sniper team "plussed up" with two additional Marines for added security) deep into the Korangal Valley region to surveil Ahmad Shah's suspected safe houses, positively identify Shah, any of his underlings, and his exact location, then pass word to the COC for the op to press ahead. A company-size force of Marines would then insert by helicopter, cordoning Shah's safe house(s) and either kill or capture the target and his men. As the helicopters inserted the grunts, two other companies of Marines would form "blocking positions," inserting either by foot or by convoy, denying the enemy an escape route.

The success of his draft plan hinged on one pivotal asset, however: helicopter support. While Keith and his small team could penetrate the region at night undiscovered, a company was simply too large to move through that area and not be seen or heard—they had to insert with blazing speed by air. Had 2/3 been part of a MAGTF, the air issue wouldn't have been a problem, but the Marines didn't own any helicopters in-country as part of a joint task force. Wood set out to get "buy-in" from Task Force Sabre, the large Army conventional aviation element that fell under CJTF-76 in command. Sabre had both UH-60 Blackhawks and the massive, double-rotored CH-47 Chinooks, renowned by helicopter pilots throughout the world as one of, if not *the* best high-altitude helicopter ever made; Sabre's Chinooks would fit the bill perfectly. 2/3 could get the *Stars*-based op done without dangerously compromising command and control, using all conventional assets. Or so Wood thought.

Sabre was stretched thin; they served as aviation support for not just RC-East, but all of Afghanistan, meaning 2/3 would have to compete with other units throughout the entire country for their help.

Furthermore, Wood realized that depending on the final target zone, troops might have to insert via fastrope if trees prohibited the aircraft from touching down—but Sabre's Chinooks would first have to be upfitted to accommodate fastropes. The major deal breaker with Sabre, however, came with the time and date of the op—Wood foresaw a possible late June launch date, possibly the twenty-eighth or twenty-ninth, which would keep in the spirit of the op tempo MacMannis had ordered, but would give Westerfield enough time to harvest and process the necessary intel to feed to Wood in order to finalize a detailed mission plan. Inserting covertly at night meant the aircraft would have to operate completely blacked out, with the pilots flying "on goggles"—night-vision gear that uses passive sensors to amplify any ambient light, primarily from moon-reflected sunlight. But while the Chinook pilots themselves were more than willing and capable of low-ambient-light ops, their guidelines stated that they could only fly with at least 25 percent lunar illumination. In late June of 2005, however, the moon wouldn't rise above the high mountains of the Hindu Kush until well past midnight—and once it was above the ridgelines, lunar illumination would fall just short of the requisite 25 percent. Sabre's Chinooks were out for such a late-June launch date.

That left Wood with two alternatives. The first would have him plan the operation with the direct-action and associated cordon phase going down during daylight hours, using Sabre. But based on Priddy's earlier counseling on the ISR of the Korangal, Tom knew that the insurgent and terrorist cells would know immediately that an operation was imminent as Marines who would form the operation's blocking positions would almost certainly tip off the innumerable "eyes" of the hills throughout the region as the grunts readied to move. Most Afghans in Kunar's mountains run their lives with the sun—up at dawn, to sleep just after dusk—a nighttime insert would best position the Marines for surprise, leaving Wood with just one option: Task Force Brown, the in-country designation of the Special Operations Air Regiment (Airborne), or 160th SOAR(A)—the "Night Stalkers."

One of the most secretive of USSOCOM's units, the 160th hails from Army SOF and primarily supports direct-action hard-hit units—inserting special operations personnel for shockingly fast counterterror and other surgical-strike operations—often by fastrope, which their helicopters have special modifications to quickly deploy. The aviators of the 160th aren't just capable of low-illum missions, they fly, with rare exception, *only* at night, seeing the world before them through the most advanced visualization equipment available. In Afghanistan, TF-Brown flew the MH-47D and MH-47E Chinooks, comprehensively modified conventional CH-47 Chinooks (hence the M designation) giving the craft higher speeds (faster than even attack helicopters), extended range, and heavier armaments and more robust onboard defense systems, among a number of other attributes. Wood saw TF-Brown as the vital cornerstone for his mission concept's success. But the 160th fell under SOF rules, and therefore, by doctrine, the Night Stalkers couldn't theoretically support 2/3. But Wood felt that CJSOTF-A could make a reasonable exception, as he wasn't seeking to control a ground SOF element, but an aviation support unit. The operations officer, fiercely devoted to the young enlisted "trigger puller" Marines who would carry out his plans, had to formulate a mission that was tactically rock solid from a command and control perspective, but one where the Marines who would undertake the actual operation would have the best available chances of success and survivability. The OpsO would have to scrap his plan for a conventional-forces-only operation and begin anew with a plan that utilized TF-Brown—but to what extent would he be forced to compromise the rigid command and control structure he knew to be vital to get support from the 160th? As the days ticked away and the intel on Shah trickled in, he would find his answer.

That intel trickle would roar to a torrent of information—actionable, specific information—that would allow Wood to finalize his plan within just a few weeks. 2/3's main element had wasted no time jumping into the campaign throughout their respective provinces as they arrived in Afghanistan, keeping at least 50 percent of the Marines of each base on patrols at all times—through the mountains, in the towns and villages of the provinces, sleeping, eating, and living with the Afghans themselves.

And while sophisticated SIGINT mechanisms churned away for Westerfield, his big payoff came as a dividend of this outside-the-wire mindset when Second Lieutenant Regan Turner, commander of Whiskey Company's Second Platoon, ventured into the village of Khewa, about ten miles northeast of Jalalabad in the Kuz Kunar district of Nangarhar province in mid-June, just after the official turnover of authority to 2/3 from 3/3. Turner, a quick-witted and disarming officer whose natural charm transcends pretty much all language and cultural barriers, scored what would be the first of a small number of pivotal interviews with credible intel sources during a meeting with elders in the small village. Removing his flak jacket, ballistic glasses, and helmet to best engage the elders at the *shura* meeting through eye contact and nonintimidating body posturing, Turner and his interpreter sat and drank tea with the locals as the group went through rounds of introductions.

About thirty minutes into the meeting, Turner met a man named L.C. (his actual name omitted for security reasons) who proudly stated that he fought the Soviets as a mujahideen and then took up arms against the Taliban—whom L.C. despised so much that he sacrificed three years with his family in order to fight against the much-hated group. Regan, a diligent student of the region's history, smiled that he was now sitting face-to-face with a warrior who not only helped fend off the Communists, but fought against those who willfully harbored Osama bin Laden after the 9/11 attacks. Taking a very easy, relatively passive approach to his HUMINT work (at first), Turner didn't ask L.C. a single intel question during their introduction—and as it turned out, he didn't have to: within a minute of their meeting each other, the former mujahideen uttered the words that Regan wanted to hear more than any others: Ahmad Shah. Westerfield had instructed Turner to be on the lookout for anything and everything on Shah, whom the intel officer personally considered to be a high value target, but warned the lieutenant that he might not hear as much as a peep about him from anyone. L.C. seemed to know everything that Westerfield didn't—information that the intel officer desperately yearned to uncover. "His family is here, in Khewa. Right *here*!" Turner's interpreter, "Bobby," yelped—not just translating L.C.'s words, but emulating his enthusiasm. "L.C. has nothing personally against Ahmad Shah—really, he just hates the Taliban and the al-Qaeda guys and these other azz-holes." Turner laughed at Bobby's reference, which he took to mean HIG and other extremist types. Regan burned through pages in his notebook as L.C. rattled off the vital details to Bobby. "Ahmad is a real azz-hole. Really. He killed another man just because he wanted his wife—and then he stole her and now she's his wife! No shitting, Commander Regan! Really, this big azz-hole, he works with the Taliban, and the al-Qaeda guys."

"Calm down, Bobby. I know. He's an *azz-hole*," Turner carefully enunciated. "But just give me the facts. This is important."

"Right. My sorries." Bobby then continued, "Shah and his three brothers, Muhummad Azam, Ruhola Amin, and Palawan, all sell opium and have illegal weapons throughout the area, and that supports Ahmad Shah's fightings. And the people around here don't like him, especially for murdering the man for his wife."

"Bobby, ask L.C. where Shah is actually from, any other names he uses, and where he operates."

"Right, sir." The normally soft-spoken interpreter jumped back into the Pashto intel dump with L.C. "He is from the Dara-I-Nur, north of here, this means 'the Valley of Light.' This is the area that was the Kafirs', but now enlightened. His full name is Ahmad Shah Dara-I-Nur, Ahmad Shah of the Valley of the Enlightened Ones."

"Wow." Turner shook his head, "Is he a Nuristani?" *Westerfield's gonna flip when he hears all this,* he thought.

"No, not from Nuristan itself, but almost Nuristan. He looks Nuristani. Thin, light-colored eyes, and has an orange beard. He is midthirties-years-old. He speaks in the Pashto, the Dari, and the Pashai—he is a Pashai. He is the only person in this entire area to have really supported the Taliban. He is such an angry man, that is why. He went to seek Mullah Omar, and he fought for the Taliban, and then also the al-Qaeda."

"And where does he do his attacks, his ambushes," the second lieutenant asked, inciting a further spate of L.C.'s hand gesturing and pointing, speaking so fast that Turner, who knew a little Pashto, couldn't pick out a single word.

"The Korangal. High in the Korangal, he has people up there who protect him, they hide weapons and supplies for him up there. It is the village of Chichal mostly, but also the lower village of Korangal, far up the valley. They are Pashai, too, and he pays them. He ambushes the Marines in the Korangal, and he sets off IEDs on the Pech Road against the Marines and the police. From the top of the Sawtalo Sar mountain he can see everything. He has a small team of about ten to twenty men with him who he directs during ambushes, using the ICOMs for communication, as he is often not part of the actual attack—but sometimes he is, and he always carries a PK machine gun. He also has phones, the Roshan cellular for when he is in the cities and the Thuraya satellite for when he is in the Korangal and on Sawtalo Sar, to talk to his contacts in eastern Afghanistan and Pakistan."

"Pakistan? Does he ever go into Pakistan, and if so, where?" Turner leaned in, sipping tea with his left hand as he shook out his right from all the note taking.

"The Shamshatoo camp. By Peshawar. He lives there much of the time when he is not out here."

"Bobby, has L.C. ever told this to anyone else from coalition forces?"

"No. He says that you are the first. And one more thing." Bobby turned to listen to L.C. speak. "He says that Ahmad Shah is calling himself a Taliban commander, and intends to destroy the elections in September. He has hired people to watch the roads for him, build the remote bombs, and bring in rockets and mortars and guns and RPGs. He is very hungry for the power. He wants many people for his army, but he only has ten or fifteen men with him now." Shah seemed to be leveraging his local ties to influence people in the high Korangal who resisted all outside influences, even the early Taliban.

"Can anyone else confirm what he is saying. I *believe* him—but I need to confirm with another source."

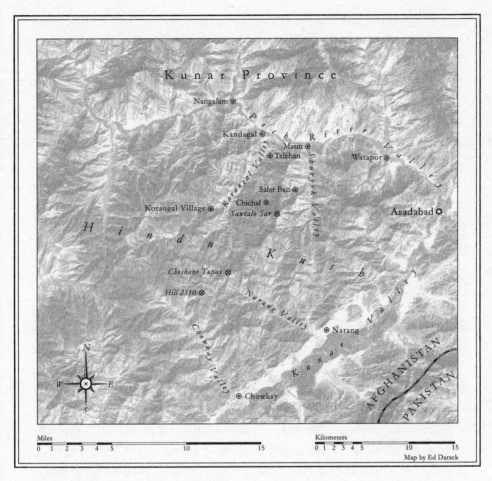

Shaded relief map of the Sawtalo Sar region, including the Korangal Valley, the Shuryek Valley, the Chowkay Valley, the Narang Valley, the Pech River Valley, and the Kunar Valley

Bobby and L.C. continued talking, then the former mujahideen gestured for Regan to jump into his truck. L.C. drove the lieutenant to the home of another man who was involved in security of the region. He confirmed everything L.C. had told Regan, adding also a list of Ahmad Shah's relatives who didn't support the terrorist, and told Regan two of Shah's aliases: Molawi Ibrahim, Ismael, Mullah Mohammed Ismael, and Commander Ismael. "Thank you, thank you both, I'll see you again." Turner noted a list of the village's needs to pass to battalion HQ, then headed back to brief Westerfield.

"You're amazing, Turner. Absolutely amazing."

"Thanks, sir. Just doing my job, though."

"Get a picture of him?"

"No. They didn't offer one."

"That's fine. What you've given me is what we need to proceed, it'll get Tommy Wood rollin' on the final op plan."

Westerfield pored over Turner's notes, compiling a detailed picture of Shah, his small cell, and his area of operation. To Westerfield, the terrorist leader clearly was using his Pashai background to co-opt the locals in the Korangal, who clung to their Safi beliefs. But Shah's connections seemed to span a broad fundamentalist spectrum, from the Pashtun-dominated Taliban to the Arab-rooted apocalyptic al-Qaeda. But because he spent time—actually lived in—Hekmatayar's Shamshatoo, Westerfield believed that Shah's primary allegiance, and substantial financial, personnel, and armament support, came from HIG or associated Pakistani connections. Hekmatyar, who was known in the late sixties to throw battery acid on women who dared to show their wrists and ankles while walking down streets in Kabul, proved to be a continuing thorn in the side of democratic evolution well into the twenty-first century in the region. Far more important—from a tactical standpoint—than his specific connections, Shah seemed to have established a firm network: safe houses, financial aid, arms caches, paid runners and observers, which he intended to utilize to dash the prospects in the Kunar that the Marines had come to secure: the upcoming safe, unfettered democratic national elections.

Gazing at 1:50,000 scale maps of the specific region where Turner reported the location of Shah's operations—in and around the village of Chichal and the summit of Sawtalo Sar—Westerfield immediately realized that he was staring at the catbird seat for any insurgent or terrorist cell in the region. Sawtalo Sar is a domineering massif, a north-south-trending five-mile-long phalanx of twisted, dark earth that rises over 6,000 vertical feet from its water-lapped base on the Pech River to

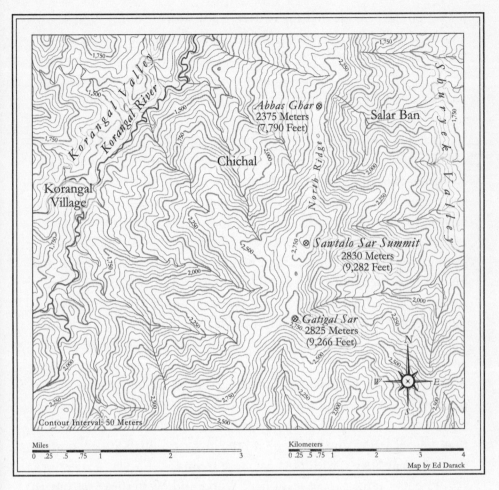

Topographic map of the summit region of Sawtalo Sar

its apex at 9,282 feet above sea level. Chichal village, a loosely defined medley of stone houses and large timber smuggler–built mansion compounds, lies near the very summit of the peak. An extensive trail network, splaying out from the main "Super Highway" trail that runs along the crest of the peak's north ridge, interconnects the village's houses, pastures, and terraces. The mountain is densely covered in Himalayan deodar cedar and broad-leaf ferns on its upper shoulders; numerous rock outcroppings grant vistas of the Pech Valley, the Korangal Valley (of which the peak defines the eastern wall), and the Shuryek Valley, of which Sawtalo Sar forms the western periphery. From Chichal and Sawtalo Sar's summit, Westerfield noted that Shah could control a number of small units of his team, ambushing convoys, emplacing rocket attacks, and lobbing mortars into villages, through his ICOM two-way radio.

Needing further detail than his maps supplied, Westerfield studied oblique (sideways, as opposed to orthogonal, or "straight down" view) submeter resolution MQ-1 Predator UAV imagery of the upper Korangal, upper Shuryek, and Sawtalo Sar summit region taken just hours earlier. Wood and Westerfield, having compiled a complete vetted intel set, noted a series of "Named Areas of Interest" (NAIs), numbered one through four where they felt Shah would most likely locate himself and his cell. They designated Korangal Village as NAI-1 (while this location represented the least likely location for Shah and his men to be found, they believed that villagers might hide weapons for him there); they denoted Chichal village as NAI-2; the duo marked a network of terraces and small structures of and around the Northeast Gulch of the Peak as NAI-3; and they designated a small section of the north ridge of the peak just to the north of NAI-2 and NAI-3 as NAI-4. SIGINT hits that continually rolled in off Shah's Thuraya and Roshan phones indicated that the cell leader and his men had the highest probability of locating themselves at NAI-3, with NAI-2 a close second.

With the target areas identified, Wood and Westerfield set out to locate observation posts (OPs) that would grant the clearest, most direct views of the NAIs, yet allow a small reconnaissance and surveillance team to remain well concealed from any roving timber harvester, goat herder, village traveler, or bad guy meandering along any of the countless trails the duo noted on the "Pred" feed. While more difficult to identify than the relatively large NAIs, the high-resolution black-and-white imagery did provide just enough detail for the two to identify two observation posts: OP-1 would lie within some dense trees at the top of the peak's Northeast Spur just over a half mile to the northeast of Sawtalo Sar's main summit, granting a view of NAI-3 and

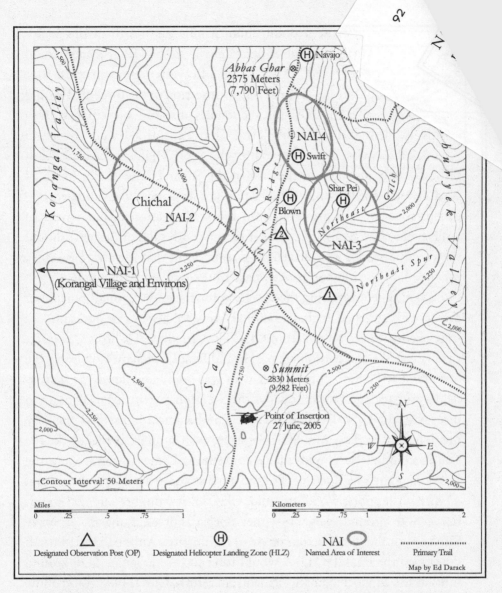

Topographic map of the summit region of Sawtalo Sar, showing named areas of interest, insertion point, designated helicopter landing zones, and designated observation posts for Operation *Red Wings*

AI-4; and they chose a point about a mile due north of the peak's main summit directly off the Super Highway to be OP-2, which would give a view of NAI-1 and NAI-2. Wood and Westerfield then chose four helicopter landing zones (HLZs) for the insertion of the force that would cordon and strike the NAI the reconnaissance and surveillance team positively identified as Shah's: HLZ Shar Pei, on a broad terrace in NAI-3; HLZ Swift, just to the east of the Super Highway inside NAI-4; HLZ Navajo, also just to the east of the Super Highway but north of NAI-4; and HLZ Blown, which the two saw as tactically advantageous— except for the trees growing from the well-positioned, flat parcel of land; those trees would need to get blown (with satchel charges) should the reconnaissance and surveillance team deem that location necessary for the main cordon and strike phase of the op, hence the name.

Wood, intent on using the battalion for the entire ground portion of the op with attached Afghan National Army soldiers for its latter phases, now needed to get buy-in from CJSOTF-A to allow TF-Brown to insert the main strike and cordon teams. He and First Lieutenant Rob Long, the Scout/Sniper Platoon commander who was "double-billeted" as Westerfield's primary assistant (known as the S-2 Alpha) ventured to Bagram to meet with the CJSOTF-A commanders and Kamiya himself to pitch the mission. But no dice. Any SOF elements, even support elements like the 160th, couldn't be employed by conventional forces—those were the rules, mandated by doctrine. For the mission to proceed with the pivotal TF-Brown support, Wood was told, CJSOTF-A would require 2/3 to utilize a SOF ground element—either Special Forces, Rangers, or Navy SEALs—for the direct-action phase of the mission. Although the Marines developed the op, CJSOTF-A would force 2/3 to designate SOF ground units as the supported, main elements; in return, CJSOTF-A would allow the 160th to support the Marines by inserting them for the cordon of the NAI inside which the direct-action team was taking down the targets. Once the direct-action team completed the hit, the Chinooks of the 160th would pull the SOF team out, and at that point, the Marines would be the "supported" element. Furthermore, CJSOTF-A mandated that the initial, shaping phase of the op be conducted by a SOF team, and not by Ronin, as they considered those first hours so critical to the subsequent direct-action team's actions on the objective in phase two of the plan that they simply could not trust a conventional team, regardless of that individual team members' capabilities, skill sets, and experience. Eggers and Team Ronin were out—without even the slightest hint of a review of their qualifications.

"This is fucking outrageous, Long. Unbelievable. They have us hamstrung. Have you ever heard of such nonsense? All these rules . . . if only we were a MEU, or some type of fucking MAGTF." The young lieutenant stared blank-faced at Wood. "If we were the BLT [Battalion Landing Team] on a MEU, the Fifty-threes [CH-53E/Ds] would fly no matter what—zero illum. Colonel would say do it and they'd fly," the major roared.

"Sir, can't Eggers and his team at least go in with their initial reconnaissance and surveillance team?"

"It's out! Eggers and his team are already out. They don't think that our scout/snipers are good enough to lay the tactical groundwork for their main element. And they got the rules on their side. We have to get air support to make this work, and this is the only way. We bring in SOF—*and give them the C2 of our op*—just to get the hand-me-down use of the air primarily tasked to their teams. What a system. We're at the mercy of SOCOM rules."

Wood took a step back and tried to calm himself. "Okay. Basically, they want us to split the C2, they got command and control for our mission for the first part of the op, then we're supposed to be 'supported' by them once they exfil . . ." Wood pondered the March 2002 Operation *Anaconda*—which he'd studied in depth—where the C2 was virtually nonexistent as was SOF-conventional-forces integration. Wood, who'd been raised as an enlisted grunt and then as an infantry officer to strictly adhere to the concept of unity of command/effort, couldn't comprehend how such a convoluted structure ever enveloped his battalion. "We got no choice. We do it their way or we don't do it at all. If we choose the latter, then we might as well be sitting back in Oahu sucking down Mai Tais at Duke's."

"Roger, sir." Long tapped his wrist slowly . . . rhythmically—*forebodingly*.

"We get the air we need, we get the op done, and they get their rules fulfilled. And hopefully things don't go haywire like they did in that goat-rope masterpiece *Anaconda*," Wood seethed.

"So, sir, do we pitch it to one of the ODAs? The SEALs? *Who?*"

"We should pitch it to both SF and NAVSOF . . . But since we already have a working relationship with Kristensen and the SEALs, we might as well go with them. It amazes me, Kristensen and the SEALs had no problem falling under our command and control when I asked them. No problem at all."

Wood contacted Kristensen once again, and although the SEALs had no problem working with 2/3 the way NAVSOF had worked with 3/3 in *Spurs* and *Celtics*—even working under 2/3's command and control—Wood knew he had no vote in the process. The Marines would take the backseat to NAVSOF for the first two phases of the operation, then work the security and stabilization and MEDCAP portions themselves with the Afghan National Army once TF-Blue had completed the direct-action phase of the operation. "We need to get this mission done, and this is the only way," Wood told Long. "I'm not happy about the split C2, but that's how it's gotta go."

"Roger that. We just keep our fingers crossed that nothing goes wrong when we're not in control of it," the young lieutenant stated with unease.

"Yeah, fingers crossed, Long," Wood said with a sarcastic tone. "Lotta good that always does." The two Marines shook their heads and laughed nervously.

5

RED WINGS
TAKES FLIGHT

Steeling themselves for the rigors of their eastern Afghan mission from the very moment their boots hit the deck of RC-East, the Marines of 2/3's main element proved both eager and indefatigably capable as they attacked every task—from the minuscule to the battalion-scale—with determined resolve. Focused on their ultimate goal of ensuring successful Afghan national parliamentary elections on 18 September and then continuing to stabilize the region after that historic event, the Marines took no task lightly, from mission planning, to splicing wires in broken radios, to drinking enough water during long movements through the mountains to remain combat capable, to ensuring that bottles of that water made their way to the respective bases—even as extremists intensified their campaign of terror throughout the spring.

Nestled in the shadows of Sawtalo Sar and its sibling peaks, Camp Blessing was the clear focus of the extremists during that spring-thaw campaign. Kinser and the other "Blessing Marines" picked up quickly on the bad guys' standard tactics—improvised explosive-device strikes on convoys near the firebase and 82 mm mortar and 107 mm rocket attacks, launched typically three or four days on either side of a full moon from well-concealed locations just behind the high ridges to the east of the camp. Terrorists used one spot in particular enough for it to earn the name Rocket Ridge, which lay in a direct line between the rooftop lookout of the base's COC and the summit of Sawtalo Sar. Providing the Marines of the firebase with a tremendous tactical advantage, however, the Afghan Security Forces personnel manned four observation posts surrounding Blessing. Hailing from throughout the slopes and valley floors surrounding Nangalam, the ASF proved themselves vital to the Marines for their knowledge of the area and its people—people good, bad, on the fence, trustworthy, and sneaky. The Afghan fighters, whom many of the Blessing Marines would come to regard as family by the end of their deployment, reflected the sentiments of the villagers throughout the Pech Valley region: they hated the attacks, the shrieks of the rockets, the out-of-nowhere deafening *crack* of impacting 82 mm mortar rounds, the IED strikes, the threats to their families, the indiscriminate ambushes, the terror. From the abhorrent slaughter of the people of the Pech in the late seventies by the Afghan Communists, to the intentional targeting of civilians of the area by the Soviets, to the infighting of the early nineties, to the Taliban, and now the "leftovers" of all those past influences, the ASF just wanted an end to it all, to close the book on the decades of war, to go back to their homes and small mountain pastures and live out their lives in peace. The ASF members would come to view the Marines' presence as a chance to finally lay down their Kalashnikovs and RPGs and go home; and for that, they would fight side by side with the grunts, with bloodlust, vehemence, and incalculable loyalty.

The day after the short-lived firefight against the snipers in the Shuryek Valley, Kinser greeted a fellow infantry officer at Blessing's front gate whose magnetically sincere midwestern charm, devotion to the COIN fight, and independent- and quick-mindedness would, as a complement to Kinser's leadership style, yield payoffs to 2/3's mission far greater than even the insightful Rob Scott—who masterminded placing the two together at the remote base—could have imagined: First Lieutenant Matt Bartels. Bartels, a standout high school football player from Bloomington, Minnesota, fought his way from near death at the clutches of viral meningitis and, once recovered, set his sights on becoming a Marine Corps infantry officer. Having proven himself a uniquely independent yet utterly trustworthy and competent platoon leader during 2/3's deployment as the Battalion Landing Team of the Thirty-first Marine Expeditionary Unit, Bartels was chosen to lead a fifteen-man experimental Marine Corps antiterror augmentation force that would work with the Navy's SEAL Team 3 as part of Joint Task Force 510 interdicting the al-Qaeda-connected Abu Sayef terrorists of the southern Philippines. Returning just weeks before 2/3 began predeployment training for their Afghan fight, Scott chose Bartels to be Camp Blessing's base commander, learning from Cooling that the vital "tip of the spear" outpost required a leader who was one independent yet regimented, compassionate toward the locals, yet coolheaded and deliberate, even under the worst of attacks.

Camp Blessing, which had once been a school, then a medical clinic in the nineties before the Taliban commandeered the small group of buildings (which they used as a command center as well as for rape, torture, and execution of the locals), was taken over by U.S. special operations forces early in the war. Marines of 2/8 spent some time at the camp—named in honor of Jay Blessing, a Special Forces soldier killed by an IED strike near the base in 2002—as did some from 3/6, who fended off a number of direct attacks by insurgents, including one assault where militants overran one of the observation posts and nearly breached the camp's main perimeter. But 3/6 had only spent a few months at Blessing, operating the firebase with Special Forces, as 2/8 had done. 3/3 would be the first battalion to occupy Blessing for their full deployment, operating it as a Marine-only camp. MacMannis and Scott looked to have a single commander run the base with a single platoon of Marines deployed there for the duration of 2/3's tour, another recommendation of Cooling's, who had cycled base commanders through "tours" of Blessing. Handing over command to Bartels was 3/3's First Lieutenant Justin Belman, who, through his and his Marines' outreach to the locals of the Nangalam area, laid the foundation for the personality-driven leadership successes of Kinser and Bartels—successes emblematic of the classic admixture of unconventional war-fighting styles historically recognized as unique to the United States Marine Corps.

Bartels wasted no time jumping into his role as commander of the base that jutted farther into the enemy than any other in Afghanistan, lying just a few miles from the frontier with Pakistan, smack on the prime insurgent corridor between Kunar and Nuristan. In total, 98 of 2/3's Marines would live at Camp Blessing—Kinser's platoon with attachments, and Marines attached directly to the firebase: heavy-weapons operators, light machine gunners, straight-leg 0311 infantrymen, cooks, Navy Corpsmen, and communications specialists. In addition to the 98 Marines, 114 ASF fighters, and 5 interpreters, or "terps," lived at Blessing, and nearly 50 local workers came and went each day from Nangalam and surrounding villages. Studding Blessing's concertina-razor-wire perimeter, a hodgepodge of captured Taliban and insurgent weapons systems, many of which dated back to the Soviet era, stood ready to be manned by ASF during attacks: DShK 12.7mm heavy machine guns, ZPU-1 antiaircraft guns pointed at the surrounding ridges, recoilless rifles, RPG-7s, PK medium machine guns, 82mm mortar tubes, even 107mm rocket launchers. Of course, the Marines defended the wire with their own tried-and-true armaments as well as more recent additions to the Marine Corps inventory: M2 .50-caliber machine guns, M240 light machine guns, SMAW and AT4 shoulder-launched rockets, MK19 40mm automatic grenade launchers, and even the Javeline shoulder-launched missile. Lobbing football-size rounds, the 120mm mortar tubes (on loan from the Army) gave outside-the-wire Marines shockingly effective indirect fire support during their missions. Based at Blessing, Marine mortarmen could move the "120 tubes" by Humvee throughout the region, ensuring that any patrol was just a radio-transmitted call for fire away from lighting up an enemy position "out of nowhere" with blazing efficacy.

The morning after Bartels's midnight arrival at Blessing (he came by way of convoy, operating blacked out to avoid IED strikes), the twenty-five-year-old lieutenant emerged from the concrete COC to a spring Hindu Kush morning. Climbing onto a rooftop lookout, he immediately thanked Rob Scott in his head. "This is it—*wow*," he uttered to himself. Before him, cathedral-like peaks stretched into the powder-blue dome of sky above. Cradled by those peaks, verdant fields, meticulously terraced pastures, and the thrashing, ribbonlike Pech River drew his attention from the heights. Ringing the lowlands at their juncture with the towering Hindu Kush peaks, Nangalam's homes rose out of football-field-size slabs of steep, glimmering stone. Framed by long arcs of exposed geologic strata, the boxy architecture looked to be chiseled from the domineering peaks on which the houses stood. Bartels saw the enclave as a hidden paradise, *from another time*—as so many other of the Marines had remarked—and was dumbfounded that such a place could know even the slightest hint of war, much less decades of such barbaric inhumanity.

In the weeks between their arrival at Blessing and that of the battalion's main element in June, Kinser and Bartels would fall into their respective, synergistic roles, having learned within a few days of working with each other what Rob Scott already knew—that the two stand-out lieutenants each brought unique capabilities to this vital and challenging crevice of the war, capabilities that would engender a whirlwind of effort by the Marines under their commands, aiding the fight in ways that few could have predicted. The duo realized that they'd feed off each other during their first patrol together, just a few days after Matt's arrival at the firebase. Bound for the home of a former high-ranking mujahideen commander, Haji Arref, they headed up the Waigal Valley, a sinewy corridor that connects the Kunar with Nuristan. As Kinser remained stone-faced, Bartels drew a wide grin upon reaching their destination—and their Marines stared bug-eyed at the sight before them: a massive, ornate private compound deep in the recesses of the

Kunar. Haji Arref invited the patrol inside his walled complex, complete with a mosque and living quarters for his personal bodyguards, then ordered one of his goats slaughtered for a feast. Through an interpreter, the jovial Bartels began discussing the Soviet war with Arref as Kinser chuckled to himself at the sight of a dummy bomb leaning up against a wall in the former commander's rear courtyard, wondering how he'd gotten his hands on Soviet practice munitions. The lieutenant tapped his knuckles on the skin of the ten-foot-long decoy, but didn't hear the hollow *bong* he'd expected. "Kinser!" Matt blared, laughing his ass off. "That's a thousand-pound bomb the Soviets dropped on his compound here in the eighties—that never exploded!" Kinser laughed, then took a step back. "He kept it as a war memento, it's one of his prized possessions. His kids played hide-and-seek behind it growing up!"

"That's fucking hilarious," Kinser barked. "Shit, what a great story. Guess he's pretty confident in the shoddy quality control of Soviet bomb fuses."

After the dinner—of local bread, okra, rice, and what Kinser decided was undercooked goat—Arref brought out two olive-drab belts. "From da killed Russians!" the lieutenants' interpreter, Rafi, chortled. "Ha ha ha!" Arref lifted up his shirt to reveal he was wearing his so that its buckle, a Russian star, was turned upside down, pointing to the ground. "Commander Arref says to wear this star Russian reversed, you'll make many friends here." Bartels threaded it on—star pointed down—and pledged to his host that he'd never be without it for the remainder of 2/3's deployment, just one of many gestures the gregarious and charming midwesterner would make to connect the locals with the Marines. Those connections would grow so strong that some villagers literally cried at the end of the Blessing Marines' stint in Nangalam.

Kinser was right. The goat meat *was* undercooked, but he didn't let the resulting dysentery slow him down. In the weeks before 2/3's main element arrived, the lieutenant ventured throughout the Korangal, the Matin, and the Pech. He learned names and faces, hammered down basic language skills, immersed himself in culture and tradition, and got to know the ASF members—whom he worked with to hone their weapons-handling and tactical skills—as close friends. By the mid-June arrival of the battalion's main element, Kinser had become a virtual expert in the greater Pech region, particularly the Korangal Valley, as well as honing his skills in the use of the various Soviet-style weapons the Afghans used for Blessing's perimeter defense and on operations. The tireless lieutenant knew that the more time he spent in the high reaches of the area, the better. He just wanted to be outside the wire with his Marines and the ASF. On the other side of the world from tiny Jonesville, Virginia, Kinser felt more in his element than he'd ever felt before.

"Seiffert, we need a name for this op," Tom Wood quipped at his assistant-in-training, First Lieutenant Lance Seiffert, at the JAF COC soon after the lieutenant arrived in-country. "3/3 was doin' mostly basketball names—Texas basketball names, but their last was going to be *Stars,* a Texas hockey team. MacMannis wants to continue with hockey teams, but from throughout the rest of the States."

"Right, sir. I'll make up a list." The diligent Seiffert jumped on the Internet and came up with a list of ten, from the New York Rangers to the Colorado Avalanche.

"Can't do New York, Seiffert, those are the Rangers. We're Marines; that'll confuse people—they'll think it's an Army Ranger op. Scratch that one."

"How 'bout number four, sir, Detroit?" Seiffert asked.

"Yeah . . . yeah, sounds good. I'll run it by MacMannis, but let's go with it. I like it. *Red Wings.*"

By 20 June, Wood had *Red Wings* mapped out in detail, a detail that would accommodate the rules to which CJSOTF-A mandated such vehement adherence. As well, the OpsO drafted an official goal for the mission: "Disrupt anticoalition militia activity in the Korangal/Shuryek/ Pech region to further stabilize the area for the forthcoming 18 September 2005 national parliamentary elections." However, since the majority of the ACM (anticoalition militia) attacks at that point had been orchestrated and undertaken by Shah and his men (intel had directly attributed eleven attacks to Shah by that point, including IED strikes, mortar and rocket attacks, and small-arms ambushes), "Commander Ismael" and his terrorist cadre were the clear targets.

The op would consist of five phases:

1. **Shaping:** A NAVSOF reconnaissance and surveillance team observes the NAIs, guiding the direct-action team of phase two to specific, prenumbered structure(s).

2. **Action on the Objective:** A Navy SEAL direct-action team inserts by fastrope from TF-Brown's MH-47s onto the target(s) positively identified by the reconnaissance and surveillance team. Just minutes after the direct-action team inserts, the MH-47s return, inserting Kinser and a group of nineteen of his hand-selected Marines to form an inner cordon. The direct-action team, having linked up with their recon unit, kills or captures Shah and any of his men as Kinser's team closely guards the objective. NAVSOF personnel then exfil on the craft that just inserted Kinser and his Marines. Simultaneously, members of Echo Company's First Platoon form a blocking position at the opening of the Korangal Valley and Echo's Third Platoon moves into the Shuryek Valley, each pushing southward, "up" their respective valleys, to interdict any of Shah's cell that may have slipped away undetected. Once the NAVSOF teams lift off the ground, the Marines assume the command, or "supported" status, of the operation.

3. **Outer Cordon:** After the direct-action hit, Golf Company, reinforced with a platoon of Afghan National Army soldiers, inserts by helicopter at Korangal Village, establishes security, then moves by foot up the northwest shoulder of Sawtalo Sar into the village of Chichal, and links up with Kinser and his Marines, sweeping for insurgents and terrorists and searching for weapons caches along the way.

4. **Security and Stabilization:** In the days following the first three phases of the operation, Golf and Echo Company Marines maintain security of the region, conduct a MEDCAP, and find out the needs of the locals—improved roads, schools, wells, mosques, etc., and pass that information to provincial reconstruction teams.

5. **Exfiltration (exfil):** Depending on enemy activity, the Marines stay for as little as one week or as long as three or more weeks, then walk out to the Pech Valley Road, where convoys of Humvees will return them to Camp Blessing or Camp Wright at Asadabad, then continue to push regular patrols out of Camp Blessing to reinforce ties the Marines made with the locals during *Red Wings*.

Wood also developed a comprehensive indirect fires plan—able to be used throughout all phases of *Red Wings*: based in part on "Doghouse 10," two 105mm howitzers of the Army's Task Force "Gun Devil," located at Camp Wright at Asadabad. The guns, utilizing RAP rounds (rocket-assisted projectile rounds) could reach just far enough to accurately hit targets on the summit of Sawtalo Sar and the upper Korangal Valley. Wood, born and raised thinking, living, dreaming, and acting MAGTF and the synergy of combined arms, detailed a number of specific locations throughout each NAI for a call for fire to aid friendly forces—be those forces the initial reconnaissance and surveillance team, the SEAL direct-action team, Kinser and his Marines, the Golf Company outer cordon element, or either of the blocking positions—so that any of those friendlies could direct the psychologically and physically overwhelming high-explosive rounds onto any number of predetermined targets should the fight go in the wrong direction.

The OpsO would also carefully integrate close air support into the *Red Wings* plan, ensuring that both fixed- and rotary-wing CAS assets would be available to ground forces, should they need them. Wood tapped Casmer "Pigeon" Ratkowiak, 2/3's air officer, to outline the specifics of the air side of *Red Wings,* although unlike the combined-arms assault they practiced back in Twentynine Palms, close air support would be included as an on-call asset only, like the howitzers of Doghouse. The reserved and complex Ratkowiak, a Marine F/A-18D Hornet aviator with nine hundred hours in the cockpit who was also trained as a forward air controller, would ensure that Army AH-64s would be ready as rotary-wing attack assets, that Air Force A-10 Thunderbolt II "Warthogs" would be able to provide fixed-wing CAS, that Air Force C-130s would be ready to parachute-drop CDS (containerized delivery system) packs for resupply of food, water, ammo, and other vital matériel, and that Task Force Sabre's transport and air ambulance Chinooks and Blackhawks were prepped for their roles as well. Pigeon was also ready to both advise and to deconflict with conventional aviation assets any SOF air platforms, such as the TF-Brown's MH-47s and the devastating Air Force Special Operations AC-130 gunships.

Communication, one of the central pillars of tactical operations, would prove particularly critical for *Red Wings.* With input from Kinser based on his experiences throughout the greater Pech region, the OpsO thought it best for ground units to use the "Cadillac" of commo gear, the PRC-117, as the lieutenant noted that other radios, particularly the PRC-148 MBITR (Multi-Band Inter/Intra Tactical Radio—pronounced "Em-Biter") tended to hit "blackout" points and often couldn't generate enough power to "bounce" a signal out of the region's deep valleys. While it was not typically used for Marine Corps combat operations, the lieutenant also had experience with the Iridium satellite phone (which he and other Marines of Blessing used to call home from base) and noted that it was prone to peculiar blackout points as well, only working semireliably in Blessing from one small courtyard near the base's COC. Powerful, capable of using a broad spectrum of networks including satellite communication (SATCOM), and able to encrypt both data and voice transmissions, the 117 virtually never failed. Those who carried the 117, however, knew it as a beast—big, heavy, and a power drain, requiring the portaging of a number of heavy lithium batteries along with the phone-book-size unit to stay in "good comms" with the rest of the battalion—as opposed to the small MBITR, about the size of a box of spaghetti, and just a few pounds, even with a spare battery.

Wood planned every aspect of phases three to five in meticulous detail, and made himself available to Kristensen during the SEAL lieutenant commander's planning of phases one and two, even offering some information about clandestine mountain operations he'd gleaned from Eggers. Kristensen struck Wood as an uncompromising tactician, every bit as committed to the success of *Red Wings* and the safety of those on the ground as the OpsO. While confident in the abilities of Kristensen and other NAVSOF planners for their phases of *Red Wings*, Wood did question a few of their decisions. First, Wood assumed that their reconnaissance and surveillance team would insert by foot, departing from one of the villages in the Pech Valley, such as Watapor, which lay just twelve hours distant for a strong team like Ronin (traveling through the mountains, not on established roads or large trails). But, he learned, they would insert by helicopter, fastroping onto a spot just over a mile from NAIs 2, 3, and 4 on the saddle between Sawtalo Sar and its sister peak just to its south, Gatigal Sar, certainly alerting Shah and his men of the close presence of American forces, Wood thought. Kristensen noted, however, that TF-Brown would conduct nighttime "decoy drops" during the week leading up to the actual insert date (which still hadn't been determined, pending final SIGINT hits positively identifying Shah's location), "acclimatizing" Shah and the locals to helicopter activity in the region. Furthermore, Kristensen explained, TF-Brown would conduct a two-ship insert, with one craft actually deploying the reconnaissance and surveillance team, while the other undertook a series of low hovers over areas outlying Chichal and Korangal Village, intending to confuse Shah and his cell. This was a standard, and proven, SOF technique; but Wood still felt uneasy about a helo insert for phase one. The prime reason he brought in special operations forces to begin with was to guarantee air for the main direct-action hit and subsequent cordon—and to do the hit with maximum surprise. With a helo insert for phase one, he felt, the bad guys stood a huge chance of learning of American forces arriving in the area before the recon team even hit the ground—and long before they would get "eyes on" the target from OP-1.

The size of the recon team also bothered Wood. NAVSOF planners chose to insert just four men for phase one. The OpsO would also learn that the four had never operated in the Korangal and Sawtalo Sar area. From Kinser's briefs, Wood knew that each small nook of the Hindu Kush held its own unique challenges, from the standpoints of terrain, weather, and the locals—and the challenges of the Korangal area revealed themselves to be of deadly serious proportions. Wood felt that the best chances of success came with a team of six, as he originally planned with Eggers and Team Ronin. Comms posed another issue; when asked about their communications gear, Tom learned that they would in fact not be carrying a 117, but an MBITR with a "Sat Fill" allowing the small five-watt radio (as opposed to the 117's twenty watts) to utilize SATCOM with encryption. As a backup, the recon team would use an Iridium satellite phone, not a piece of comm gear Tom would approve for any of 2/3's operations, particularly after hearing Kinser's experiences with the unit at Camp Blessing, just eight air miles from Sawtalo Sar. Also related to potential communications problems, NAVSOF chose to command their phases of *Red Wings* from their COC in Bagram. While the SEALs would place liaisons at the JAF COC housing the Marine command—to ensure no "blue on blue" (fratricide) incidents, and to help coordinate any rescue attempt, should one be needed—Wood regarded this as an absolute, and potentially disastrous split of *Red Wings'* command and control, not only a bifurcation of the employment of C2, but a physical separation of the two command elements. Regardless of his trepidations, however, Wood knew of the successes of NAVSOF teams, particularly in Afghanistan, and understood that their tactics, techniques, and procedures differed from those of conventional forces. Still, the details of the first two phases irked the fiery Marine Corps officer. He'd raised all his concerns with NAVSOF, but they seemed to have their strategy squared away—and the details of phases one and two were theirs to plan, not Wood's. *This just isn't the way to put together an op,* he thought. *But it's the only motherfucking way we can do it in this operational environment.* Tom, whose father fought in Vietnam as a Marine—and who designated the Marine Corps University as his sole beneficiary should he die in Afghanistan—felt as if he was selling his soul to the "joint devil" just to get something as basic as air support (that he'd have with a snap of a finger and without any compromise in a MAGTF). Wood briefed the mission to higher command, directly to Kamiya himself. The major general asked just a few questions before approving the mission. Now the op just needed the final, decisive SIGINT hits, then *Red Wings* would launch.

"Bradley, we got something good here." Kinser approached Corporal Justin Bradley, a six-foot-five-inch, 270-pound wall of concrete of a Marine from the mountains of northern Montana, on 22 June. "Just got word from higher that some big, high-speed op with Navy SEALs is goin' down and we're tasked with the inner cordon and security of the direct-action hit on some terrorist cell."

"Sounds pretty cool, sir," Bradley, the twenty-three-year-old leader of First Platoon's First Squad replied in his typically relaxed drawl.

"I'm gonna hand-select the best of the platoon's Marines for this— making twenty total, including me. It's gonna be a fastrope insert somewhere in the upper Korangal or even the top of Sawtalo Sar, so we're gonna have to get qualled [qualified] for fastrope."

"But, sir, everyone in the platoon's already qualled," Bradley responded with confused exasperation.

"Army doesn't recognize our quals. We'll have to go to Asadabad to get the qual, then we push out from there for the op."

By that evening, Kinser had collected his group of nineteen that included Bradley; Bradley's close friend from boot camp Corporal Cody Fisher (squad leader of Third Squad); William "Red" Davidson, a feisty expert in Marine Corps martial arts never without a golf-ball-size wad of tobacco between his lower lip and gum; the reserved but witty Lance Corporal Christopher Burgos; the utterly selfless Navy Corpsman HM3 Luis "Doc" Anaya; and Lance Corporal Kevin Joyce, who hailed from the Navajo Nation town of Window Rock, Arizona, and was the grand-son of one of the fabled Code Talkers of World War II.

The team of twenty arrived at Asadabad late in the afternoon of 24 June, just as Westerfield prepared to snap the final pieces of Shah's intel picture into place. Having deciphered the extremist's identity, his asso-ciates, his financial backing, and his general patterns of movement, Westerfield just waited on the last critical SIGINT hits to reach his desk so he could process the information and then enable the recon team to get their eyes on the exact set of homes and/or farmhouses to positively identify Shah.

That intel came, by way of the Army's SIGINT teams, late in the eve-ning of 24 June: on 26 June, Shah and members of his small cell would move to a location denoted simply as "11," a farmhouse set a few meters off the Super Highway on the edge of some trees at the opening of a broad, gently sloping field on the northwest aspect of NAI-4, almost exactly two hundred meters to the south of the designated helicopter landing zone "Swift." *This is perfect,* Westerfield thought, *within direct line-of-sight of OP-1, almost exactly one mile from, and 250 meters lower in elevation than, the observation post. They'll look right down on it.* "Gotch-YOU!" Westerfield uttered menacingly as he poked his index finger onto the yellow-circled 11 on his Predator imagery sitting on his cluttered desk.

But at that point, the battalion really only had a plan set to go and intel that *indicated* Shah's likely position on the night of the twenty-sixth. Wood and Westerfield knew all too well how the innumerable variables governing mission execution changed—changed—and changed again and again. The first changes would come just as Westerfield's SIGINT rolled in: Task Force Brown, while able to support the reconnaissance and sur-veillance team, the direct-action hard-hit team, and Golf Company's outer cordon, now wouldn't be able to also support Kinser's inner cor-don unit—the timing just wouldn't work. BUT, the moon would be shed-ding just enough illumination on the twenty-sixth—a day earlier than Wood initially projected to be the earliest launch date for *Red Wings*—to utilize Task Force Sabre's Chinooks. Kinser and his team would still qual for Army fastrope, but conventional Chinooks, known by their call signs as the "Big Windys" would insert them, not the MH-47s. But then, just as two Chinooks roared into Asadabad on 25 June, word came that Sabre's birds were too "tasked out," and couldn't support the insert of the twenty Marines. Kinser couldn't believe what he was hearing. "Sir, do we convoy back to Blessing now?" Bradley asked the lieutenant.

"I'm trying to get a grasp of what the fuck is going on here. At our level, we only have limited visibility on the overall mission," the lieutenant said, then pondered for a moment. "I bet we walk in. The Chinooks go back to Bagram, we wait for a night convoy to Blessing, and then we walk into the Korangal or Shuryek as part of a blocking position. Fuck, I don't know." And then, perfectly on cue for what Kinser jokingly began calling "a saga of combat governed by stream of consciousness," Kinser's company commander radioed him that an intel pop indicated fifty ACM fighters had just passed through the border and were headed toward a terrorist training camp about two and a half miles to the northeast of the village of Matin. "That's across the Pech River, way up on the side of some pretty steep mountains," Kinser said to Bradley, who stared at the lieutenant with a smirk.

"*Fifty* terrorists, huh, sir?" the squad leader said as he wiped a slick of sweat off his brow. "Thought you said they usually run in teams of around four to eight at a time, never more than twelve."

"That's right. *Fifty* . . . come on. That intel is *bullshit*. The ACM do this all the time; they talk to each other over their ICOMs, saying that fifty or one hundred fighters have just arrived, fresh with training and arms from Pakistan, and that they're planning some big attack—knowing full well that we're listening to 'em. It's just their ghetto-ass version of psyops [psychological operations], trying to scare us. It raised my hair the first time I heard it, but I learned to pretty much dismiss that trash after a few weeks of hearing it." Kinser shook his head. "Guess the Army SIGINT guys picked up on that chatter, and now we got no choice but to move on it. So we wait to hear if one of the CAATs [Combined Anti-Armor Team, a convoy of heavy-weapons-fitted Humvees and troop transport Humvees] will pick us up and insert us. Then we go on a hunt for an enemy that doesn't even exist. *Fuck*."

"Don't worry, Lieutenant Kinser," Bradley began, trying to hold back laughter. "At least we have each other," he enunciated slowly, moving his head back and forth as he gazed skyward.

"Go fuck yourself." Kinser couldn't help but laugh with everyone else. "And gimme one of those cigarettes, dammit," he barked.

Within an hour, Kinser learned that his team wouldn't be inserted at the base of the mountain by convoy after all—but by the very Chinooks on which they'd planned to practice fastroping. "So they can't support us for this op, but I guess the consolation prize is they insert us for a goat rope in the hills on their way home. Hey, at least we're in the mountains and we have guns. Fuckin' love this shit. Bradley, get everyone ready to load up."

"Okay, Girl Scouts! We're about to go on a helicopter ride into the mountains in Afghanistan. How 'bout that? Check your weapons—condition *one*!" With a *snap-click* of a charging handle, each grunt checked that his weapon was condition 1: magazine inserted into the weapon's well (or rounds in the feed trays of squad automatic weapons and M240s), round in the chamber, bolt forward, weapon on safe—ready to fire with a flick of a thumb on the fire selector. Drenched in sweat, the grunts hauled their gear up the loading ramp of the big Chinooks, the torrid blasts of jet exhaust knocking the wind out of some as they passed by the sides of the burly aircraft. Inside, the *thwack-thwack-thwack* of the chunky rotors spinning at idle added an almost soothing effect to the banshee whine of the engines and gearbox. Strapped down to the red webbing of the benches running the length of the "bird," the grunts heard the engines spin up as the rear ramp rose off the ground a few feet, allowing the ramp gunner to drop his M240 light machine gun into its mount, then arm it with a hasty *ker-CHUNK* heave on the bolt. The side gunners armed their 240s as well, locking 7.62 mm rounds into place, and as two Task Force Sabre AH-64 Apache gunship escorts screamed past their flanks, the Big Windy pilots coaxed the two beasts into the air, as smoothly as a couple of helium balloons rising in a gentle morning

Some of the most important work in the area would be done by the Marines led by 1st Lieutenant Rob Long (left), 1st Lieutenant Matt Bartels (middle), and the amazing 1st Lieutenant Patrick E. Kinser (next to Bartels). The three, dressed in local garb, led a tremendous outreach campaign with the locals, ultimately responsible for the rescue of Marcus Luttrell.   *USMC/Task Force KOA*

Scott Westerfield, the battalion's genius intel officer. *USMC/Task Force KOA*

1st Lieutenant Matt Bartels flanked by members of the ASF.
USMC/Task Force KOA

1st Lieutenant Matt Bartels in
local garb with his friend C-Put,
Camp Blessing.
USMC/Task Force KOA

1st Lieutenant Rob Long hands out much needed materials to girls of the school in Nangalam. This outreach made tremendous inroads to helping stabilize this restive part of Afghanistan. *USMC/Task Force KOA*

Lieutenant Matt Bartels flanked by two of his Marines in front of the girls of the school in Nangalam. *USMC/Task Force KOA*

A good view of Ahmad Shah, wagging finger. Note the guy with the video camera. There were two videos made of the ambush, one that made some rounds on the Internet, and was "produced" by As Sahab in Peshawar, Pakistan, and the one that was never released, from which I got this screen capture. *Digital Version courtesy Ed Darack*

Ahmad Shah speaks into his Icom during the ambush
Digital Version courtesy Ed Darack

Remains of a rotor assembly of the 160th SOAR(A) MH-47D helicopter shot down by Shah's men on the summit region of Sawtalo Sar, Shuryek Valley in background.
USMC/Task Force KOA

Shah's men with weapons and equipment captured after they ambushed the SEALs.
Digital Version courtesy Ed Darack

Lance Corporal Phillip George (left), and an Afghan soldier.
USMC/Task Force KOA

One of Shah's men making an IED. Notice the child in the background holding a handgun.
Digital Version courtesy Ed Darack

Making an IED, likely in the Korangal Valley.
Digital Version courtesy Ed Darack

Remains of a Humvee after an IED strike by Shah's men, from the convoy carrying Donnellan. *USMC/Task Force KOA*

Donkeys used for Operation *Whalers*. *USMC/Task Force KOA*

Keith Eggers, holding his M-40A3, on Sawtalo Sar.
USMC/Task Force KOA

Pigman and Roy on Sawtalo Sar, near where they were ambushed by Shah's men during *Whalers*.   *USMC/Task Force KOA*

Lieutenant Colonel James Donnellan, the Battalion Commander of 2/3 after *Red Wings*, in the Korangal Valley.   *USMC/Task Force KOA*

Wilson, getting help up to the LZ for the inbound Dustoff.
USMC/Task Force KOA

One of the amazing Dustoff medevacs, getting Marines of Fox-3 off the ground after "Armageddon" during *Whalers*, just after nearly getting shot down by Shah's RPG gunner.   *USMC/Task Force KOA*

Marines carry Corpsman Jamie Pigman to the Dustoff that just put down on the side of Sawalo Sar.   *USMC/Task Force KOA*

Ben "'Dorf" Middendorf, Pigeon, and Konnie during *Whalers*.
USMC/Task Force KOA

Captain Kelly Grissom, Op *Whalers*, Chowkay Valley.
USMC/Task Force KOA

Captain Kelly Grissom.   *USMC/Task Force KOA*

SAW gunner. *USMC/Task Force KOA*

Hauling the heavy 81mm mortars into the steep Chowkay during *Whalers*.
USMC/Task Force KOA

The Chowkay Valley. *USMC/Task Force KOA*

Ben Middendorf. *USMC/Task Force KOA*

breeze. As the helicopter's rotors dug into the summer sky, lifting the Marines above the dusty landscape, cool puffs of air swirled through the side gun hatches. The Marines lifted the fronts of their helmets, getting a few spates of relief—Kinser measured the temperature inside the Chinook with a small thermometer attached to his flak jacket: 121 degrees Fahrenheit, and it was barely noon.

The grunts strained their necks to catch a glimpse out the rear of the Chinook. The door gunner, his restraint strap perfectly measured (and double-checked), sat with his legs dangled off the edge of the ramp, scanning side to side, looking for tracer rounds arcing up toward the craft from the ground. The Apaches, swinging back and forth relative to the straight flight line of the Chinook, kept even closer watch for ground threats through their targeting optics. Between the two ribbons of exhaust, the Marines could trace the path of the turquoise Kunar River as it struck west toward Nangarhar province, then once over the confluence of the Pech and the Kunar, the aircraft banked west, into the steep-walled Pech Valley. Kinser, forever in love with the ground "side of the show," felt mildly envious of military aviators, getting to see the complex landscape from an eagle's perspective, day in and day out. At an altitude well below the highest ridges and summits of the mountains framing the narrow Pech, the side and ramp gunners now craned their necks upward as well as side to side, as with each *thwack* of the helicopter's blades, they drew farther into territory roamed by the enemy, an enemy often intimately familiar with all those ridges and peaks under which the Chinooks streaked.

Their target sighted—a single mud-brick–and–stone building on the side of a grassy slope—the pilots spun the craft around, dropped each Chinook's loading ramp as the rear gunners detached their 240s, and the aviators gently connected the edges of the ramps with the steep slope. "MOVE—FUCKIN' *GIRL SCOUTS*! Get out and hold perimeter!" Bradley roared over the stentorian scream of the jet engines. The grunts bolted onto the steep ground, spellbound at the expertise of the Army aviators—the rearmost aspect of the aft rotors spun just feet above the slope, the Chinooks' landing gear dangling in the air; only the helicopters' ramps made contact with the ground. Overhead, the Apaches carved tight arcs through the sky, the pilots always keeping their eyes on the ground below, ready to unleash their crafts' 30 mm canons and 2.75-inch Hydra rockets on any threat that popped up.

"Damn, that's fuckin' amazing," Burgos muttered to himself at the sight of the Chinooks "backed into" the mountain, the rotor wash blowing small tornadoes in the long, flowing, green grass. "How the hell do they do that without crashing?" he asked Kinser.

"Very carefully, that's how. They're fucking badasses. Wish they could support us for that op we were gonna do." With twenty cases of MREs and fifty cases of bottled water off-loaded, the Chinooks' pilots spun the engines up and eased the two birds back into the heights, disappearing into the eastern distance with the Apaches, leaving only the sounds of gentle breezes on the airy slope—and some ringing in the grunts' ears.

"Wow, look at all these extremist fighters here at this big-ass training facility," Kinser began as he searched for a cigarette, examining the eight-foot-by-eight-foot-by-five-foot-high rock hut. "Think there's fifty midget Taliban in there, Bradley?"

"Let's find out." Bradley lifted a latch and swung open a rickety wood door, exposing piles of harvested corn kernels.

"Oh . . . *shit*. Somebody gimme a cigarette," Kinser ordered, shaking his head. "Great intel." For the next four hours, the twenty Marines fanned out over the entire mountain above them, finding nothing—no weapons caches, no signs any bad guys had ever even been in the area. Then an old shepherd rounded a corner, the owner of the small storage shack. As the Marines greeted the Afghan, Kinser's company commander radioed the lieutenant. "Nope, no monkey bars, no guys with black masks running through an obstacle course, no Osama bin Laden, just a nice old man and some corn." Kinser gave a quick brief over a secure net.

"Okay. Then get back to Blessing, and take all that chow and water with you. Get back immediately, I mean *now*." Kinser tried to explain the situation on the ground—the very, very steep ground below his feet—and that portaging the hundreds of pounds of chow and water would be virtually impossible without making a number of trips up and down the slope. After more back-and-forth, Kinser's commander finally acquiesced, and the lieutenant gave all the supplies to the shepherd, which the Marines stacked inside and around his storage shack. Then, communicating more with hand gestures and facial expressions than in Pashto, Kinser apologized for "dropping in" on him and invading his space. The Marines followed their new friend down the mountain, on their way stopping by his small house, from which the shepherd brought out a large jug.

"I think he wants to give us something," Kinser said with mock trepidation, still reeling from the undercooked goat at Haji Arref's compound. As the shepherd poured cups of the creamy liquid, Burgos and Bradley looked at each other with fear for their commander.

"Sir, you aren't gonna—"

Kinser gulped it down. "This shit is damn good. Goat's milk! First time I've ever had milk from a *goat*. Well, from a goat rope mission, we get goat's milk! *Mmm*." He finished off the cup, remarking how cool the drink felt in his throat.

"Sir, I think it isn't that cool; it's just that it's so freakin' hot out that even something that's a hundred degrees tastes cool," Fisher added, then drank some himself.

With the sun closing on the jagged western horizon, Kinser and his Marines fanned out and started down the mountain. "Keep thirty feet of dispersion, Girl Scouts!" Bradley shouted repeatedly as the Marines clumped up on their passage down the peak. "Remember, it's a lot easier for them to hit us if we're all fuckin' clumped together. Keep dispersed!" Many of the grunts had never faced such a grueling physical challenge before; each carried from eighty to one hundred pounds of gear and Kinser's thermometer showed the temperature to be 105 degrees just as the sun kissed the horizon. Their body armor wasn't just heavy, it compressed their chests, bound into their shoulders, and their Kevlar helmets acted as convection ovens, literally cooking their heads in the intense heat. "This isn't fuckin' boot camp! And this ain't training!

This is for *fuckin' real,*" Bradley roared. "Stay damned dispersed and look alive. We can get shot at at any moment!"

Kinser, who bounded down the mountain at the head of the patrol, got tired of Bradley and Fisher constantly reminding their Marines how to be Marines.

"Listen, motherfuckers," he finally said. "I love you all. But if you didn't want to worry about twisting your ankles or getting fucked-up knees and backs by the time you're twenty-five, then you shouldn't have joined the fucking Marine Corps. Understand? I'm tired of hearing Bradley and Fisher have to tell you how to act like Marines. Let's rest for five, then when we step off again, stay fucking dispersed and keep up with me!"

Burgos, who'd kept up with Kinser for the entire movement, proclaimed during the break, "Sir, I think we're gonna have to start calling you the centaur."

"The centaur, huh?" Kinser responded. "Fisher, gimme another cigarette."

"What the fuck is a centaur?" "Red" Davidson asked.

"It's one of those white horses with a horn sticking out of its head, runs out of crashing waves with twinkly stars and a rainbow in the background. My ex-girlfriend's little sister used to have posters of them all over her room," Fisher stated with a wry grin as he handed the lieutenant a cigarette.

"No, dumb-ass, that's a fuckin' unicorn," Bradley interjected. "A centaur's a—"

"Half *man,* Half *stallion,*" Kinser roared as he exhaled a long plume of smoke from atop a boulder, then broke a huge grin—causing everyone else to fall down in laughter. "Now let's get movin'" But while Kinser time and again showed his bravado in a joking, almost self-effacing way, he knew from Officer Candidate School and now in the field that great leadership stemmed in large part from physical ability. The dysentery had thrashed the young lieutenant from the inside out. He'd lost nearly twenty pounds, and could easily have just lain in bed for much of his days. But as an infantry officer, he didn't just have to keep up, he had to set the pace—a strong pace, no matter how difficult the terrain or weakened his condition. He had to charge ahead not fearlessly, but with honest confidence and deliberateness, never revealing even the slightest hint of discomfort, pain, or trepidation. Marines watch their commanders, they pick them apart, notice their weaknesses, and Kinser valued stalwart leadership of grunts in the field above all else.

"Oo-rah." All nineteen Marines sounded off in consonance.

"Hey, Bradley. Just to let you know, I know what a unicorn is. I was just jokin' around." Fisher enlightened his close friend.

"Sure you do, Fish. I'm sure you're a real expert on unicorns."

"Hey, sir, how do you know that the shepherd back up there wasn't a Taliban or al-Qaeda supporter?" Burgos asked as the group neared the floor of the Pech Valley, now cloaked in the shadow of dusk.

"Well . . ." Kinser thought as he bounded onto easier terrain, sighting the Pech Valley Road a few hundred meters ahead of him, "I suppose since we can't read minds, we don't really know. But we didn't find any weapons caches in the little storage house, and there was no dunnage [leftover material from rocket or mortar attacks] anywhere on the mountain, and the guy's little one-room house had nothing in it any of us could see, so then he's just a regular Afghan, living his life." The lieutenant, who, like many of his peers, possessed wisdom years beyond his age, continued: "I mean, look, we got bum intel, and you have to remember that the only real intelligence is gathered once boots hit the deck, and we get eyes on. Our boots hit the deck, we got eyes on, and the guy was clean—even gave us some kick-ass goat milk. We're deep in the counter-insurgency part of this war. We can't treat every Afghan like a bad guy. Far from it; it's all about restraint. We can't be pissing off the locals who the bad guys are tellin' that they'll be around long after we leave, and to trust them and not us. Read your ROE [rules of engagement] card. Read it, memorize it, and read it again." Kinser was referring the "CJTF-76 Operation Enduring Freedom-VI Rules of Engagement Card," a three-by-five-inch document published on 15 March 2005 detailing how all forces under CJTF-76 (both conventional as well as SOF) could and couldn't engage known or potential enemy combatants. "I got that shit memorized, Burgos, and you should to. Points seven and eight are two of the most important: 'Civilians Are Not Targets,' and 'Respect Private Property.'" The lieutenant continued to explain the ROEs, which Burgos knew, but didn't understand to the depth Kinser wanted. "You've only been here a short while; you'll pick up the subtleties pretty quick."

Rule number one on the ROE list—"You have the right to use force, including deadly force, to defend yourself"—obviously ranked as the most critical, and the one onto which battalion leadership focused the attention of the grunts during their predeployment training more than any other. In the COIN fight, however, only in-the-field knowledge, of the kind Kinser had gained through trial by fire during his first month in-country, could provide a basis for distinguishing an elusive enemy hiding in the hills and among villagers from a civilian. And that enemy was as much a mind-set as a group, cell, or even individual, for example a villager who supported a terrorist, but who would then help Marines locate that terrorist (possibly because he'd mistreated others in the village). "Those SOF dudes beat the Taliban's asses in a matter of weeks in 2001. They crushed their fuckin' nuts, slaughtered them like pigs. The enemy we have now hides among the people, and looks for support from them. So we gotta ensure that those villagers know that we're on the side of their security—that they can trust us and the new government completely—and at the same time kill the motherfuckers who are trying to use those villagers for their own purposes," the thoughtful lieutenant, who graduated at the top of his class from Michigan State University with a degree in physical chemistry, added. "Marines have to be the pros, the real fuckin' pros, Burgos. Can't act like cowboys; that time's come and gone—a long time ago in *this* war."

But determining friend from foe would prove frustratingly difficult to do; Kinser taught himself to rely on a sixth sense he'd gained through experience and from members of 3/3. Having run patrols throughout the Korangal, Pech, and Shuryek, the lieutenant knew all too well about the "soft compromise," where a local noncombatant—often a goat herder or a woodcutter—appears out of nowhere. "And then you never know what he's gonna do once he rounds the bend in the trail—just keep tending his goats or pull out an ICOM and let his insurgent buddies know our pos [position], or maybe just start humming loudly, or tapping a stick to a certain beat—there are all sorts of ways they can alert the bad guys to our presence. The only way to really know is to make sure everybody in these hills *knows* that we're here to help 'em, and simultaneously kill or capture the terrorists and insurgents. I prefer killing over capturing," Kinser stated with a grin. "Don't have to worry about prison breaks and all that." But after decades of slaughter, the locals were wary of outside military forces, and Kinser knew that getting them to trust American intentions was a tough sell; only staying outside the wire, living with the villagers themselves, was the answer. "If it were up to me, Burgos, me and you and Bradley and Red, and everyone here would never see the inside of Camp Blessing for the rest of our deployment. We'd eat chicken and rice every night with the locals and run the hills for the next six months, drinkin' goat milk, makin' new friends like that old man up there. I fully expect one day to come back here with my wife and kids and go on vacation, maybe at the 'Nangalam Mountain Resort.' That'd be pretty fuckin' cool."

"Yeah." Burgos laughed. "That would be pretty cool, sir."

"Okay, Girl Scouts, keep sharp!" Bradley commanded as the group of twenty reached the Pech Road—Camp Blessing's "MSR," or main supply route, and Kinser got on the radio to call for a CAAT. "Three guys. That's all it takes." The burly corporal thrust his index finger at three positions on the mountains above them that he'd identified as ideal platforms from which to set an ambush. "Three of those motherfuckers, all in superior [higher] positions from us, two guys on PK machine guns, and one with an RPG." Bradley was referring to a standard ambush technique frequently seen in the area: often beginning with an RPG hit, two machine gunners from different positions "open up" so that their respective lines of fire meet exactly on the target, "interlocking" those streams of rounds, forming a triangular "tip of death" as RPG rounds rain down. Such an ambush can make three bad guys seem like thirty—or even a hundred and thirty—and had been preferred by the mujahideen as a way to hold up massive columns of Soviet armor. Although in the event of an ambush, Kinser would immediately start a call for fire from Doghouse, potential ambushers need just five seconds to send enough rounds downrange to kill a small group of Marines standing close together. Dusk was a preferred time to strike, with enough light to see a target with the naked eye, but not dark enough for the grunts' night-vision goggles to work.

There would be no ambush that night, however. Kinser stared out at the Pech River, its thunderous roar fed by the massive snowmelt of one of the wettest winters on record. Like clockwork, CAAT-Alpha arrived, with an additional local Toyota truck to help carry the Marines and their gear. Having spent the past month up and down the Pech Road, Kinser had seen the water level slowly climb, nearing the road in some places. He also knew that the road itself was in bad shape, making night driving all the more dangerous with its washouts and deep ruts. He wanted the CAAT drivers to run with headlights, not have to operate blacked out on NVGs (night-vision goggles). But his commander had mandated running dark. So they loaded their gear into the Toyota and the highback Humvee (a troop transport Humvee fitted with benches, surrounded by light armor high enough to protect Marines while sitting), then jumped into the trucks.

"You know, Joyce, you never complain about anything," Bradley said to the young lance corporal, who, at just 135 pounds, was one of the smallest in the platoon. "I love that about you." A SAW gunner (squad automatic weapon, or M249, a fully automatic weapon much heavier than an M16), Joyce quickly developed a reputation in the platoon as one of the best Marines of the bunch, one who never once complained about any patrol, food, living quarters—anything—and who always volunteered first for any mission or project. He was tough, but with a magnetically kind demeanor; shy but absolutely reliable. He smiled at Bradley and jumped into the highback. "Okay, bitches, let's get the fuck back to that wonderful wonderland of Camp Blessing!" Bradley slammed the heavy doors shut on the highback and jumped into the Hilux, then the convoy slipped into the pitch darkness of the June night.

The condition of the road proved even worse than Kinser had remembered. The drivers, who sped the convoy along as fast as possible to minimize time windows for any IED triggermen to set off explosives, slammed the Humvees into ruts and potholes, sending the Marines in the highback flying off their benches. They hit one pothole so hard that the Marines thought they'd been struck by a small IED. Then a slam into a rut knocked the NVGs off the driver of the highback, blinding him as he veered into a deep rut on the edge of the road. The violent jolt flung three of the Marines out of the rear of the truck, over the steep riverbank, and into the icy, roiling waters of the Pech, ten feet below the road. The convoy screeched to a halt. Bradley, Fisher, and the other Marines jumped into action, scrambling down the embankment and wading into the numbing water as Marines who'd fallen into the river clung to rocks and boulders, fighting off the crushing cold and gasping for breath, the weight of their flak jackets with heavy ceramic plates and helmets filled with water adding to their struggle. "Gimme a fuckin' HEAD COUNT!" Everybody was there, but one: Joyce.

"Where the FUCK is he?" Fish yelled over the thunderous rush of the pitiless river. Kinser immediately got on the hook with Matt Bartels. "Start droppin' illum rounds. Drop 'em NOW!" The lieutenant passed Matt their coordinates and within seconds the river lit up under the blinding-white light of parachute-suspended 120 mm phosphorus illumination mortar rounds.

"We're fuckin' findin' him!" Kinser roared.

"JOYCE!" the Marines bellowed into the night as they locked arms and waded chest-deep into the water, their breathing crushed by the water's iciness. "*JOYCE!*"

"We got two Apaches and a Dustoff inbound to you guys," Bartels passed to Kinser. The Dustoff, the call sign for the Army's famed Air Ambulance units, was a UH-60 Blackhawk, and came equipped with a powerful spotlight. The mortarmen lobbed the illum rounds at perfect intervals; just as one died, another popped open hundreds of yards higher. Once the Dustoff roared in zone, the mortarmen ceased dropping, and under cover of the Apaches, the pilots of the UH-60 flew the craft just ten to fifteen feet above the river, beaming the penetrating spotlight into the water. But the air crew could see nothing, not at the site of the accident, or downstream, during their hours-long search. Lance Corporal Kevin B. Joyce, so young, vital, capable, and recognized by his peers and his commanders as such a great Marine, yet so reserved, kind, and utterly selfless, was gone.

"Sir, everyone's gonna get hypothermia. We can't keep goin' into the water," Doc Anaya told Kinser. Both soaked from head to toe, they struggled to keep from shivering. The lieutenant just stared at Anaya in the darkness, then nodded. Anaya—a member of one of the most important cadres of U.S. Marine Corps units (and most distinguished groups in the entire U.S. military)—attached Navy Corpsmen—who not only fight side by side with infantry, but stand ready to drop their weapons even in the thickest of battle to save Marines' lives (as well as those of civilians, and even injured enemy combatants)—realized that each of the group had overtaxed himself, and might go missing in the torrent as well. Anaya's struggles that night, shoulder to shoulder with the others, proved that although the letters on his camis spelled out *U.S. Navy*, he was a grunt through and through.

"Call just came in that we need to mount up in the convoy and get back to Blessing," Kinser stated firmly. Kinser's company commander wanted CAAT to keep moving. The Marines solemnly loaded up and headed back home.

But just a couple hours after arriving at Blessing, Bradley and Fish organized a foot patrol to continue searching for the missing Marine, keeping their hopes alive that he'd washed ashore and survived the ordeal. Under the steel-blue glow of an eastern Afghan dawn, the Marines passed once again outside the wire, and hiked down to the spot where they last saw their friend. Then again, with arms locked, they waded into the river, combing for the young Marine for hours. But no sign of Joyce.

Later that day, a local farmer noticed that the furrows in his fields, normally inundated with slowly flowing irrigation water, had gone dry—something had clogged a main feeder channel. Walking his land, the local noticed an odd bundle of items blocking one of his main canals. Up close, he found what he recognized to be gear from Marines he'd seen in the area. He gathered the gear—a SAW, a belt of 5.56mm rounds for the weapon, a flak jacket, and a Kevlar helmet. The helmet had a name tape: JOYCE. The villager immediately brought the items to Blessing, dimming the Marines' hope for the lance corporal's survival. Days later, Joyce's body was found twenty miles downstream. The Marines at Camp Blessing held a memorial; with no requisite trumpet available at the small firebase, one of the Marines used his harmonica to play taps. The moment was somber and wrenchingly emotional, but one that left the incredible Marines with ever-greater resolve for their still-long road ahead. Joyce would forever occupy a place in their hearts.

"So the intel hits died off again?" Tom Wood looked at Westerfield like he wanted to punch the intel officer in the face.

"Didn't die off, Tommy. Just changed. Relax. He's *gonna* be there on the night of the twenty-seventh and stay there for at least two days. Structure 11, it's an IED factory and weapons-cache location. With those SOF guys heloing in—basically announcing their presence—we don't want the recon team lingering around any longer than they have to. They gotta insert on the twenty-seventh, not tonight. That'd be a day too soon, especially in that area." Wood sat down and dropped his face into his hands.

"And we still figure that he's got between six and twelve guys with him?" the OpsO asked.

"At the very, very most, he's got twenty fighters, and some other nonfighters he pays for support. Realistically, though, from the latest hard intel, we know he has between six and twelve. But those six to twelve are well-trained foreign fighters with experience," Westerfield responded.

"Okay. They helo-insert on the twenty-seventh. Brown's been doin' decoy drops all week, so let's hope that Shah or any of his lookouts figures its just another unlit helicopter buzzing around the villages up there." Westerfield stared back at Tom blank-faced, just as uneasy as the OpsO about NAVSOF's planning decisions for phase one, as well as what both felt to be a tenuous at best command structure that was inviting disaster. Even if disaster were to strike, however, the Marines had their component of *Red Wings'* quick reaction force (QRF) in place, prepared to speed to the rescue of NAVSOF personnel during the first two phases of the op. The QRF would consist of twenty-four Marines from Golf Company, led by Captain Pete Capuzzi, who would form the main effort of phase three of the mission with their job of outer cordon.

With the Marines of the QRF fastrope qualled and ready to act with lightning speed, *Red Wings* stood ready to launch on the night of 27 June 2005. Just hours prior to the scheduled insert of the reconnaissance team, Kristensen and other members of NAVSOF met with 2/3's commanders at the JAF COC and "rock-drilled" phase two and the segue into phase three. Confidence swelled at the meeting—the SEALs impressed with the Marines and the grunts confident in NAVSOF's fighting prowess—as they hashed out the final air support, indirect fires assets, deconfliction, and QRF details. By 6 P.M. at Jalalabad Airfield, as the scorching sun sank toward the dusty plains to the west, *Red Wings* seemed destined to become yet another success in joint operations in the area, despite the hardened stance on USSOCOM doctrine at the CJTF-76 and CJSOTF-A levels.

Just after sunset, as the orange glow of dusk began to succumb to night's grip, pilots readied two MH-47Ds of the 160th at a remote hangar at Bagram for another mission into the darkness. The modified Chinooks were some of the most impressive of Aviation's creations, and their crews looked after every maintenance and operational detail with an eye for perfection—the "birds" were masterpieces, and the maintainers sought to keep them in prime condition, despite innumerable combat flights. The two ships ready, the pilots "spun up" the large craft and lifted into the night, one a decoy bird and the other carrying seven NAVSOF personnel, including the four members of the recon team: Lieutenant Michael P. Murphy of SEAL Delivery Vehicle Team 1 out of Pearl Harbor, Hawaii, who would lead the team; Petty Officer Second Class Danny P. Dietz from SDVT-2 (based in Virginia Beach, Virginia); Petty Officer Second Class Matthew G. Axelson from SDVT-1; and Navy Hospital Corpsman Second Class Marcus Luttrell, of SDVT-1. Landing at JAF to refuel, three of the NAVSOF passengers jumped out to aid in liaising, while Kristensen and Wood climbed aboard. Ever concerned about the small team's success and safety, Wood made certain to pass to both Kristensen and then directly to Murphy six ten-digit grid reference points (a ten-digit grid reference point indicates a location on the ground to a resolution of one square meter) for calls for fire from Doghouse, who had those six coordinates preset into their mission package. If all went according to the detailed plan, in just over twenty-four hours, the direct-action team of *Red Wings*—composed primarily of members of SEAL Team 10—would envelop Shah and his operations, and that restive nook of the Hindu Kush would take yet another leap forward in stability. The powerful jet turbines roared to launch power under the control of the seasoned aviators, the big rotors dug into the night air, and the sounds of the "invisible" craft melted into silence. *Red Wings* had taken flight.

6

AMBUSH

With the waning glow of dusk a faded memory and the moon still hours from cresting the high, serrated complex of mountains to their east, the aviators piloting the two MH-47s guided their Chinooks through the darkest of Hindu Kush nights. Bound for Sawtalo Sar, they sped ghostlike over the village-dotted expanses of the lower Kunar Valley, then pressed ever higher above the vicious peaks surrounding the target zone. Viewing the world around them from behind the eerie green glow of their NVGs' reticules, the Army special operations aviators drove the powerful, heavily armed helicopters deep into the heart of the very worst of the enemy's lair. Intimate with the terrain from previous nights' decoy drops, the pilots once again hovered their craft over insert zones surrounding the village of Chichal and the summit region of Sawtalo Sar before the lead ship peeled off, arcing to the south of the mountain's uppermost triangular bulk. As the decoy bird roamed near more populated areas above the upper Korangal, the

Chinook carrying the recon team slowed as it approached a point about a third of a mile south-southwest of, and three hundred feet in elevation lower than, the peak's true summit, the "saddle" between Sawtalo Sar and Gatigal Sar. With the *clak-clak-clak* of the craft's twin rotors resonating in muffled *ka-klatter-ka-klatter-ka-klatter* echoes off the walls of the Korangal and Shuryek valleys, the SOAR(A) aviators eased the muscular bird into a perfect hover about thirty-five feet above a patch of lightly treed ground as the MH-47's crew chief lowered the Chinook's rear ramp and deployed a single three-inch-thick fastrope. The four members of the recon team, laden with a broad array of gear from food and water to weapons, donned their lightweight Pro-Tec helmets and calmly stood in anticipation of their phase of the mission, then approached the very rear of the craft. Both "torquing" with stacked clenched hands and pinching the line with their boots' inner soles, the SDVT SEALs slid into the abyss of the night's dimensionless pitch dark-ness and connected with the ground just seconds later, fanning out away from the MH-47's rotor wash as soon as their boots hit the deck. Feeling the fastrope go limp once the last of the team reached firm ground, the crew chief—trained for and accustomed to direct-action raids where he'd jettison the fastrope as soon as a team hit the ground—instinctively detached the line; the olive-drab fastrope snaked to the earth with a dull *whump* as the crew chief alerted the pilots that all four had suc-cessfully inserted. As the Chinook's turbofans' screams and its rotors' *clak clak clak*s melted into the silence of the staid night with the MH-47's quick departure, Murphy, Dietz, Axelson, and Luttrell moved to-ward OP-1. But the four didn't know about the dropped fastrope—this *wasn't* a direct-action hard-hit raid, but a covert insert, necessitating as small a footprint as possible. And for the SDVT recon team on the ground that night, that meant *no* footprint whatsoever, given that they were operating on Sawtalo Sar, literally in the den of some of the most viciously determined extremist fighters in the world. Relatively unfa-miliar with each respective unit's comprehensive standard operating procedures, neither the SOAR(A) planners nor those of NAVSOF dis-cussed the post-insert fate of the rope during mission planning. The

SEALs assumed the SOAR(A) crew would retract the fastrope, as this was a covert insert; but the TF-Brown aviators assumed that the SEALs would cache the line, as they felt—based both on their doctrine and experience—that lingering over enemy territory, even for a few extra seconds to reel in a fastrope, invited disaster. It allowed time for an enemy to put rounds into the large craft, and the attached fastrope presented a snagging danger (on trees or buildings) as the bird moved to exfil. The result of a seemingly small communications oversight during the planning phases of *Red Wings,* the rope just might prove the undoing of the entire operation . . .

Just over a mile away from their destination, the SEALs wasted no time putting the insert point well to their rear. The four moved quickly and with utmost stealth, despite portaging a full suite of gear: desert-camo "SOPMOD" M4 carbines each fitted with a flash/sound suppressor, an M203 40 mm grenade launcher, a visible wavelength laser pointer (producing a red dot on a target), an ACOG sight, and a PEQ-2A infrared floodlight/IR laser pointer (to be used with their night-vision goggles). Of course, they carried dozens of 5.56 mm thirty-round magazines and 40 mm high-explosive grenade rounds for their M4s and 203 launchers, as well as hand-lobbed fragmentation grenades should they make contact with Shah and his force. They also carried the MBITR, the Iridium satellite phone, infrared strobes to mark the insert point for the following night's direct-action raid, red and white pen flares, a GPS unit, laser rangefinders, Steiner binoculars, a large Leupold long-range spotting scope, a tripod on which to mount the scope, a digital camera, and a Panasonic "Toughbook" laptop on which they could process digital images of possible target individuals then interface with the MBITR to pass the photographs to the COC for positive identification via secure satellite transmission. The team also carried a "Phraselator," a wallet-size device loaded with prerecorded Pashto phrase files selectable in English on a menu screen, with the ability, through a speech recognition algorithm, to also translate phrases from English to Pashto by speaking into an attached microphone. As well, the team carried a 7.62 mm semiautomatic sniper rifle, similar to one Eggers had tested (designated an MK11 by the Marine Corps), to use for acquired targets of opportunity during phase two of the op. Should the unthinkable happen, and Shah's force overrun the small team, they carried incendiary grenades, which would render their valuable and sensitive gear useless in a white-hot conflagration as they egressed from harm's way.

The team maneuvered through the complex terrain of Sawtalo Sar's upper ramparts through the dark night. With dense carpets of low-lying ferns, steep rock outcroppings, fields of dead upright and fallen trees, and large deodar cedars reaching into the thin air at over nine thousand feet, upper Sawtalo Sar presents confusingly treacherous navigational challenges during the height of midday, much less during the depths of a moonless night. Further complicating operational difficulties, this time of year sees the influx of moisture from the Indian monsoon, fueling volatile, unpredictable thunderheads that lash the slopes of the peak like angry clenched fists, leaving the mountain's reddish-brown soil and sharp chunks of shale dangerously slick, even to daytime-traveling locals who know Sawtalo Sar and its trails, trees, outcrops, and villages like their own backyard. By midnight, however, with no sun to infuse convective energy for thunderheads to thrive, these storms typically disintegrate, revealing effervescent fields of stars, the brilliant view occasionally dashed by roving threads of dissipating clouds, the seasonal moisture then lying in wait for the pounding sun's energy to once again engender the powerful, capricious, and operationally vexing storms. The recon team traversed some of the earth's most unforgiving land that night, a forbidding yet uniquely beautiful labyrinth on which extremists could create a storm of fury for the Americans.

"They dropped the rope! I can't believe it! They dropped the *fucking* fastrope!" Lieutenant Rob Long overheard one of the Navy SEAL operational liaison officers exclaim hours after the insert at his post at the Jalalabad Airfield Combat Operations Center. Long, who, like Wood, viewed the decision to helo-insert what he thought to be an insufficiently manned team for phase one with skepticism, felt his heart drop at the news—news immediately conveyed to the recon team once the MH-47s returned to base and Kristensen learned of the rope's jettison.

This is their backyard, Long thought, referencing the locals whom Shah was known through intel to pay to keep tabs on Sawtalo Sar's many facets. Long knew that even tightly coiled, the fastrope would occupy a volume similar to that of a good-size moving box, something like three large suitcases stacked one atop another. *Where are they going to hide it?* Long wondered as he observed the commotion of the COC ramp into a near uproar. He imagined his own backyard, wondering how an outsider would conceal such a large package without him noticing. *They couldn't. Period.* And villagers throughout the Kunar lived far more intimately with their mountainous environment than the lieutenant did with his backyard. But with all the gear the SEALs already had with them, they couldn't pack that "anaconda" of a piece of gear as well. *Besides,* Long thought, *they must be far downrange of the fastrope. Would they break out of their concealed hide at OP-1 and risk being seen on their route to or from caching the rope?*

But the dropped fastrope could very possibly reveal itself to be a complete nonissue, Long realized. Regardless of the number of decoy drops in days past, Shah certainly would push out patrols to see what a dark night's clattering helicopters left in their wake each following day, as well as to get the word out to all the locals either paid by him or scared of him to look for signs of the presence of American forces. *Where are they and what are they looking for?* Long imagined Shah's thoughts. With his rigorous training as both a ground intel officer and a sniper platoon commander, the lieutenant viewed the first two phases of *Red Wings* as "duct-taped together—*at best*" from a command and control perspective, and completely haphazard from an on-the-ground operational standpoint. Long kept wondering how the four would dispose of the dropped fastrope—go back and try to conceal it as a full team, just leave it and hope it wouldn't be discovered, or have two SEALs remain at OP-1 while the other two dealt with the problem, breaking an already undersize team in half. Or call for an extract, which he thought to be the best option, based primarily on the loud helo insert, which he regarded as a huge neon sign proclaiming AMERICAN FORCES ARE HERE. But like Wood, Rob Scott, and even MacMannis, Long had no say. This phase of *Red Wings* was completely controlled by USSOCOM rules—and nobody in that chain of command, Long knew, would want any input from a young Marine Corps lieutenant.

Then, late in the morning of the twenty-eighth, the inevitable transmission Long had feared crackled over the radio in a barely audible voice: "We've been soft-compromised." The exhausted Long's ears pricked up; his heart pounding, he rose from his chair and lunged to the corner of the JAF COC occupied by the Navy SEAL *Red Wings* liaison officers. "Goat herder," Long thought he heard at the tail end of the weak, thready transmission. *Herder or herders?* Didn't matter. *Had they seen the fastrope, or found it buried—then searched for the team? Or just spotted the four by chance? Or were they Shah's operatives, locals earning a little extra money as yet another set of the terrorist's eyes?* Didn't matter. *Mission's blown. Get the FUCK outta there!* Long screamed in his head at the news of the "soft" compromise, a term referencing a unit's discovery by *apparently* noncombatant locals. Had this been Team Ronin, Keith and his team would have photographed the locals, asked them a few questions, then sent them on their way—then called the COC to discuss options; but given the current circumstances now, there would have been only one choice: extract, extract immediately. *Call for extract,* he barked in his head at what he wanted done with the recon team. *Do it. Do it NOW!* Too many of the mission's variables looked to be going south in too short a time. Long, Wood, and then Rob Scott and Pigeon—all out of the command and control loop at this stage—wished to just reach out to any air available and get them back to base. They immediately contacted Capuzzi, who stood ready with the quick reaction force at the Jalalabad Provincial Reconstruction Team base, and told the captain that the order to launch the QRF might likely be imminent.

"I don't feel good about this, not at all," Tom Wood uttered under his breath.

Then, after what seemed to Long like just a few minutes from the soft-compromise call, icy chills ran down his spine as the next of the recon team's transmissions echoed through the room: "CONTACT!

We're *hard*-compromised!" No longer simply discovered by unarmed locals, machine-gun, RPG, AK-47, and possibly 82 mm mortar rounds tore downrange from members of Shah's cell, who focused on killing all four of the SEALs, howling *"Alla-u Akhbar!* [God is the Greatest!] *Alla-u Akhbar! Alla-u-Akhbar!"* repeatedly between trigger pulls. A call from the team crackled through the COC again, but their PRC-148's five watts just couldn't kick a sufficient signal from Sawtalo Sar to Jalalabad to carry an audible voice. The transmission melted into splintered pops and squeals of static noise, indecipherable to Long and everybody else in the room. *Do a call for fire from Doghouse!* Long mentally screamed as every muscle in his body flexed. *Do it now! Get rounds impacting on the ACM!* Long practically shouted aloud as the liaison SEALs crowded around their comm gear. They shot message after message to the recon team. "Your transmission's breaking up. It's breaking up! Can't READ YOU!" they yelled.

Then the Iridium rang. Long stepped closer to the SEAL liaison crew as the COC fell vacuously silent. "We're in heavy contact, commencing our E-and-E [escape and evasion], going down the gulch below the OP." The lieutenant heard the words as well as the chilling *crack! crack! crack!* of gunfire buzzing from the handset's tinny receiver. *They're in the gulch, no wonder their MBITR doesn't work*, he thought. The SEAL liaison then asked for a ten-digit grid marking their position. "Do you hear us!" came the transmission from the recon team. "We're in HEAVY CONTACT!"

"WHAT'S YOUR POS?!" the SEAL liaison roared.

"HELLO!" Screamed the voice from the lonely mountain over a background of explosions and clatter of automatic weapons. Long instantly realized that the sat-phone had hit a partial blackout spot, allowing just one-way communication—the SEALs on Sawtalo Sar couldn't hear a single word from the liaison officers at JAF. Like Kinser and the Blessing Marines had discovered in the area, the phone required perfect placement when operated in the steep mountains and deep valleys of that part of the Hindu Kush, something the recon team didn't have the luxury of seeking at that desperate moment. Long, his eyes bugging out,

stared in silent horror as the SEALs at JAF ended the call, then immediately called the four-man team back. The call went through, and *maybe* the recon team could hear them, but the liaison officers couldn't hear the SEALS on the ground. They hung up; seconds later, the phone at the COC rang again, the SEAL liaisons answered, but heard just the booms of RPG impacts and the distant rattles of automatic weapons, then nothing but a terrible, bleak silence. *Those poor souls,* Long thought, cracking his knuckles.

Meanwhile, the four SEALs of the recon team lunged down the chutelike northeast gulch of Sawtalo Sar—leapfrogging with bursts of covering fire to protect one another during their egress—as RPGs exploded around them and interlocking PK machine-gun rounds cracked just inches overhead. Shah, loosing bursts of 7.62×54 mm rounds from his PK, directed his RPG gunner and two other AK-47-toting fighters at his side as well as controlling a small number of his other men at different positions through his ICOM. This was the real-life incarnation of the hypothetical ambush about which Justin Bradley had warned his Marines just a few days prior. Shah's assault sent streams of coordinated deadly fire onto the retreating team, "funneling" the four down the steep gulch. The SEALs fired back, but four men, with no comms for indirect fire support, no mortars organic to them, who were unable to even see the muzzle flashes of the insurgents' weapons through the steep ravine's dense trees, couldn't take down Shah's team, roughly ten strong, who leveraged their advantage of superior ground, terrain familiarity, and use of RPGs and possibly 82 mm mortars to overwhelm the SEALs with downward 'plunging' fire, making their ambush seem as if perpetrated from a team of not ten, but fifty—or one hundred—*or more*. The number in Shah's team didn't matter; their superior, multiple positions geometrically amplified their numbers and weapons' effects by many orders of magnitude—a basic, albeit relatively unknown, principle of mountain warfare. The four could only hope for a swift QRF as they struggled for survival.

"We need to launch the QRF right fucking now!" an exasperated Tom Wood barked to Rob Scott.

"We can't. We don't have the authority," the executive officer answered what Wood already knew. "The react order is in the hands of SOF." As the SEAL liaisons rushed to make a series of desperate calls to Bagram and continued attempts to raise the recon team by radio and Iridium, Capuzzi and his Marines of the QRF waited anxiously near a wooden guard shack at the east end of the PRT airstrip. Wood, Long, and Scott burned with frustration while the four men on the ground fought as desperately and valiantly as any U.S. military unit ever had in the history of American warfare. Outgunned, but far more important, *outpositioned*, the four continued to stave off the extremists and move farther down the northeast gulch into the Shuryek Valley, closing on the village of Salar Ban.

Forty-five minutes after the hard-compromise call, the Marines couldn't believe that the order to extract the team hadn't yet been issued. "By now, we could have birds in the air, eyes on the four SEALs, and grids of Shah and his men's positions—and then have Apaches run close air support, and get the team the fuck outta there," the OpsO raged. But the Marines could only stand by, hamstrung by the obscenely convoluted command structure. At a time when every second counted, the Marines in the COC felt helpless. *This can't be happening. Who's in control of this? What the fuck is going on?* Long felt almost dizzy; everything he'd been taught as a modern U.S. Marine seemed to swirl into dissolution around him: airpower was out of their control at that point, as was Doghouse (which couldn't fire anyway because the gun team didn't have grids on friendly positions since their comms were down); even the Marine portion of the QRF—composed of grunts from Golf Company—while theoretically under 2/3's control, couldn't launch unless the SOF lead element was under way. Scott and Wood, older and more attuned to the pitfalls of "joint discord," themselves felt the black hole of emptiness in their guts; there were four Americans falling down some sinuous throat of death into the bowels of a monstrous hell. And nothing was being done to stop it. No actionable decisions were being made. Insanity in warfare was supposed to manifest itself as some out-of-control commander slaying innocent locals, incinerating schools,

and decapitating children. But that was for the movies. This was real
modern war insanity. It was like returning home to find one's home en-
gulfed in flames and firefighters obliviously playing a game of cards in
the driveway. Each of the Marines stood shocked and blindsided by the
command and control paralysis—the insanity of inaction at a moment
requiring steadfast leadership and resolve. Out of the command and
control loop, they could only observe the SEAL liaisons themselves observing the Bagram SEALs at their COC trying to get *their* higher command to authorize a QRF. Long imagined the scene on Sawtalo Sar that
afternoon. Were the four even alive still? How could they survive more
than a couple of minutes with rounds raining down on them from
above? RPGs detonating with deafening, concussive blasts? PK and AK
rounds pummeling the dirt, rocks, and trees of the ravine—and the
SEALs, too? Then he imagined their families, so immensely proud of their
decisions to join the fight against extremists; worried yet confident in
their Afghan deployment—but now completely oblivious to their feverish fight for their lives. Thoughts of their friends and family made the
lieutenant even more crazy with frustration that no authorization had
come down the pike for a QRF launch for the eternity of hours.

"QRF ready to launch! Two MH-47s out of Bagram," one of the SEALs
yelled to the Marines in the JAF COC.

"Finally." Wood was seething—the stocky OpsO shook his head.
"Hours after it should have gone in," he said, noting that the time was
three in the afternoon. As Wood, Scott, and MacMannis looked to "build
their SA" (situational awareness) on the rescue about to launch, Pigeon
worked to mitigate any possible disaster involving air.

"We don't know what the ground situation is like," he glibly told
Wood. "We haven't heard from the recon team in hours," the Hornet
aviator, who graduated at the top of his class from flight school at Meridian, Mississippi, stated; he feared the worst about the four SEALs.
As a Marine aviator, Pigeon pushed for a QRF flight plan based around
a threat that he instinctively sought to avoid more than any other:

antiaircraft guns, surface-to-air missiles, even lucky small-arms fire taking down the helicopters; "barn doors in the sky," he called them. "Before any bird comes in zone [approaches a landing or fastrope-insert zone], they're gonna have to get positive comms with the guys on the ground, or get positive visual on them—or both—and we need to prep the HLZ first, either with Doghouse or with Shock." Pigeon referred to running a SEAD—Suppression of Enemy Air Defenses—package by bombarding the intended helicopter landing or insert zone with 105 mm high-explosive rounds from Doghouse, or by having Task Force Sabre's AH-64s (call sign Shock) clear the area with 30 mm gun runs and 2.75-inch Hydra rocket attacks, to ensure that a bad guy couldn't pop up from behind a tree or rock and nail the helicopters as they roared in to land or hovered to deploy fastropes.

"I agree with you one hundred percent," Wood responded. "But it isn't our call, Pigeon. SOF is the lead on the QRF."

"With their MH-47s. But I'm going to do whatever I can to work with conventional air, to ensure that the aviators and the passengers— *our Marines*—keep out of harm's way," the captain snapped back to the OpsO. In short order, however, through one of the Task Force Brown liaisons at JAF, Pigeon got a handshake deal—among all the aviators, those of Brown, as well as Task Force Sabre, who would be flying the UH-60s packed with the Marine QRF element and a small number of SEALs. All agreed that they would either acquire visual confirmation of the recon SEALs on the ground, get positive comms with them, or both, before coming in zone. Otherwise, they wouldn't insert, either by landing or by fastrope.

The aviators of the 160th, however, looked to fly without Shock escorts, aiming to move onto Sawtalo Sar alone. By culture and doctrine, the "Night Stalkers" sought to keep their aerial footprint as small as possible; in other words, the fewer aircraft, the better—giving the enemy less chance of catching wind of an impending attack. Operating in heavily armor-plated Chinooks defended by multiple .50-caliber machine guns, the pilots and crew of the 160th's MH-47s felt that they didn't need Shock escort. The MH-47s also could fly significantly faster

than the Apaches and even the swift Blackhawks, due to 100 percent of
the Chinook's engines' transmission power moving the two counterro-
tating blade assemblies that provided both lift and directional thrust, as
opposed to conventional helicopter designs exemplified by the 64s or
60s, where raw physics mandated a tail rotor to counteract the inertial
force of the single lift/thrust assembly, a substantial power drain (upward of 30 percent). Furthermore, they would be flying at altitudes of
nearly ten thousand feet—in the afternoon, meaning a density altitude
of nearly fourteen thousand feet (density altitude being a function of
actual altitude and temperature—the warmer the ambient temperature,
the thinner the air, and hence the more power required to maintain normal performance), conditions easily manageable by the big Chinooks,
but that posed serious speed and handling problems for the Blackhawks
and Apaches. But the lightly armed and relatively thin-skinned Blackhawks *did* require Shock escort, and since the QRF would consist of
both Task Force Brown Chinooks and Sabre's Blackhawks, by default,
the Apaches would run with the pack—or so the handshake agreement
dictated.

At roughly 3:30 P.M. local time, as streaks of grayish-white clouds
knifed into the baby-blue sky above Nangarhar province, three Blackhawks, call sign Skillful, streaked over the pastoral lands surrounding
the Jalalabad PRT base with two Shock Apaches flying close cover. A
scene just moments earlier defined by gentle breezes under the blistering
sun and murmurs of small talk among the grunts was now an adrenaline-
infused uproar of five powerful U.S. Army aircraft on approach that
incited the Marines to stand ready for an insert into the monstrous unknown. Flaring steeply just before contacting solid ground, the Blackhawks touched down with blazing speed and razor precision, each kicking
a doughnutlike ring of roiling dust out from under the craft. After refueling, the 60s "hopped" a few dozen yards, and Marines piled inside the
sleek craft, then together with the Shocks, they made the short flight to
Jalalabad Airfield, where, as the helicopters idled, the Marines made final preparations for the launch onto Sawtalo Sar.

A total of twenty-four Marines of Golf Company would embark on the rescue mission: ten, including Capuzzi in the lead Blackhawk; another ten, including First Lieutenant John Bambey, commander of Golf Company's Third Platoon, in the second bird (following USMC protocol, the two spread out in multiple craft to ensure that if a helicopter went down carrying one commander, another officer would survive to lead the fight forward); and four Marines accompanied by three members of SEAL Team 10 jumped into the third, "light" Blackhawk, which kept enough room onboard to load the four recon SEALs. With all of the Marines having fastrope-qualled during the days leading up to the launch of *Red Wings,* the Blackhawk aviators would fly their craft with their doors off, ready to insert the grunts with lightning speed— to get onto the ground and save the members of the recon team. With morale high, the Golf Company grunts felt rush after rush of energizing adrenaline, excited to insert onto the high slopes of Sawtalo Sar and take care of business, ultimately reuniting the SDVT SEALs with friendlier ground.

And with as much ardor the grunts felt for saving the foursome, Erik Kristensen, the commander of the ground aspect of the rescue operation, burned with even more resolve to save the team. As the Golf Company contingent of the QRF loaded into the Skillful Blackhawks at Jalalabad, Kristensen and four other members of SEAL Team 10 (Chief Petty Officer Jacques J. Fontan, Petty Officer First Class Jeffery Lucas, Lieutenant Michael McGreevy, and Petty Officer First Class Jeffrey S. Taylor) accompanied by three members of SEAL Delivery Vehicle Team 1 (Senior Chief Petty Officer Daniel R. Healy, Petty Officer Second Class James Suh, and Petty Officer Second Class Eric Patton) boarded the lead MH-47D, commanded by Major Stephen Reich of the Third Battalion of the 160th SOAR(A), commander of the air side of the QRF, at Bagram. Seven other members of the 160th also crewed the command ship: Staff Sergeant Shamus Goare, Chief Warrant Officer (3) Corey Goodnature, Sergeant Kip Jacoby, Sergeant First Class Marcus Muralles, Master Sergeant James Ponder III, Sergeant First Class Michael Russell, and Chief Warrant Officer (4) Chris Scherkenbach.

But the order to launch from Kristensen's higher command, for reasons still unknown, never came. Kristensen, as great a hero as America has ever produced—intensely driven to save the team of four recon SEALs—ultimately gave the order to launch the QRF himself. He simply couldn't wait any longer. At three-thirty local time, the two Task Force Brown MH-47Ds of the *Red Wings* QRF spun up and lifted into the crystalline skies above Bagram—an extremely rare daytime launch for the 160th—bound for the dark unknown swirling about Sawtalo Sar.

With the MH-47s roaring inbound, the Marines and SEALs in the three Skillful Blackhawks made their final preflight checks—all their gear was secured, their "spiderweb" multipoint restraints were locked in tight yet ready to release with a robust twist, and nothing would snag, not even a shoelace. With the thoughts of everyone of the Quick Reaction Force focused on the SEALs on the ground, the collective seismic howls of ten turbine engines thundered across Jalalabad Airfield as the five craft rose into the sky in a deafening, tornado-like symphony. The birds then carved steep turns above the billowing dust storm that rose in the wake of their launch to merge with the MH-47 Chinooks rocketing toward the Kunar Valley. Bambey, sitting in the rearmost right-side seat of his Blackhawk, made sure that his M16A4 was pointed out the door, then focused on the terrain below as he monitored the nets with his PRC-119F radio. As cooler, cleaner air swept out the ground-level smoky odors of rural Afghanistan, Bambey could see storms building ahead of him—hazy gray cumulus bunching up atop the dark, shadowed mountains toward which the craft sped. Soon, he knew, those gray clouds would turn black, and begin shedding curtains of drenching rain. No matter, the group had lives to save, American lives in duress—he imagined the recon team's plight, careening down the steep gulch, each keeping the others in sight, fighting both the onslaught of their attackers and the raw environment. The collective assets of the QRF—aircraft, the aviators and crew, the SEALs, and the stone-faced, ultrafocused grunts, shot ahead like a clenched fist.

The five Sabre birds never merged into formation with the MH-47s, flying only within about a half mile of the Chinooks. Bambey recognized the craft as MH-47s by the "stinger" refueling probes he

could see protruding from the nose of each, the telltale profile difference between the M and the conventional version. The lieutenant's attention then reverted to the ground below—his chosen realm as a grunt.
The attentive Marine officer immediately pinpointed the craft's exact
location by terrain features he'd traversed by foot and Humvee, and
could mentally plot the course the seven aircraft were taking. But
when he looked up again, he could only count five birds total—the two
MH-47s had disappeared. With dark curtains of rain careening ground-
ward on all points of the compass, Bambey wondered why the two
SOAR(A) Chinooks had slipped away—then he heard over the pilots'
net one of the Skillful aviators remark, "They're pushing ahead"—
referencing the MH-47s.

"Let's move up to eight hundred AGL [feet above ground level],"
another stated. "That'll give us enough space to keep out of SAFIRE
[small-arms fire] range but still close enough to the hills to spot the SEALs."
Bambey kept studying the ground features—ridgelines, peaks, dry washes.
And then he felt a mild jolt of déjà vu. *Those peaks,* he thought, *we just
went over them—we're flying in circles!* The lieutenant craned his neck
around to spy the view from every possible window in the Blackhawk as
the pilots torqued the powerful craft into steeply banking turns. He saw
the other two Blackhawks as well, the two Shock Apaches, but still no
sign of the TF Brown Chinooks—nor of Sawtalo Sar; just the same terrain, over and over. *What are we doing? Why aren't we moving toward
the mountain?* While he could listen to the pilots, he didn't have a microphone hookup at his seat, so he couldn't ask them what he burned to
know. Bambey glanced at his gear, his Marines, then to the ground
below—ever darkening under a thickening deck of storm clouds. Then
he felt the first drops of rain strike his cheeks.

"I just got two Shocks to break off from an op south of Asadabad
and head toward Sawtalo Sar," Pigeon told Wood. "They should be up
there right about the time the MHs get in zone."

"Good. Hopefully they'll let the Shocks prep the LZ for 'em."

"Let's hope. I know the SOAR(A) community likes to work alone;
they don't typically like having conventional air around."

The aviators of the two Shocks coming from south of Asadabad tore through the skies to reach Sawtalo Sar in time to run an ad hoc SEAD package for the inbound Chinooks. Their cockpits rattling from the speed, they tried furiously to raise TF Brown on their nets. But no luck. With miles of Hindu Kush terrain blurring below them with each minute, the pilots of the lead Shock finally established comms with one of the Chinooks—with the help of two Air Force A-10 Thunderbolt II "Warthogs" that just checked in on station, orbiting at fifteen thousand feet above Sawtalo Sar, awaiting a call for close air support runs. "Let us prep the LZ for you!" the Shock pilots pleaded.

"We're already in zone. We can't wait."

"Let us get in there. Orbit the peak. *Orbit the peak!* Don't drop in! We'll be there in less than two minutes! *LET US GET IN THERE!*"

"Thanks, brotha," came the calm reply. "But we don't have two minutes. We don't have two seconds." Then, after a brief pause: "You can prep the LZ when we're on the ground." The bravado sent chills into the spines of the Shock pilots, now forming up and preparing to roll into the potentially hot LZ.

The TF Brown aviators tore through the air at nearly 180 knots—faster than any other helicopter in the air that day by a long shot. Kristensen, the other SEALs, and the Army crew of the command ship must have been more ardent to save the recon team than anyone could have imagined back at JAF, now that they had eyes on the hulking massif. With the summit now in clear sight, the crew chief lowered the loading ramp and readied a fastrope. All available eyes focused downward, looking—looking—looking for any sign of the four on the ground. Kristensen and the others kept on their radios, trying to raise the team on every net possible. They neither saw nor heard anything. Holding out hope that the team was still alive—fending off the attackers—Kristensen gave the order to roll into final approach. Pigeon's "handshake deal" wasn't even a thought at that point.

But it was too late, far too late for three of the four. Murphy, Axelson, and Dietz all lay dead, deep in the chasm of the northeast gulch. Luttrell, having fought both against the fighters as well as to save his teammates' lives, took a near-direct hit from an RPG—knocking him unconscious as the blast's concussion threw him behind a large boulder, out of sight of the attackers, where he slowly bled toward death.

"Small-arms fire! Taking small-arms fire!" the Shock pilots heard over their net as they closed on Sawtalo Sar and could just make out two dots roving above the peak's summit. The Chinooks had made a low pass over the point where the recon team had inserted, and would come back for another attempt to get Kristensen and the other SEALs on the ground. The command bird powered up and banked steeply to the north, and circled around the mountain. Ready for a lightning insert, the lead MH-47 came in fast and flared hard, directly over the insert point. As the crash of thunder resonated through the shadowed valleys radiating about Sawtalo Sar and black curtains of rain swept the peaks of the Hindu Kush on all sides, Kristensen firmly grasped the fastrope and awaited the word from the aircraft's rope master. As the Chinook's airspeed dropped to near hover at less than fifty feet off the deck, Kristensen looked down and prepared to quickly and fluidly insert onto the rough patch of ground—just as Shah's RPG gunner emerged from behind a rock, loaded RPG-7 resting on his shoulder. Perfectly aligned with the bird, the gunner aimed at the open rear of the craft, cried *"Alla-u Akhbar! Alla-u Akhbar!"* and then as time seemed to stop, squeezed the trigger. *Click.* With a *boom! hiss!* and a puff of white smoke, the rocket sailed toward the Chinook—self arming after eleven meters in flight—then a fraction of a second after that, streaked inside the helicopter and connected with the transmission under the rear rotor assembly of the MH. The explosion sent a stream of molten metal into the gears and shafts of the complex beast, incinerating and shattering the precision hub assembly. The Shock pilots watched in horror as the nose of the craft pitched up, then the girthy Chinook fell out of the sky onto the steep, rocky terrain below, erupting in a massive orange-and-yellow fireball as it tumbled 120 feet down the Shuryek Valley side of the peak, coming to a rest under a mushroom cloud of black smoke on a small ledge, instantly killing all sixteen aboard.

"CHINOOK DOWN! CHINOOK DOWN!" the lead Shock pilot

called out. Bambey, hearing the message, struggled to find Sawtalo Sar, to see what had just happened, to find a plume of smoke—to see *something*. But he could see nothing but the sweeps of perdurable Hindu Kush mountains and an ever-darkening sky. The Skillful pilots of the Marine QRF element immediately thrust their craft into hard, evasive maneuvers, pressing the grunts deep into their seats under G-loading, and forcing one side sharply into the center of the craft while the other side pulled toward the open doors of the bird like a wild roller-coaster ride during hard evasive maneuvers. The Skillful pilots didn't know at that moment what had brought the Chinook down—just that it *was* down. For all any of them knew, the craft could have had mechanical failure—or Shah could have gotten his hands on an SA-7 shoulder-launched antiaircraft missile, one of the greatest fears of pilots in Afghanistan; hence the hard, evasive turns. But with sixteen more Americans down, Bambey felt that much more eager to insert. *Let's just get in—get in and do something. Americans are down,* the twenty-six-year-old thought. *Why are we just circling?* He shook his head in frustration. *What* . . . Bambey then noticed features not of the terrain over which the two Apaches and three Blackhawks had been in a holding pattern, but of the Kunar Valley. *We should be going in! We're headed back to Jalalabad?!*

7

STORM OF CHAOS

After nearly an hour in the air, spending most of that time carving tight, steeply banked turns over the same parcel of the Hindu Kush in a feverish holding pattern, Bambey realized that the Skillful Blackhawks were bound not for Sawtalo Sar but for Jalalabad. Capuzzi, too, recognized the dustier, flatter terrain on the city's outskirts as he gazed down at the shadows of the QRF's helicopters. *We're gonna re-fuel, recock, and get back up there. Four guys are down, and now also a Chinook and all its crew. We gotta get back up there!* The thoughts raced through Capuzzi's mind. The Skillful aviators landed their Black-hawks in perfectly orchestrated formation, rousing a blinding tempest of dust into the sky; the Marines squeezed their eyes shut and clenched their jaws tight as gritty swirls of air punched through the open doors of the 60s. As the whine of turbine engines grew lower and the roiling brown fog enveloping the craft bled away to reveal typically clement afternoon conditions at Jalalabad, Bambey squinted at the sight before him, wondering if the helicopters had landed at an airfield other than JAF. He recognized familiar landmarks of the base, but couldn't see a single Marine—just crowds of SOF personnel—most sporting their signature beards and baseball caps—heatedly preparing . . . something. *Preparing what?* the lieutenant wondered. As the Hawks idled, Capuzzi raised the lieutenant over the net: "Bambey, we're off. We're done. Outta the loop."

"*What,* sir?" Bambey responded with shocked disbelief.

"You and your Marines exfil the bird. We're convoying back to the PRT, where we wait for further orders," Capuzzi responded in a pissed-off tone.

"Roger." Bambey, feeling insanely piqued, burned to argue with his company commander—to plead to get back into the air, to race back to Sawtalo Sar, to hit the ground and rescue any survivors. But he quickly realized that Capuzzi felt just as bewildered, just as frustrated, just as sucker-punched as he, and he figured that the order originated from a level far, far above even the highest ranks of 2/3. *We were right there— right fuckin' there! Twenty-four Marines. Four SEALs. Two Apaches to rip the shit out of an LZ for us to insert onto!* his thoughts screamed. The lieutenant shook his head, trying to wake himself out of the surreal nightmare he was living, then motioned for the Marines in the Blackhawk to move out of the bird. "We're convoying back to the PRT base!" he yelled over the drone of the idling engines.

"WHAT?!" the Marines bellowed in near unison before releasing their spiderweb restraints and jumping out of the helicopter. But once the MH-47 went down, returning to JAF was really the Golf Company Marines' only feasible option, as the downed Chinook carried not only the QRF's on-site ground commander, Kristensen, but its on-site air-element commander, Reich, leaving the rescue team literally with no leadership. With no contact with the four recon SEALs on the ground, and an insert zone made deadly to unknown proportions by Shah and his men, rolling in was out of the question. The Blackhawks and overwatching Apaches had actually been orbiting at a position well away from the destruction on Sawtalo Sar: Task Force Brown had requested that Pigeon hold back the three UH-60s and their escorting AH-64s when the MH-47s pulled ahead of the group of five helicopters during the initial push to the mountain; the five birds waited in their holding pattern over the Narang Valley region, seven miles to the south of Sawtalo Sar. Pigeon, his imagination full of nightmarish scenes the instant he learned the horrifying news of the MH-47's downing—scenes ranging from slow, choking deaths inside the burning craft, to Shah and his men torturing and then beheading survivors—at that point acted solely to mitigate further bloodshed. He'd been outraged upon learning that the Shock aviators had been waved off when they requested to prep the insert zone for the now-downed craft, and felt adamant that not another mistake, of even the slightest consequence, would be made. When he learned from the aviators of the second MH-47, after they made a fast flyby high above the crash scene (again taking small-arms fire), that nobody could have survived the explosive downing, and with no comms with the recon team, Pigeon made a quick analysis of the QRF's options. Since the "invisible" enemy had just proven it could melt into the very geography of the peak, rendering a thorough SEAD prep virtually impossible (with the exception of a massive artillery bombardment on the entire upper chunk of Sawtalo Sar, possibly killing any surviving Americans and innocent Afghan civilians), the skilled aviator realized he could make only one decision: he called the three Skillful Blackhawks and their two Apache escorts back to JAF. The second MH-47 lingered in the area to try to gain visual contact with the recon team, but was unsuccessful. In addition, they were low on fuel, and with violent weather closing in fast, the crew had no choice but to return to their base at Bagram.

Inside the JAF COC, MacMannis, Rob Scott, and Tom Wood literally watched from a corner as planners from an array of SOF units—ODAs, ODBs, and SEALs—heatedly argued about the next move in the operation, an operation now called *Red Wings II* (the primary intent of part two being the rescue of the recon team and the recovery of the bodies from the crashed MH-47). If the command and control situation had been convoluted just a few hours prior, it became indecipherable to the Marines once the various SOF teams of CJSOTF-A started planning *Red Wings II*. But the C2 would morph into even more outrageous contortions within just minutes.

After a quick meeting with planners from yet another SOF unit—the Army Rangers based at JAF (Task Force Red, which, commanded directly by CENTOM's special operations element—SOCCENT—fell completely out of the command structure of even the highest echelons of Afghan-based command, including CJSOTF-A)—Wood briefed Mac-Mannis and Scott: "SOCCENT just slapped down a JSOA [Joint Special Operations Area—an ad hoc SOF geographic operating area superior in command to any area of operation already in place], and the Rangers are going to take the lead in the recovery effort from here out." The command of *Red Wings,* initially intended to be placed with the Marines at JAF when Wood built the mission plan, then relocated to Bagram with NAVSOF (with special operations liaisons placed at the Marines' COC), now shifted half a world away—to Tampa, Florida, at CENTOM's headquarters at MacDill Air Force Base.

"That's fuckin' great, Wood. We're all the better for it—aren't we?" Rob Scott sarcastically began. "I mean—" He stopped and half laughed as he shook his head. "They have some great fucking golf courses there at MacDill, don't they? I hear the op planners *love* sunny Florida—and the orange juice. Makes up for the hurricanes and summer humidity."

"You're just a dumb grunt, Rob. *Shut up.* What do you know?" Wood responded, the two majors resorting to humor as their only outlet as they watched the mission's last gasps of operational rationality shatter into stunning absurdity before their eyes. "Didn't the same sort of thing happen just a few years ago . . . *Anaconda*, wasn't it?" Wood, maintaining the sarcastic tone, referenced the operational melee that resulted from poor command and control and essentially nonexistent SOF-conventional-forces integration during March 2002's Operation *Anaconda*. "We should've just had 'em walk in. We should have just had Eggers and Team Ronin walk in for this, and then had Kinser and his crew *walk in*, and then had Golf Company *walk in*, too—anything would have been better than what we got with this setup.

"This is way worse than *Anaconda*, Tom—on a whole lot of levels," Rob responded.

"No shit."

Despite the storm of chaos raging at the JAF COC before them, the fate of the now essentially abandoned recon team continued to dominate the Marines' thoughts. They not just hoped, but expected, that all four had survived the ambush, and were holding firm somewhere on Sawtalo Sar. But they knew that as plans for *Red Wings II* were devised, discarded, augmented, and argued over, the SEALs of the recon team had to cling to life completely on their own that evening, doing anything and everything they could to reunite themselves with friendly forces, including seeking refuge with locals—a frightening proposition given the inimical allegiances many of the people living on the slopes of Sawtalo Sar had forged.

Knowing that survivors of the ambush could have traversed to virtually any point on Sawtalo Sar's many facets by late on the twenty-eighth, MacMannis, Wood, and Rob Scott worked up 2/3's part of *Red Wings II* in short order. They developed a simple scheme of maneuver: Golf and Echo companies would push south into the Shuryek and Korangal valleys, sweep for surviving members of the recon team, hunt for Shah and his men, and continue their campaign of outreach toward the local population—granted that their plan was approved within the new command structure. While SOCCENT designated *Red Wings II* as a rescue/recovery mission, the Marines still hoped to attain some of the goals of their original operation.

Wood contacted Kinser early in the evening of the twenty-eighth. "You and Eggers and your best guys take some ASF and get into the Korangal. There are some missing personnel, four of them, and they're somewhere on Sawtalo Sar. Some may be injured, some may be dead— or all of them may be dead—for all I know. But right now we're assuming that they're all alive and well. That's all I can tell you right now. The

worst place they could be is in the Korangal, and that's why you're going there." Kinser immediately drafted a detailed op order, submitted it
to Wood, and gathered his twenty best Marines. At one o'clock in the
morning on the twenty-ninth, Wood gave Kinser the go-ahead: "Move
your ass, Kinser. Get up into the Korangal, establish a patrol base,
then I'll push you out as needed." Wood felt a dire urgency to save the
lives of any surviving members of the recon team, knowing that the
convoluted command structure, long mission-approval processes, and
individual-unit egos at the planning levels would just continue to delay
the rescue operation. With Kinser, Eggers, and crew located at an ideal
spot from which to pounce onto a position anywhere throughout the
Sawtalo Sar massif to vector onto the position(s) of the missing personnel, the survivors might not be so abandoned after all.

Under pitch darkness, the force of thirty-seven slipped outside
Camp Blessing's wire and moved quickly down the Pech Road on foot.
Every one of the group carried enough MREs and bottled water to last
at least three days; while nights were often cold, particularly after heavy
thunderstorms, the temperatures of the summer days would reach well
in excess of 115 degrees, so each carried as much water as possible. The
group, which included some of the best of the Blessing Marines—Doc
Anaya, fully laden with extra supplies to aid those they searched for;
mortarmen with two 60 mm mortar tubes and rounds; SAW gunners;
M240G light machine gunners; and Corporal Joe Roy, Eggers's spotter
from Team Ronin—moved quickly along the shores of the treacherous
Pech River, entering the mouth of the Korangal Valley after just two and
a half hours of stiff walking. Also moving with Kinser and crew were
"Hamchuck" and "Henrietta," Blessing's two loyal "Afghan war dogs"—
local strays, trained by a SOF direct-action team temporarily stationed
at Blessing before 2/3's arrival—that the team lowered in specially made
harnesses when they fastrope-inserted on hard-hit raids, using the dogs
to help flush out bad guys. Kinser planned to use the two well-behaved
canines to locate the as-yet-unidentified lost personnel. In addition, the
friendly Hamchuck and Henrietta proved great companions to the

grunts. The group set up a camp near the village of Kandagal, at the mouth of the Korangal, and awaited Wood's order to move into action.

Unknown to the Marines, only one of the four recon-team SEALs had lived through Shah's ambush. And hours after the last of the attackers' rounds had been loosed from their weapons, he barely clung to life. With all his teammates dead, suffering from multiple penetration injuries throughout his body and massive blood loss, Marcus Luttrell fought off almost certain death as he regained consciousness. Deep in the bowels of the northeast gulch, his position on the declivitous slope provided him with one glimmer of hope: the people of the Shuryek Valley, into which the gulch fed, had traditionally been at odds with villagers of the Korangal Valley, particularly those of Chichal, bumping heads over grazing-land boundaries. And while not overly friendly to American forces, people on the Shuryek side of Sawtalo Sar hadn't proved nearly as supportive of anticoalition militia forces as those of the Korangal. Furthermore, Luttrell had roughly just one mile of downhill travel in order to reach one of the Shuryek's largest villages, Salar Ban. Best of all, relations between American forces and people not only of the Shuryek Valley, but throughout the greater Pech region, had very recently taken a quantum leap forward—a quantum leap that had been launched eight miles to the northwest of Luttrell's position, at Camp Blessing.

The change began during 3/3's Afghan tour and quickly accelerated toward the end of the Third Battalion's deployment with First Lieutenant Justin Bellman and his Blessing Marines' outreach to the locals of Nangalam and beyond. When 2/3 arrived, Matt Bartels—the keenly perceptive, gregarious, and ever-welcoming twenty-five-year-old first lieutenant whom Rob Scott had hand-selected to run the show at "the tip of the spear"—took off not running, but sprinting, to continue the building of close ties with the villagers of the historic region. Often working with Kinser on patrols and operations outside the base's wire,

Bartels took note of the young children of Nangalam, who often mobbed the Marines, always looking to make eye contact and conversation, and often offering tea and sometimes even flowers—a welcome surprise to the grunts on patrol. Adult villagers also quickly warmed up to the always-smiling Bartels, and most would get to know the lieutenant on a first-name basis.

Deciding from day one that he was going to leave an indelibly positive mark on the war-ravaged area, Bartels set out to better the lives of the area's people through any means at his disposal. While Task Force Devil's Provincial Reconstruction Teams kept busy with construction and improvement of wells, roads, schools, and mosques, Bartels focused on the locals' simple day-to-day needs and wants. A village elder who came to the entrance one morning to speak with him noticed the lieutenant drinking from a paper cup; the local asked Matt if he could have the cup once he was finished. "No," Bartels replied, disappearing momentarily, "but you can have eight hundred unused, brand-new ones for you, your family, and your village," and with that, he handed over an unopened case to the stunned elderly Afghan. The lieutenant also made personal friends with a number of the area villages' merchants and craftsmen, including a local baker, whose son—whom the Marines knew as "C-Put"—would bring fresh "sugar bread" to the camp every morning and often stuck around the camp and followed Matt, who helped the eight-year-old learn English. Matt also ensured that word got out that anyone in need of medical care should immediately come to Camp Blessing, where the camp's "saints"—the tireless Navy Corpsmen—diagnosed problems, doled out appropriate medication, set broken bones, disinfected blisters and lacerations, sutured deep wounds, even saved an elderly man during a heart attack, medevacing him to Bagram Air Base for emergency heart surgery. The corpsmen didn't limit their work to humans, either, stitching up the leg of a villager's donkey after a fall on a steep trail one afternoon.

Recognizing that a clothing staple Americans take for granted was one of the commodities most coveted by the region's men—shoes— Bartels jumped online and registered a request with a number of websites that organize aid drives to deliver care packages to deployed American troops, stating that he wasn't procuring for Marines, but for the locals of Nangalam and the Afghan warriors who fought side by side with the grunts on missions. Shoes, sizes seven to nine (the most common range for men in the area), poured in; Matt and the Blessing Marines immediately distributed them to the grateful locals. He then continued the shoe drive through his friends and family, who donated both brand-new and used sneakers and boots. Still short of the village's needs, the lieutenant used his own money to purchase a final fifty pair from a major discount shoe company through its online store.

The Blessing Marines' most notable outreach achievement came from providing items not to adult Afghans, however, but to young girl students of the school adjacent to the camp's entrance, which often took the brunt of Shah's rocket and mortar attacks during the terrorist's spring offensive. Noting the girls' lack of basic supplies—pencils, paper, uniforms, and backpacks—as he watched the storage facilities of Blessing bulge with the unused care packages delivered by Sabre's Big Windy Chinooks during weekly mail runs, Bartels hatched a plan to ensure that the students of the Nangalam Girls' School would never be without their vital matériel. He e-mailed friends, family, even distant relatives and old classmates, asking for both financial donations and shipments of pencils, pens (a treasured implement for both adults as well as children throughout the mountains of the Kunar province), backpacks, folders, and notebooks in lieu of typical care packages. The resourceful lieutenant, whose father served a stint as a Peace Corps volunteer in the southern African country of Lesotho before driving a Volkswagen Beetle from that landlocked country to Afghanistan in the late sixties, also noted that he had a surplus of money distributed to him from Task Force Devil for "base improvements." *Well,* he figured, *improving the girls' school is a clear improvement of the base.* The request for donations spread like wildfire back home. Churches held fund-raisers, businessmen friends of Bartels's father kicked in, even the National Football League ponied up some supplies. The Big Windys had to make extra trips in mid-June to handle the influx. By late June, through combining the "base improvement" funds with donations from home, Bartels had five hundred schoolgirls' uniforms crafted locally, paying five thousand dollars for their manufacture. The students proudly showed up at the school in brand-new outfits, carrying their brand-new school supplies in brand-new backpacks that sported such team logos as the Steelers, Jets, and Broncos. It was an almost tearful sight to behold for the Marines.

One of Bartels's most important assets in his campaign to improve the lives of the locals of the Pech region arrived one rainy June afternoon in the front seat of a white, slumped-suspension Toyota Corolla. To glean information about anticoalition militia weapons caches in the region, Bartels had been working with a local elder named Nawab (who had proven to be instrumental in bringing in Najmudeen during 3/3's tour, and with whom Bartels and the Blessing Marines would continue to work to outwit the area's bad guys during 2/3's deployment). "This is pretty shady stuff," he told his small security element before meeting an information source brought in by Nawab. "I'm gonna be carrying just my Nine [Berretta M9 9mm handgun], that's it. No helmet, no flak. I'm gonna have to get into the small car with this guy, his driver, and the source's terp, and if the car takes off, light up its tires with the 240 and the SAW. If somethin' happens to me—if I'm killed—light the entire car up. If things go bad and I make it outta the car, light it up on my mark," Bartels coolly instructed his M240G light machine gunner and his squad automatic-weapon gunner, punctuating his order with a wry grin. He also had Ronin for support, with Keith on the M40 sniper rifle, prepositioned to take out individuals inside the car if things went south. Nervous, but never showing it, he sprinted through the pounding monsoon rain and hopped in the backseat next to his contact. As if the shutting door were his cue, the man sitting in front of the lieutenant spun around, and with a wide, toothy, and gummy smile, exclaimed, "Hello! I am Sultan! I am the interpreter!"

"Your English—it's perfect!" Bartels responded, stunned.

"Yes, that is right!" the hoarse-voiced man stated, sporting an ear-to-ear grin below a shock of jet-black hair. Bartels, who had been suspicious of two of the five terps attached to the base whom he felt to be corrupt, had been on the lookout for new translators, ones without recent ties to Pech region (Matt figured outsiders were less susceptible to nepotism-inspired corruption).

"What's your story? Where you from?" The lieutenant fired off questions to Sultan, ignoring the man sitting next to him—the one he'd arranged the potentially dangerous rendezvous in order to meet. Bartels learned that Sultan grew up in Asadabad during the seventies and eighties; but he, like many of the Kunar, fled to Pakistan during the height of the Soviet occupation.

"My brother, when I was seven, was executed. Right there!" He pointed toward the building that housed Camp Blessing's Afghan Security Forces contingent.

"Huh? Right . . . *there*?" Bartels gestured toward the building. "Inside the camp perimeter?"

"Yes! The schoolhouse. The Russians tortured and then shot my brother in the head!" Sultan emotionally responded, his voice beginning to quiver. He explained that for years, he and his family had survived a number of wretched Pakistani refugee camps, where he taught himself English by reading newspapers and magazines (although not broadly spoken, most major print media use English, Pakistan's official language). When he was sixteen, Sultan stowed away on a Canadian military C-130 cargo aircraft and made his way to Toronto. "I lied, and told them I was eighteen. The crew was nice to me. They brought me to Canada, feeding me potted meat on the plane. Once there, I got citizenship while I worked in a factory, and brought my family over."

Bartels stared with incredulity at his new friend—as Eggers pegged his M40's scope on the driver's head and the SAW and 240 gunners kept their weapons' iron sights trained on the Corolla's tires. As cold, heavy drops of rain thumped against the car's thin exterior, Sultan told Matt of his childhood aspiration of gazing at New York City with his own eyes, to trace Manhattan's brilliant night skyline from the shores of the Hudson River, a view he'd seen reproduced in a magazine he found in a refugee camp. The Afghan stowaway saved enough money from his factory job to buy an old Honda Accord, then made the long trip to New York to find a job in the shadow of the skyline of his childhood dreams. The resourceful Sultan quickly landed work as a nightshift worker at a fast-food chicken outlet. Deep into the night, he served up greasy deep-fried thighs, legs, wings, and breasts from behind thick bulletproof glass—but always with an ebullient smile—and quickly rose in the company's ranks to become a regional manager, overseeing a total of eleven restaurants in Brooklyn and Queens, as well as adjacent spots such as Elizabeth, New Jersey. But Afghanistan's ruggedly beautiful Kunar never left his mind. Inspired and invigorated by America's 2001 liberation of Afghanistan from the Taliban—who not only oppressed the people of his birthplace, but aligned themselves with those responsible for the permanent gash in the skyline he'd journeyed so far to experience—and with a healthy chunk of savings, he returned to Asadabad, began construction of a home, and repatriated his family. "I never want to leave now. I see the hope of the fight against the Taliban and al-Qaeda fuckers. I'm never leaving my home again. I kill them all myself—maybe with a little help from you Marines . . ." Sultan folded his arms and struck a confident grin, lifting his thick, dark eyebrows.

"Whatever they're paying you as an interpreter, I'll triple it right now. You've got two days to get back to Asadabad to let your family know that you'll be working in Nangalam, then get your ass back here to be my personal terp."

"Right, sir. I can stay right now. I'll let my family know with a phone call. Fuck this shit I'm doin' now for *this* guy." Sultan motioned with his head toward the sweaty, overweight "source" sitting next to Bartels in the Corolla's backseat. "I'm with you now, my man!"

Word of the Marines' magnanimity quickly spread throughout the valleys surrounding Nangalam, including the Shuryek. During a patrol in late June, while assessing the need for a MEDCAP in the village of Matin, a quiet, slightly built man approached Bartels, extending his hand in a show of friendship as he drew a confident grin. Matt shook the villager's hand, then began to introduce himself, but the local cut him off. "Commander Matt!" the villager blared, nodding excitedly. "Commander Matt!" Through Sultan, the lieutenant learned the villager's name: Gulab; Mohammad Gulab Khan, of the village of Salar Ban.

"He says he's scared to talk to the Americans. He hasn't had good experiences with them from Asadabad, but he knows of what you have done with the Nangalam Girls' School, and he and the other villagers of Salar Ban want to know you," Sultan translated.

"Tell him that he's welcome anytime. He is our friend now. Come to Camp Blessing. Our home is his home."

"Yes . . . yes . . . yes!" Gulab exclaimed after Sultan translated Matt's words. "My friend! My friend! *My friend!*" As the convoy roared back to Blessing, Matt felt a deep sense of gratitude for the unexpected rewards of his deployment in Afghanistan. And those gains would extend broadly through the region—beyond the Marines themselves—inspiring feelings of goodwill for American forces of all services.

Marcus Luttrell—dehydrated, bleeding, and literally shot full of holes— made the grueling descent down the northeast gulch of Sawtalo Sar in a superhuman push. With each step, more of the village of Salar Ban, three miles "up-valley" from Matin, emerged into view. Struggling to maintain consciousness, Luttrell sought shelter from the enervating sun under a shade tree just outside a cluster of mud-and-rock homes on the morning of the twenty-ninth. Then, rounding a bend in a nearby trail, a local emerged—of all people, it was "Commander Matt's" new friend Gulab, who immediately recognized Luttrell as an American. The Navy SEAL brandished his weapon and a hand grenade; Gulab, seeing that the American was in dire need of aid, raised his hands and gestured to Luttrell that he wanted to help, then led the SEAL to his home in Salar Ban, where he fed and rehydrated him. Surmising that the lone American was being pursued by men Gulab knew to be linked to the outside forces of the Taliban or al-Qaeda, he brought Luttrell into his home and pledged to treat and protect him just as he would close family in the tradition of *Pashtunwalli*, a "blood code" passed down through generations of Pashtuns.

Luttrell had used his corpsman training and first-aid kit to treat his own wounds, but still required extensive medical attention; with deep-tissue injury and unknown amounts of shrapnel lodged in his body, every minute counted—most people would have been long dead by this point. Gulab, who made his living primarily as a goat herder, but was also a farmer and woodcutter, knew that whoever had assailed the American would very likely continue to hunt for him in Salar Ban, and pledged to stick by Luttrell's side until rescuers arrived, providing anything within his means to help him survive.

Luttrell pulled out a three-by-five inch all-weather "Rite in the Rain" notepad and scratched a quick message, then tore off the green page and handed it to Gulab, asking him to take it to the Americans at Asadabad, an easy (for a local) jaunt down the Pech Road. But Gulab refused to leave Luttrell's side; instead he called on the service of a distant relative, an older man named Shina, who dwelled in another part of Salar Ban. Gulab instructed Shina to go not to Asadabad, but directly to Commander Matt at the American base at Nangalam, a longer, more grueling journey to the opposite end of the Pech Valley from Asadabad. Gulab and others from the Shuryek, having endured decades of brutality at the hands of outside forces, viewed the American military at Asadabad with suspicion, having had just a few experiences with them. Shina, hesitant even to leave the Shuryek, much less make the arduous trek to the Marine base at Nangalam, finally acquiesced to the pleas of Gulab, who even paid his elder relative a thousand afghanis (about twenty U.S. dollars) to make the trip to see Bartels. And so on the night of the twenty-ninth, the lone Afghan, carrying the small piece of green paper in one of his pockets, journeyed down the meandering trails of the Shuryek Valley into Matin, where he hired a cab to drive him along the Pech Road to Nangalam.

"Commander Matt! Commander Matt!" Sultan ran into the COC at Blessing around midnight. "There is a man at the gate saying that there is a dying American! In Salar Ban! He wants to talk with you! He is very scared of the Americans, but he wants to see just you, and not anyone from Asadabad. For him to come in the middle of the night is pretty crazy around here."

Matt, unaware of the SOF tragedy that had unfolded just a few miles from Blessing, sprinted to the camp's entrance, where he met the gray-bearded Shina. "Sultan, make some tea, and get this guy a blueberry muffin or something. He looks tired."

"Yessir," Sultan gruffed. Matt led Shina into what Bartels knew of as the "tearoom," where he took all camp guests to converse about a range of topics, from a family member's medical needs to the location of an ACM weapons cache. Sultan bounded through the door just as Matt and Shina sat down on red-and-yellow floor mats, with the lieutenant pouring tea and handing Shina one of the chow hall's blueberry muffins. The initial meeting lasted just minutes, Matt learning through Sultan that an American "doctor" was hiding in Gulab's home, somewhere in Salar Ban.

"An American doctor?" Bartels shot a puzzled look to Sultan.

"Yes, and he says that he is shot, bleeding a lot. Dirt all over his face. Very bad condition. He is a doctor who is doing work on *himself*!" Bartels immediately realized that the survivor must have been a Navy Corpsman—possibly connected to the search Kinser was awaiting orders to undertake from his patrol base at Kandagal, many miles and thousands of feet of elevation gain from Salar Ban, but still closer than any other American troops in the region. Shina then remembered the note. He handed the folded green paper to Matt.

"I can barely read this . . . what is this? *It isn't even legible,*" the lieutenant muttered to himself. After a few moments, Bartels managed to decipher the glib message scratched in black ink:

BEEN SHOT
VILLAGE PEOPLE TOOK ME IN
NEED HELP
SIGNED

Below *signed,* he read the name Marcus and then struggled with what he thought spelled "Little" or "Lateral." *Is this some sort of a hoax? Is someone trying to lure us up the Shuryek?* the lieutenant wondered. Bartels, intimately familiar with U.S. military protocol for "blood chits," knew that all units, conventional or SOF, mandated the inclusion of some uniquely identifying personal information, such as mother's maiden name, name of a first pet, name of a high school, etc., in order to confirm the identity of personnel in duress; the lieutenant even looked for some hidden message, but couldn't decipher anything. Still, he sprinted to the COC with the note, where he immediately scanned it, then sent it by SIPR (secure e-mail, pronounced "sipper") to Rob Scott and Tom Wood, and then called the OpsO.

"What's the note say, Bartels?" Tom barked.

"I just e-mailed it to you, sir. You should have it now. But it's a real short type of blood chit." Matt read the message to Wood. "If it's real, somebody's in really, really bad shape. I mean, this is barely legible— like its written by someone gasping their last breaths."

"Is there a name on it?" Wood asked.

"Marcus something . . . maybe Marcus *Little* or Marcus *Lateral.* I can't read the last name."

"Hold on." The OpsO, now at Asadabad with a contingent of SEALs under the command of an O-6-level SEAL (a Navy captain, a full-colonel equivalent in the Marine Corps—one rank higher than MacMannis) in Bagram, made a quick inquiry. "Marcus *Luttrell?*" Wood asked the lieutenant.

"Yeah. Yeah! I can just barely see it spelled that way."

"Okay, Bartels. Make sure that that walk-in doesn't fuckin' walk *out.* And hold on; someone at Bagram, a SEAL captain, wants to talk to you. He'll be calling any second now." The SEAL asked Matt a litany of questions. Bartels could only tell him the few facts that he had before him, and quickly sensed that the captain didn't believe a word he said.

"Well, sir. We have this note, and we have the walk-in who has seen one American in the village of Salar Ban—that's all I can say." The SEAL ended the conversation, then Matt returned to the tearoom with Sultan and Shina. Back at Asadabad, a line of SEALs, clutching their M4s, launched a verbal attack against Wood, demanding to gain access to Shina and get a grid on Gulab's house in order to launch what Wood sensed the SEALs planned to be a direct-action raid/hostage rescue mission.

"Look, this is just a friendly local somewhere, helping one of your guys. Hopefully there are more survivors that other villagers are helping, too—"

"As far as I'm concerned, your career as a Marine is over. Fuckin' over. Gone. You'll be out of theater in less than twenty-four hours!" the SEALs spat at the shocked OpsO.

"We have a Marine patrol literally one valley over from Salar Ban, in the Korangal. They can push into the village within two or three hours, get your guy outta there—have him within six hours, possibly, if we can identify the exact location of the house. Maybe have him within two or three hours, but we need to determine the *exact location* of the house first," Wood stated, flanked by the Marines who faced down the SEALs along with him.

"Marines won't have anything to do with this. This is a SEAL mission. We're gonna get our men outta there! Give us the walk-in. You don't gimme the walk-in and I'll—"

"He's with First Lieutenant Matthew Bartels, at the base he commands—Camp Blessing—at Nangalam," Wood stated, then stormed out of the "meeting."

Shina stayed with Matt and Sultan through the daylight hours of the thirtieth, during which time the lieutenant and his terp worked with the elderly Afghan to pinpoint the exact location of Gulab's home on a map. Salar Ban, like most villages in the Kunar, sprawls across a huge expanse of rugged terrain; even a large American force would need to spend upward of a week to locate Luttrell if a search-and-rescue operation required comprehensively sweeping individual houses (many of which blend into the mountainous surroundings so well that outsiders can stare directly at them from just thirty feet away without noticing a "house" at all). The Afghan, who knew his land intimately, knew *just* his land—and not a graphical representation of it, like a map. He couldn't even give directions; he just had to *physically show* Bartels or Sultan—or a SEAL rescue team—himself.

"What if we took him up in a helicopter?" Matt asked Sultan.

"No way, his eyes have never seen the landscape around him without his feet planted firmly on that land, just like a large piece of paper printed with squiggly lines showing the terrain around his home means nothing to him. He needs to kick his own steps up those trails he's walked for decades, with any outsiders who want to know the secrets of the villager's mountainous world paying good attention as they follow closely behind him."

Bartels and Sultan quickly established a rapport with Shina, who, despite the drama of their introduction, now saw the two as friends, and extended an invitation to the duo to come to his home in Salar Ban. On the evening of 30 June, Bartels, now partially briefed on the SOF disaster, received another heated call from the SEAL captain in Bagram, who demanded that Bartels disclose the location of Gulab's house.

"I don't know, sir. But as you know, the guy who can take a rescue team to him is sitting here at my base."

"Get him to point it out on a map!" the SEAL thundered.

"Been trying all day. He doesn't even know what a map is, sir," Bartels explained. "He can't even vaguely describe where the house is, sir. He just has to walk there himself, and show someone firsthand."

"What if we get him in the air? He can point out the location to a team from the air, right?"

"No. He's not used to seeing the world from the air, just from the trails he's walked his whole life," Bartels replied.

"Keep him there. Don't let him move. Absolutely don't let your eyes off him!" The SEAL captain then tersely ended the conversation.

Later that evening, a helicopter swooped onto Blessing's landing strip, carrying two unidentified, bearded SOF personnel who charged into the tearoom, demanding, "That him?" as they pointed to Shina. Matt nodded, then the duo threw a black bag over Shina's head, tightly flexicuffed the villager's hands behind his back, and dragged him into the helicopter, which then roared into the night. Bartels and Sultan shot each other stunned looks.

"I guess that's why he didn't want to go to Asadabad," Matt said with a tone of disbelief and embarrassment, astonished that fellow American military servicemen would treat a local clearly trying to help with such unnecessary brutality.

"Too bad we couldn't keep Asadabad from coming to him, sir," Sultan replied.

Earlier on the twenty-ninth, as Shina journeyed to Camp Blessing, Ahmad Shah and his men descended upon Salar Ban. They'd seen a total of four Americans during their ambush, but counted only three bodies in the aftermath of the attack, and knew the only possible egress route off that part of the mountain struck through Salar Ban. Capturing a survivor, whom the terrorist could use in a videotaped beheading spectacle, would make Shah's cavalcade of death and destruction complete. Through intimidation of villagers in Salar Ban, Shah learned of Gulab and the injured American he harbored, and immediately came to the shepherd's door. But the reserved Gulab refused to turn over the SEAL. Had Luttrell descended into Chichal or any other of the Korangal Valley's villages, he would almost assuredly have been handed over to the terrorist. But the SEAL had made his way from the heights of Sawtalo Sar onto the mountain's Shuryek Valley flank, and Shah had just a few men in his band; violence against Gulab almost certainly would incite the entire village of Salar Ban to take up arms against the wannabe Taliban commander, and Shah knew it. After threatening the lives of Gulab and his family, Shah departed, having come just feet from Luttrell; only an earthen wall separated the two.

As the SEALs interrogated Shina at their COC in Asadabad—and Luttrell continued to cling to life—the Task Force Red Rangers finalized their plan to move onto Sawtalo Sar to recover those in the downed Chinook and locate the survivors of the SDVT SEAL recon team. With air unavailable for inserts throughout the area in the wake of the MH-47 shoot-down, the soldiers drafted a plan where they would move onto the objective area by foot, starting from a point west of Camp Wright along the road connecting Jalalabad with Asadabad. Rob and Tom scrutinized the Rangers' plans. The soldiers had done a "route recon" assessment of their intended movement onto Sawtalo Sar using 1:50,000-scale map sheets of the region, and determined that they could reach the crash site, roughly ten miles in a straight line from their starting point, within twelve hours; thus, they planned to have individual Rangers carry less than one full day's worth of food and water, keeping light to move fast, with the intention of resupplying via CDS drops [Containerized Delivery System—pallets of food, water, and other supplies dropped from the rear of high-flying C-130s] once at the crash site.

With raised eyebrows, the two Marines openly questioned what they felt to be an unrealistically low approximation of the time the Rangers would need to traverse the incredibly steep and rugged terrain, particularly when factoring in the temperatures the area experienced at the height of summer. "These guys are used to short, helicopter-inserted hard-hit ops, which they're great at," Rob Scott explained to a representative at SOCCENT. "But as far as we have seen, they haven't done many—if *any*—long-distance movements through the mountains out here. Their plan just isn't realistic." But the advice of the Marines—to man-pack at least seventy-two hours' worth of food and water and to take a closer look at the densely packed contour lines on the section of the map representing the ground they would follow—fell on deaf ears. Commanders in Tampa, Florida, approved the mission, and approximately one hundred special operations soldiers, including members of Task Force Red Rangers and various ODAs, embarked on their journey.

Two days later, after soldier after soldier went down with heat-and-dehydration-related afflictions necessitating a number of emergency CDS drops, less than a third of the original force staggered onto the crash site. The daytime-high temperatures deep in the convection-oven-like dark rock valleys just west of Asadabad rocketed past 120 degrees, sapping the troops' energy and depleting their water. Meanwhile, Kinser, Eggers, the Marines, and the ASF along with Hamchuck and Henrietta, waited at Kandagal, while Tom Wood awaited approval for 2/3's portion of the recovery effort. With the crash site secured, the restriction on helicopter flights into the region was lifted, and the grisly job of recovering the bodies began. Finding the fastrope wrapped around the rear rotor assembly, and with the stench of burned flesh and jet fuel hanging low in the air, the recovery team quickly determined that all had died instantly, the pilots' hands still clutching the controls of the big Chinook.

By 1 July, with no sign of Dietz, Murphy, or Axelson, and with Luttrell clinging to life under the care of Gulab (just four miles to the southeast of Kinser and Eggers's location), 2/3 was approved to move. With Eggers and Joe Roy bounding ahead to establish well-concealed overwatch positions, Kinser led the larger group of Marines and ASF (flanked by Hamchuck and Henrietta) south into the depths of the Korangal Valley. With the larger group armed with light machine guns and mortars, they could provide immediate fire support to Eggers and Roy—who, in turn, kept a sharp lookout for any ambush Shah may have put in place. Of course, both units maintained solid comms with each other, as well as with Camp Blessing, the battalion COC at JAF, and Wood at Asadabad.

Having been passed a series of grids of the possible locations of the recon SEAL team, Tom Wood contacted Kinser and had him race into action. Kinser grabbed three Marines, and with Hamchuck and Henrietta, they bounded south two miles to the village of Taleban (no relation to Mullah Omar's group, the *Taliban*) and up one thousand feet from there in a matter of hours. "Nothing, sir. Not a damn thing. Not even a broken branch," the lieutenant reported.

"Here's another grid. Keep going." Wood knew that he could keep the tireless lieutenant racing throughout the entire mountain—just not in the vicinity of Salar Ban, as mandated by *Red Wings II*'s command.

For days, the Marines combed the entire Korangal Valley, searching, climbing, descending, linking up with other platoons of Echo, thrashing their feet, enduring biting-cold monsoonal rainfall at night and blistering, humid heat during the day—without success. Golf Company, too, raced throughout the eastern and southern aspects of the Shuryek Valley, but also discovered nothing. Finally, with help from Shina, a SOF team made it to Gulab's house and brought Luttrell back to safety on 3 July. A day later, the Rangers discovered the bodies of Murphy and Dietz, lying next to each other deep in the chasm of the northeast gulch. Axelson, who had separated from the others of the recon team, possibly to find an open area to establish comms with the MBITR during the height of the ambush, was found almost a week later, on 10 July, with the help of cadaver dogs helicoptered onto the mountain's slopes.

The American military threw a tremendous amount of assets at the search-and-recovery effort. Air Force Special Operations AC-130 gunships lit up the mountain at night with their onboard 105 mm howitzer, miniguns, and 40 mm Bofors guns; A-10s tore up ridgelines both day and night with their 30 mm cannons, and commanders back at MacDill watched it all, fed imagery from MQ-1 Predator UAVs circling high above the Hindu Kush. Closer to the disaster site, a forward command post was established on Sawtalo Sar's summit, a post that included four different unit leaders, including Lieutenant Colonel MacMannis; all of them, however, fell under the control of commanders back in Florida. Far removed from the SOF information flow, Kinser, Eggers, and the other Marines wondered what the aircraft had been targeting—or if the barrages were just called in for SEAD prep.

Early in the second week of July, the lieutenant was ordered to link up with SOF near the crest of Sawtalo Sar's north ridge, above the village of Chichal. Once on scene, he directly spied one of the targets of a recent drop. Below him, at the outskirts of the village, a home on the edge of a cliff smoldered in ruin. A few hours earlier, based on time-sensitive intel indicating that Shah and his men had been hiding at the house, a B-52 from an altitude of forty-five thousand feet had released three GBU-38 five-hundred-pound GPS-guided JDAMs. "We did an off-site BDA [battle damage assessment, "off-site" meaning that no-body had actually physically inspected the damage, just observed it from afar]," one of the Ranger lieutenants told Kinser. "We have twenty enemy KIA [killed in action] and nineteen of their local supporters, for a total of thirty-nine."

Kinser shook his head in acknowledgment, then requested permission from Wood to do his own, *on-site* BDA, after Task Force Brown Chinooks pulled the beleaguered special operations soldiers off the mountain. He found a slew of dead farm animals and nine dead civilians, but nothing to indicate that any of Shah's men had been there; although he did find evidence, in the form of written notes, that illegal RPGs and PK machine guns had been kept and sold at the house. The lieutenant stared at the destruction before him, the stench of rotting flesh wafting around him, and shook his head at what he felt to be rank overreaction—and once again, very, very questionable intel.

In fact, Shah and his men had been nowhere near Chichal, or anywhere else on Sawtalo Sar by the first of July, having fled into Pakistan days before the GBU-38s careened into the stone walls of the home. The terrorist, looking to propagandize his way up the ladder of global extremism, clearly looked to follow in the publicity-through-powerfully-shocking-imagery vein of the 1993 extremist attack of U.S. Army Rangers in Somalia, where dead U.S. servicemen were videotaped being dragged through the streets of Mogadishu. During the ambush of the four SEALs, Shah had with him not one, but two videographers. Once in the Peshawar region of Pakistan, most likely at the Shamshatoo camp, Shah edited and distributed footage of one tape, but essentially shelved the second tape he had in his possession, although a few copies slipped into the hands of U.S. intelligence (he possibly withheld the second tape because his image could clearly be seen on certain sequences). The distributed video, with the al-Qaeda-linked "As-Sahab Media" logo superimposed on the lower right side of the clip, shows a shot of the early-afternoon firefight after a computer-animated introduction depicting the destruction of the United States of America and a graphic of Koranic verse. As the videographer descends into the densely treed northeast gulch, the sounds of a heated firefight resonate in the background audio. Three of Shah's men, but not Shah himself, then approach the bodies of the fallen SEALs in a clip apparently spliced onto the first part of the footage. The clip shows Shah's execrable henchmen stealing the boots and wristwatches off the dead Americans. The final portion of the ambush video shows the gear that Shah was able to pillage from the recon team, including four helmets; three M4s; stacks of magazines and M203 40 mm grenade rounds; spotting scopes, including a high-power Leupold scope; laser rangefinders; night-vision gear; the MBITR; binoculars; and fragmentation, smoke, and incendiary grenades. Shah even got the team's Panasonic Toughbook laptop, which can be seen to have taken a round to its upper screen. The video then shows a technician pulling the hard drive from the Toughbook, installing it into another machine, and booting the drive. He then downloads maps of the U.S. embassy in Kabul as well as a U.S. military paper on the ACM's tactics, techniques, and procedures, one among a host of sensitive information kept on the computer.

The second video shows Shah himself descending into the gulch with two of his men (in addition to the videographer). The audio pops with loud 7.62 rounds rifling downrange from AK-47s, then rattles with short, controlled bursts of automatic 5.56 mm rounds sent back by the SEALs. The terrorist, clad in traditional Pashtun clothes, including a Pakol hat, is carrying his PK machine gun and speaking into his ICOM radio, and one of the two men at his side is clearly a designated RPG gunner—undoubtedly the man who would shoot down the MH-47 a few hours after the footage of their descent was shot (the second video included time code, and showed a time of 1:57:02 in the afternoon of the twenty-eighth at the beginning of the sequence, hours before the launch of the QRF). Apparently, Shah ordered one videographer to accompany each team of three men—essentially two fire teams—coordinated by Shah through his ICOM. The sounds of the firefight end literally seconds after the start of the clip—the last of the SEALs M4 shots can be heard ringing out at 1:59:25 P.M. on the video.

The two groups of Shah's men meet shortly after two o'clock in the afternoon, chanting *"Alla-u Akhbar!"* as they rifle through the SEALs' gear. The videographer shooting footage for the distributed video can be seen holding his camera and chanting *"Alla-u Akhbar! Alla-u Akhbar!"* repeatedly, then the camera zooms to a wide-angle, clear shot of Shah, holding his PK and one of the SEALs' backpacks, with the steep, sunlit northeast gulch in the background. At 2:15, Shah, one of his men, and both videographers walk back up the gulch, where the time then jumps to 2:38. Under now-overcast skies, one of Shah's men can be seen rummaging through one of the SEALs' gear racks on a well-worn trail striking through greener, higher ground as the second videographer steps into the frame. Plucking hand grenades, magazines filled with 5.56 mm rounds, a strobe, and then a map and a compass, he exclaims in Pashto, "Look, an American compass! God is the greatest!" He then finds a pen and shouts at the camera held by the second videographer, "Look, an American pen! God is the greatest!" The man then runs its ink across his left palm, and with a look of australopithecine wonder, proclaims, "And it writes! God is the greatest!" The translated diatribe gives lucid insight into the depths of humanity from which extremists such as Shah cull their underlings.

At 2:40:50, Shah receives a transmission on his ICOM from his second team requesting more rounds for their weapons. As the sky turns darker, a deep boom of thunder echoes throughout the ridges and valleys of Sawtalo Sar, apparently signaling Shah and his men to seek shelter from the impending storm. The footage ends with Shah throwing his PK over his shoulder at 2:43, then moving to head down the trail, possibly to search for Luttrell.

In the distributed video, the producers included a clip of a standard, conventional "ring flight" of Task Force Sabre CH-47 Chinooks (clearly conventional Chinooks, as they lack refueling probes) heading up the Pech River Valley with Apache escorts, included possibly to intimate the upcoming MH-47 shoot-down. However, since both videographers traveled with Shah after the linkup, and since his RPG gunner can't be seen in the video after the entire crew pillages the SEALs' bodies, the man who downed the MH-47 probably returned to the summit of the mountain with one or two of Shah's men (and no videographer), and possibly under orders from the terrorist leader, waited for the rescue helicopters with the intention of shooting one down. More likely, however, the RPG gunner and the others in the cell went to the SEAL insert site to find other gear, gear that the recon team may have cached (such as the fastrope), and then just chanced upon the Task Force Brown Chinooks attempting to insert the SEAL rescue team. Had Shah reasoned that a rescue attempt by helicopter was imminent, he assuredly would have sent at least one of his videographers with the RPG gunner to capture the fiery downing for his propaganda campaign. In the end, however, Shah and his crew really just hit a dark, disastrously spectacular streak of luck. With a total of nineteen servicemen killed in a matter of hours, 28 June 2005 went into the history books as not only the greatest single-day loss of American life in Afghanistan since the beginning of the war nearly four years prior, but the greatest disaster for the 160th, Navy Special Operations Forces, and all of USSOCOM since the command's founding in 1987.

Shah instantly rocketed into the stratosphere of global terrorist infamy, boosted there not only by the Web posting of his As-Sahab Media video (which never circulated very broadly), but by embarrassingly flawed global media accounts of the tragedy. News outlets printed, televised, and broadcast a host of errors, from the actual name of the operation, calling it "*Operation Redwing*" or "*Operation Red Wing*" to calling Shah "one of Osama bin Laden's chief lieutenants" or a "top Taliban commander," to claiming that Shah commanded an army of hundreds or even thousands of Taliban fighters (both videos, later analyzed and authenticated by U.S. military intelligence, showed eight, including Shah himself; furthermore, extremist "commanders" typically lie and exaggerate about how many fighters they command, often multiplying by tens, even hundreds). Media reports also initially claimed that the MH-47 had been shot down by an SA-7 shoulder-launched, heat-seeking, surface-to-air missile, and after being struck by the warhead, the Chinook lumbered through the air for a good mile before setting down on a cliff edge, which crumbled beneath the craft, sending the MH-47 plunging to its destruction. Even a relative neophyte like Shah was able to leverage the error-laden media coverage to his benefit, claiming, after learning of American forces rescuing Luttrell and discovering the bodies of Murphy and Dietz, that he had the fourth member of the team (Axelson) in hiding with him, and would behead the SEAL in a videotaped spectacle. The global media even got the Gulab story wrong, never mentioning Shina, Matt Bartels, or Camp Blessing, and claiming that Gulab himself walked to American forces—at Asadabad.

In the days following the rescue of Luttrell, Marines of Golf Company's First Platoon, under the command of First Lieutenant Kyle Corcoran, entered Salar Ban and made a brief visit with Gulab as part of the company's sweep up the Shuryek. The villager seemed to be doing well, but was terribly worried about retaliation from Shah, and had asked to be moved to Asadabad with his family, but was unable to get a response from any Americans at Asadabad's Camp Wright. In mid-July, as *Red Wings II* wound down, Gulab showed up at Camp Blessing; he met with Matt Bartels and discussed Shina's harsh treatment at the hands of SOF interrogators, then revealed that while Shina was given money and a number of valuable items as payment for aiding in Luttrell's rescue, he had received nothing. Gulab also told Matt of a number of death threats against him and his family, and showed him a list, left with a death threat on his doorstep, of the Taliban's most wanted dead. Number one was George W. Bush; number two, the commander of Camp Blessing; number three, Afghan President Hamid Karzai. Matt, laughing at the list— but not at the death threats against Gulab and his family—immediately got on the line with Rob Scott, who pushed a request all the way up the channels to CJTF-76. Within weeks, Gulab had a job and house in Asadabad, and received a reward for helping save Marcus Luttrell.

Many of 2/3's grunts had spent nearly three weeks in the field by the time *Red Wings II* had come to an end. Their feet bloodied from tromping up and down endless miles of mountainous terrain, their bodies enervated from the heat of the day, the cold and wet of the night, the dehydration, and for some, dysentery, the Marines nevertheless came out of the campaign much tougher and much fitter, ready for the next challenge.

And while *Red Wings* had been marred nearly from its beginning by tragedy, the battalion did uncover a few weapons caches—the lifeblood of cells such as Shah's—during their tromps through the Korangal and Shuryek. But the most notable gash in the region's network of ACM support during this time came from a simple patrol led by Bartels, a small mission not even theoretically part of *Red Wings* or *Red Wings II*. As all eyes focused on Sawtalo Sar for the recovery effort, Matt decided to act on some intel that Westerfield had given him in early June, intel that he'd been instructed to act on only if he found the time—it wasn't considered priority. The information pointed to a possible cache of weapons, a potentially large number of munitions in a home owned by a man who at one time supported the Taliban and whose brother had been hauled off to Guantánamo Bay as an active Taliban fighter; he was also someone Westerfield believed could be supporting Shah's operations. With a lack of activity around Camp Blessing during the recovery effort on Sawtalo Sar, Matt deliberately chose the Fourth of July to pay a visit to the house, located northeast of Nangalam in the Waigal Valley, the corridor linking the Kunar's Pech Valley with Nuristan, and check for any ACM fireworks. He passed the request to Rob Scott, who approved it, provided he stay outside the wire no more than twelve hours. Arriving during midmorning of the Fourth with a small contingent of Marines, including Justin Bradley, and ten ASF, Matt, speaking through Sultan, bluntly asked the man if he'd been hiding any weapons—mortars, rockets, RPGs, machine guns, rounds, etc. Responding with a resounding *no*, the Afghan invited Matt, Sultan, and Justin into his home, and offered them tea. As Bradley spoke with the onetime Taliban supporter, the sly Matt counted off the length of interior walls with his footsteps. Asking to be excused to speak with the waiting members of the ASF, the lieutenant then counted off the length of the home's exterior. When the numbers didn't add up, Matt produced a wad of cash, telling the man that if he put a hole in the wall before him, and sunshine came through, he'd give him the money. The Afghan began sweating profusely and took a step backward. "Bradley," Matt said, motioning to the stocky corporal, "can you—"

"I'd be delighted, sir." The Montanan stood in front of the rock wall, and with a stiff kick knocked a hole big enough for him to stick his head through. "No sunlight, sir. Got a match?" Matt gave him a momentarily stunned look, then realized the joke. "Just kidding," Bradley said. "I know it's the Fourth of July and all, sir."

Inside the wall, illuminated by the corporal's small flashlight, stacks upon stacks of 107 mm rockets—the type that Camp Blessing had been receiving for the past month—stood in dusty waiting. Bradley and Marines of his squad knocked man-size holes in the house's other false walls, finding a total of two hundred Chinese-made 107 mm rockets, two hundred 82 mm mortar rounds (another favorite munition of Shah's for attacking Camp Blessing), mortar tubes and base plates, RPG launchers, RPG rounds, AK-47s, PK machine guns, boxes upon boxes of ammunition—literally *tons* of munitions, requiring four convoys to remove and transport to Blessing (Matt would designate much of it to be used by the ASF for camp defense). Enough weapons had been removed to keep an operation like Shah's running for years. Bartels, knowing full well that ACM supporters rarely kept all their weapons in one location, returned to another of the man's properties, a small store, the dimensions of which the lieutenant again determined didn't add up. This time around, however, Matt had with him a Marine Corps combat engineer, who recommended against Bradley kicking any holes in walls housing old, potentially unstable explosives. With everyone a good distance back, the engineer set off a small charge of C4, leveling half of the store and revealing another ton of rockets and mortars. In the days following, the now-exposed ACM supporter had his grandchildren haul five truckloads of dangerous munitions to Camp Blessing. "He's had enough of you. He's decided that you can have it all," one of the grandkids told Matt.

"Sorry, took longer than twelve hours, sir," Bartels informed Rob Scott.

"Not a problem, Bartels. You did good there at 'the edge of the empire.' That's by far the biggest ACM cache yet. That makes you the *cache king*, Lieutenant."

Matt laughed, but Rob's pronouncement would hold true to the very end of the deployment, as the 4 July find remained the single largest the battalion uncovered during their entire tour. But it wasn't the last for the Blessing Marines, who would uncover a total of thirty-four stores of weapons during their seven months in-country.

Although Shah had been deprived of a massive store of weapons, his exploits brought him assets far more valuable—notoriety and hence fighters. With the world's eyes focused on the tragedy in the Kunar, and with hate-filled Islamic extremists, both well seasoned and fresh out of ideological madrassas, looking to achieve fundamentalist glory for themselves, Shah looked to see his ranks swell in numbers. And even as the dust settled from the tragedies of *Red Wings* and attacks quieted in the area with Shah's absconding to Pakistan, the clock continued to tick ever more loudly toward the Afghan national elections of 18 September, just two months in the future.

8

REDOUBLED EFFORTS

Arabs, Chechens, Yemenis . . . and from many other countries. They're all grouping in Peshawar and will come into Kunar very soon, to help Ahmad Shah." Bobby translated the words of a confidential source, introduced by L.C., during Regan Turner's second trip to Khewa, in July. "Ahmad Shah will soon have maybe sixty to one hundred fighters with him," the source revealed. Regan learned that indeed, the tragic events that had befallen the SOF personnel and the subsequent worldwide media attention given to the ambush and fiery shootdown of the MH-47 had greatly enhanced the cachet of the cell leader. "The fighters will be here for three months, to help Shah in stopping the elections in Kunar, Nangarhar, and Nuristan with road bombings, mortar, and rocket attacks. Shah even now has an Egyptian who commands the Arabs for him. He is also hiring some locals—not regular fighters—along the Asadabad–Jalalabad road and in the Korangal and other valleys, to look out for him, and some to shoot for him."

Turner further learned that Shah had been giving financial support to an al-Qaeda operative who would be placing his name on the ballot as a representative of the Kuz Kunar district in the September elections; the extremist clearly sought a multipronged assault on regional stability, intending, on the one hand, to disrupt the elections with violence, and on the other, to sully the democratic process with an al-Qaeda candidate. To vet the accuracy of the source's information, Turner asked a question about the shoot-down. "He says that it was not shot down by an SA-7, but with an RPG." With that piece of information, and with the source's confirmation of other details that had not yet made it into media reports, the lieutenant felt confident in the reliability of his source.

"The picture . . ." Bobby held up a widely distributed Army-produced "wanted" flyer of Ahmad Shah as he translated the source's information. "The picture is wrong. That is one of his assistants." The source ducked inside his house and then emerged seconds later, holding two small, grainy color photographs. "These, he says, are actual, real pictures of Shah." After the meeting, Turner asked a number of other Khewa locals to identify the man in the photographs; all responded with the same name: Ahmad Shah. "He will be back in the Chichal area, many villagers throughout there will help him. He won't go into Chichal by going up the Korangal Valley, though." The source motioned with his hands as he spoke to Bobby and Lieutenant Turner. "He'll be coming in from the Chowkay Valley, the way he just escaped from the Korangal before he went into Pakistan, and then when he returns, he will come up the Chowkay Valley, over the summit of Sawtalo Sar mountain, and down into Chichal in the upper Korangal. If he has to run again, he'll go through the Chowkay or possibly the Narang Valley—no Marines there!—then move up to hiding not in Pakistan, but in Nuristan. No Afghan Army in Nuristan, no police, no Marines—nobody!" The Afghan man chopped his hand through the air, accentuating his statement. "Ahmad Shah really believes that he is the new, *reborn* Taliban, that he can bring them back into power, and that he can be a big leader. If he returns to Pakistan again, he'll be seen as weak, because he'll be running away. He has to stay here now—and scare people off from the elections in the area to show that the Taliban is the only way."

"Coalition forces have no presence in Nuristan? *None?*" Lieutenant Colonel Jim Donnellan asked CJTF-76's chief intelligence officer during a series of briefings shortly after arriving at Bagram Airfield on 4 July. Donnellan had been scheduled to take over 2/3's command from Andy MacMannis on the fifteenth of July, and so he had immersed himself in the history and culture of the region, with an emphasis on 2/3's three-province area of operation. But it was only after he arrived in Bagram that he'd seen the big picture of the battalion's higher command.

"No, there's nothing going on up in Nuristan," the intel officer confidently replied. "There's no reason for any of our forces to get up there." Having finished his comprehensive historical overview of Nuristan, Kunar, Laghman, and Nangarhar provinces, Donnellan instantly put himself in the enemy's shoes—and knew just where he'd go were he on the run from coalition forces (other than the tribal areas of Pakistan). To Nuristan. Neither Afghan nor foreign units were present in the province that abuts both Kunar and Laghman.

Donnellan, who like Cooling with 3/3, would lead the Island Warriors through a successful seven-month tour in Iraq's Anbar province following his tour in Afghanistan, was fully prepared for the rigors of the Afghan fight, but had been placed in the difficult position of taking over the command of a battalion that was already in-country without having trained with, or even having met, the vast majority of 2/3's officer and enlisted ranks. But the six-foot-six, focused yet personable Donnellan had spent time with Tom Wood and Rob Scott prior to 2/3's departure for Afghanistan, and given the instant confidence both majors inspired in everyone they met, the lieutenant colonel knew that his transition into the Afghan fight would be smooth and quick.

The *Red Wings* debacle weighed heavily on the command levels above 2/3, however, creating operational obstacles both in planning and battle that would challenge and stress the Marines to the limit. Using Turner's latest intel, which Westerfield and his staff immediately dove headlong into, Tom Wood and Rob Scott began piecing together a new mission, the foundation of which they'd conceived even before the dust of the *Red Wings* disaster had settled, an operation that would have the Marines continue the fight for stabilization of the region with redoubled efforts.

By the time Colonel Gary Cheek and the 25th Infantry Division departed Afghanistan in the spring of 2005, Afghanistan's top Army commanders (bolstered in large measure by the successes of 3/3's Operation *Spurs*) took the position that organized, violent resistance in RC-East was finished, and only small pockets of terrorists remained—tiny (albeit deadly and possibly al-Qaeda-linked) cells that possessed neither the means nor the desire to become organized movements like the Taliban. The *Red Wings* tragedy had shocked CJTF-76's command, proving that elements remained in eastern Afghanistan that actively sought a broad resurgence of the Taliban or a Taliban-like regime, however unrealistic such a goal may have been.

With so much worldwide attention focused on the Kunar after the *Red Wings* tragedy, CJTF-76 Command assumed a decidedly risk-averse stance for ops on or around Sawtalo Sar, leading to their virtual grounding of what Marines know as assault support—helicopters for the insertion of troops (although they'd still allow, on a very restrictive basis, Air Ambulance support). Whatever scheme of maneuver the battalion would undertake, the grunts themselves could move only by land, and because Shah based his operations far above and beyond routes navigable by any means other than feet and hooves, 2/3's Marines would spend much more time pounding their boots up and down steep ground than bracing their backs against the jolts of rutted roads. However, as this new op began to take form, Wood and other senior battalion staff realized that the logistical constraints were actually an advantage, moving the plan away from a reliance on a covert direct-action team to pure conventional-maneuver warfare.

As his first order of business, Donnellan set out to visit every base in the battalion's area of operation. After a brief stay in Bagram, the

lieutenant colonel experienced the blast-furnace summer heat and choking dust of Jalalabad Airfield, then made a quick visit to the forward
operating base at Mehtar Lam in Laghman province, home of Fox Company. An ardent tactician, forever observing the strengths and weaknesses of both friendly and enemy personnel and facilities, Donnellan
carefully noted the condition of each base he visited. The massive Bagram struck him as virtually impenetrable—a small city complete with
a Taco Bell, Pizza Hut, and other fast-food restaurants, a huge PX,
and, of course, a miles-long heavily defended perimeter encircling aircraft, weapons, and personnel of all types. JAF, too, he found to be
well fortified and defensible, as did the forward operating base at
Mehtar Lam. A week and a half after the official 15 July change of command, Donnellan ventured northeast from 2/3's COC at JAF to Camp
Wright in the frontierlike town of Asadabad, lying in the heart of the
Kunar Valley barely eleven straight-line miles due east of Sawtalo Sar.
Surrounded by the sepia faces of the steepest mountains on which he'd
ever laid eyes, the stoic Donnellan didn't quite know what to make of
the scene at "A-Bad." Flip-flop-clad Afghans in combat fatigues worked
on heavy machine guns mounted to old Toyota pickup trucks; bearded,
M4-toting SOF types in civilian garb coolly gazed at passersby from
behind expensive black wraparound sunglasses; OCF (Other Coalition
Forces—a term for CIA, DEA, etc.) mulled around, often toting leather
briefcases; Special Forces soldiers zipped by on quad runners; even
regular Army—and of course, Marines—counted in the ranks at A-Bad.
While well defended, the camp—an accretion of tents, zigzagging rock
walls, old stone buildings, all stitched together by concrete bunkers—
struck Donnellan as a heavily armed trailer park.

"We can't help you with security outside of Asadabad," Kunar's provincial leader, Governor Wafa, told him during a meeting with the battalion commander after visiting Camp Wright. "We need more money
for police here."

"How often do you visit Nangalam?" Donnellan asked.

"Never been there. Hear it's *interesting*, though. Haven't been past
Watapor. Wouldn't travel *that* road. Especially if I were you!" The cagey

Wafa, whom Donnellan quickly began to think of as the "mayor of Asa-dabad," responded through an interpreter. Even the open-minded Don-nellan, who'd been warned about Wafa from the provincial reconstruction team commander at A-Bad, quickly felt uneasy about the man. "Really, we need more money for police here in Asadabad before we can get out into those other areas. I don't know why you even go out there. I wouldn't go on that road if I were you." The evasive Wafa seemed almost complicit with the ACM—maybe not directly, but possibly through intentional ig-norance of their activities. Or maybe he *did* have direct ties to insurgent cells; maybe even Shah's. Donnellan couldn't read minds and afforded the governor as much benefit of the doubt as was reasonable. He loaded into his Humvee and his convoy headed west, into the Pech River Valley, bound for the last of the bases on his list, Camp Blessing.

Partway into the chasmlike Pech Valley, the convoy stopped at Watapor, a village designated as one of the ballot centers for the Sep-tember elections. Out of a plume of dust, the line of six Humvees pulled off the deeply gashed dirt road next to a small complex of buildings—an old schoolhouse and a police station. To the east, a matrix of boxy rock houses stacked one atop the other on the face of a steep cliff loomed above a field of corn that swept to the edge of the road the Marines had just exited. To both the north and south, the minuscule specs of man-made structures dissolved into the furiously honed Hindu Kush; to the west, the brilliantly sunlit Pech Valley melted into pitch-darkness. The convoy drivers powered down their diesel engines and the passengers dismounted for a brief meeting with the locals and Af-ghan National Police in the small village. With the mildly pungent odor of burning agricultural fields hanging in the air, the group headed to the police station, passing a crumpled mass of rusting metal on their way. This rusted ball of steel and aluminum, now overgrown by weeds, stood as an eerie warning; those who'd seen Ahmad Shah's distributed video of the SEAL-team ambush had noted footage of a massive IED strike on a white SUV-type truck. That vehicle, the remnants of which the Marines brushed past that day during their visit, had been carrying the chief of Watapor's police, who was instantly killed just a few miles

west of Watapor on a section of the Pech Road known as IED Alley
when one of Shah's men remotely triggered the deadly blast.

After a short introduction and lunch inside the police station's mud-
and-brick-walled inner courtyard, the Marines headed west, on the final
leg of their journey to Camp Blessing. As the pastoral landscape surrounding Watapor blurred into the background and the convoy sped
toward the heart of the Hindu Kush, Donnellan pondered just what he'd
find at Camp Blessing; after hearing so many stories about the lonely
outpost, he wondered which of the many tales would reveal themselves
as fact and which exaggeration.

Coming around a turn, the convoy rumbled into view of the domineering Sawtalo Sar, and the Marines soon eyed the village of Matin at
the mountain's base. The broad, flat plain they traveled narrowed to a
corridor barely wide enough for a Humvee to traverse, with sheer cliffs
on both sides and the frigid Pech River almost a hundred feet below. As
the convoy slowed, each driver made sure to stay well behind the vehicle
in front of him as he approached a blind turn in the road, a bend marked
by a large, diamond-shaped boulder. Unbeknownst to the drivers, a couple hundred feet above the boulder, two of Shah's men, one with a video
camera, and another with a modified cordless phone, hunkered down in
sinister wait.

Days, weeks, or possibly months earlier, most likely in one of the
small houses high on the slopes of Sawtalo Sar in the Chichal area, one
of Shah's paid operatives carefully enhanced two blasting caps by squeez-
ing C4 around them, then poured high-explosive powder into the bottom of a pressure cooker. After attaching the blasting caps to a modified
cordless phone (cordless phones sold in Asia have greater transmission
power and hence range than those sold in the United States), the man,
who was known to work with his young son at his side, placed the
detonator assembly inside the pressure cooker, filled the pot with charge,
then sealed it with a crank atop its lid. Before the convoy rolled through,
almost certainly at night, one of the extremist's hired helpers buried the
device twenty feet east of the diamond-shaped boulder, a point marked
by a flat tan rock that, visually contrasted against the darker earth of

the slope against which it was propped, was visible from hundreds of meters distant. After the ambush of the SEAL recon team and then the shoot-down of the MH-47, Shah was clearly looking to continue his reign of terror.

The first two "hardbacks" (standard, four-seat Humvees), one of which carried Donnellan, rounded the bend as the third, carrying eight Marines and an interpreter, approached the point of the road marked by the tan rock. Moments later, Shah's triggerman rose from his hide and depressed a single button on his phone's keypad, arming the device. Just as the driver of the third highback rounded the bend, the world before him went black as a concussive wave of earth shattered the Humvee's windshield and enveloped it and its nine passengers in a boiling orange-and-yellow fireball. The powerful blast crushed the Humvee's undercarriage and mashed the heavy diesel engine onto the laps of the driver and front passenger as it launched the vehicle airborne in a reverse summersault. Not a second later, the vehicle lay upside down, pointed east. Donnellan's vehicle skidded to a halt; immediately the call went over the net that a Humvee had been hit by an IED. Bartels, constantly monitoring the radio at Camp Blessing, sprang into action, yelling for his quick reaction force to mount up in their heavily armed Humvees; within sixty seconds, the lieutenant had his convoy screaming out the camp's gate. When Donnellan called Bartels with an urgent request for assistance, Bartels replied, "Sir, I'm already on my way!"

Three of the Marines had been instantly ejected from the highback's open-topped rear; another three grunts and the interpreter lay beneath it. Hot oil, diesel fuel, coolant, and then blood showered the Marines in the front compartment, choking them as they hung upside down, suspended by crushed, hemorrhaging legs. As Donnellan sprinted to the smoking highback, he wondered just how many Marines had been killed by the immense explosion, then how many would be maimed for life.

Methodically chanting *"Alla-u Akhbar, Alla-u Akhbar"* as he watched the plume of superheated dirt and rocks settle around the annihilated vehicle, the videographer zoomed in on the destruction—then focused the video camera's lens onto the scene's magnified image projected by a long-range scope, possibly the Leupold pillaged from the SEAL recon team, and videotaped the 'keyhole' view of individual Marines, including Donnellan, fighting to save their comrades amid the twisted debris. Within days, Shah had the gruesome footage prepared for his next propaganda video. Released by As-Sahab, the video begins with Koranic verse and a computer graphic of an exploding and burning American flag, then shows footage of an interview of Osama bin Laden interspersed with old clips of mujahideen fighting the Soviets as well as bin Laden mulling about a training camp. The producers then spliced a translated interview of Ayman al-Zawahiri discussing how America was falling into the "abyss" in Afghanistan, just as the Soviets had, but at a much faster rate. Ironically, the next spliced sequence after Zawahiri's declaration shows a nighttime ACM attack against Camp Blessing—where the videographer clearly sees his ultimate demise at the business end of a .50-caliber machine gun—followed by footage of Ahmad Shah (with his face blurred out) launching 82 mm mortars at Camp Blessing. The producers then ran a quick clip of two of the fallen SEALs of the recon team and a brief shot of part of one of the MH-47's gearboxes that one of the locals of the Chichal area must have recovered after *Red Wings II*. Then the viewer sees the highback rolling up to the tan rock . . . and the huge ball of flame that completely engulfs the Humvee. The scene immediately following the highback hit shows the Watapor police chief's vehicle, the remains of which the Marines of the convoy passed just an hour before the attack, as Shah's triggerman makes a direct hit on it, instantly killing the chief. In the propaganda video, the explosion of the highback attack is clearly larger and more powerful.

But while Shah's triggerman timed the hit against the Watapor police chief perfectly, he struck the key that sent current into the blasting caps of the highback's IED a half second too early—an eternity when trying to destroy an up-armored Humvee, even with a large IED. As Donnellan emerged from his vehicle he eyed the disorienting sight of a Humvee flipped over, facing the wrong direction. He looked up to see three Marines already on their feet, digging to get the trapped grunts and the interpreter in the rear compartment freed. The driver and front-seat passenger were both conscious—and calm. The powerful explosion missed direct-hit status by about six feet, causing the vehicle to flip over instead of disintegrating completely. As Bartels and the Marines of the quick reaction force roared to a halt, the last of those in the rear of the vehicle crawled to safety, with only the interpreter seriously injured; he had a broken leg that healed fully in a few months. The driver and front passenger, now completely coated in oil, diesel fuel, and blood, cracked jokes and even struck up a conversation with Bartels as the lieutenant worked with other Marines to extricate the two—which they did within minutes of the QRF's arrival. In the end, as everyone in the Humvee fully recovered, the IED strike had failed to do much of anything significant. But the explosion was dramatic for propaganda purposes, like Zawahiri's words in the same video.

Why Shah chose this convoy, however, remains a mystery; Marine Corps convoys plied the Pech Road virtually every day. Killing 2/3's commander would have been a monumental victory for Shah, heaping even more attention on the extremist. But how could he have known that the lieutenant colonel was in the convoy? Shah had very likely been tipped off that the new battalion commander was on board; possibly by Wafa, or possibly by someone in the governor's entourage, or possibly by a Watapor local paid by Shah as a lookout. Neither Donnellan nor any of the other Marines of 2/3 would ever know.

Relieved that everyone would fully recover from their injuries, Donnellan walked back to his Humvee as he mentally scrolled through the destruction that Shah had caused: the IED attacks, the mortar and rocket attacks, the police chief, the SEAL recon team, the MH-47. And now this, *his own convoy*. Unemotional, consummately professional, the battalion commander icily resolved that afternoon to do everything within his ability to allow his Marines once and for all to destroy Shah's cell. As he reached to open the door of his Humvee, Donnellan scanned the ridgelines throughout the area—unbeknownst to him, two of Shah's men stared right back at him and the other Marines from

their hide—pulled the heavy door shut, then continued the journey to
Blessing.

When the shortened convoy arrived in the late afternoon, the three rear
Humvees returning to A-Bad with the injured Marines and the interpreter, the shadows of the peaks rising to the west of Blessing had smoth-
ered the camp in cool shade. Donnellan emerged to the greetings of
Kinser. "Welcome to the edge of the empire, sir," the lieutenant belted
out as he rigidly saluted the new battalion commander. Having closely
monitored the events that had just unfolded, by radio, and knowing
that everyone had survived the ordeal, Kinser felt the urge to ask sarcastically, "So, what took you so long?" But the lieutenant realized that
it was too early to start joking about the attack, especially with a lieutenant colonel he'd never met.

"Well, I've finally made it. Camp Blessing," Donnellan remarked as
he gazed at the various lookouts perched atop surrounding ridgelines,
then took a deep breath and studied the scene at the camp: grinning
members of the ASF washing their feet in buckets of water; Hamchuck
and Henrietta lounging in the dirt of a boxing ring the Marines had
constructed in front of the base COC; living quarters built not according to any master plan, but simply *into* the steep terrain; old Soviet and
Chinese recoilless rifles, RPG launchers, heavy machine guns, and AK-
47s *everywhere,* not just dotting the zigzagging, razor-wired perimeter,
but leaned against tables and chairs, suspended as decorations in the
chow hall, even used to prop open a door. Next to the Humvees, intri-
cately adorned, "jingled out" Toyota Hiluxes, with an array of weapons
systems bolted and welded into the trucks' rear beds, stood ready for
some outrageous battle. Camp Blessing looked like some bizarre cross
between a set in *Apocalypse Now* and a set in *Thunderdome.*

"EEEE!"

"Kinser. What's that red—"

"EEEE!" From inside the COC, Molly, the base's resident monkey,
loudly emerged.

"What is . . . that? And why is it red, with a Mohawk?"

"That's Molly, sir. Molly the monkey. She was here when we arrived. She used to have a friend, Mr. Peepers, but he disappeared one day. Not sure, but one of the locals may have lured him out."

"Mr. Peepers?" Donnellan paused. "I think Molly needs to move along, too."

"Tried, sir. Tried giving her away a few times, once to a villager five miles up the Waigal Valley, toward Nuristan. I got back from a patrol one night a few days later and found her dragging one of my frag grenades around by its pin. Lucky I had it taped!" Kinser laughed nervously. "One of the Marines' moms heard about her and sent some red hair dye, then Bradley gave her a Mohawk one day after a combat patrol. She loves it here. But we gotta make sure she keeps away from grenades!"

"What's with those dogs?" Donnellan asked. "In that boxing ring?"

Kinser recounted the "Special Forces dogs" story. "We have boxing matches, every Friday—so long as we're not getting attacked, that is. If you stay long enough you'll get to see the 107mm rockets land just short of the perimeter. Pretty exciting, sir!"

As much as he wanted to remain at the "tip of the spear," however, Donnellan left the unorthodox fire base a few hours later, having noted a few suggestions for changes.

"Work with Tom Wood to get an op together. Get a full suite of concepts—*conventional* schemes of maneuver," Donnellan instructed Captain Matt Tracy, with whom he'd arrived in Afghanistan on the same flight. "We're not gonna get him through any high-speed, sexy, helo-inserted raid in the middle of the night."

"Roger," responded Tracy, who personally likened 2/3's situation after *Red Wings* to a third-quarter 20–0 enemy advantage . . . and after the IED hit to a fourth-quarter, 30–0 near shutout. Tracy, who came in to work with Tom Wood as the assistant to the OpsO, had just finished the nine-month-long Expeditionary Warfighting School, or EWS, in Quantico, Virginia. Designed to prepare USMC infantry officers at captain level for combat operation planning and development, the course work had covered a compendium of skills, from maneuver strategy to fire support, to deconfliction, to a comprehensive knowledge of the Marine Corps Planning Process, a regimented methodology of formulating combat operations rooted in traditional conventional-maneuver war fighting. Central to this process is the development of multiple "courses of action," so that the command staff has a pool from which to choose the very best course, or the capacity to construct one with the best aspects from the pool. Tracy developed two and Wood devised one. And while the battalion would ultimately choose Wood's, Tracy had shown that he possessed both an uncanny instinct for tactical planning and a quick-firing mind that was ideal for tracking the complexities of an ever-developing combat operation; this led to his designation by the battalion as the fire-support coordinator for the upcoming op, a crucial role requiring the interface of the key elements of artillery, mortar, and close air-support fire with ground-troop maneuver. He also came up with the name of the operation: *Whalers,* after the New England Whalers hockey team.

"We're gonna squeeze him out—slowly, and force him into contact right where we want him," Wood began his brief of *Whalers* to Donnellan. The OpsO swept his hands over a map of the Sawtalo Sar region, up the throats of the valleys that radiated about the peak like gnarled pinwheel blades. "We know from intel that his egress route will likely be here, down the Chowkay Valley, or possibly the Narang." Wood paused for a moment. "So we insert troops simultaneously into the Korangal and the Shuryek, pushing Shah and his men south toward either the Narang or the Chowkay as our guys march up the valleys. Twelve hours after the first Marines head into the Korangal and Shuryek, we insert troops up into the Narang, blocking his route there; and twelve hours after that, we send grunts up the Chowkay, and literally force him into a fight somewhere in the high Korangal, where he's completely surrounded on all sides."

"When was the last time American troops went up the Chowkay?" Donnellan asked.

"To my knowledge—" The OpsO abruptly stopped. "I don't know of *any* patrols or missions into the Chowkay," Wood continued to ponder. "But that doesn't mean we haven't made forays up there, at some time, that I just don't know about."

"As we develop the specifics of this operation, we'll need to send a patrol up there, to probe the valley, to see how the locals react—maybe even harvest some intel." Donnellan believed that a mission not so much of reconnaissance but of "feeling out" the valley, although risky, was necessary.

On the evening of 30 July, with the battalion leadership's eyes focused on the second week of August as the kickoff for *Whalers*, First Lieutenant Jesse "Chiz" Chizmadia, commander of Whiskey Company's First Platoon, ventured into the Chowkay with sixteen of his Marines along with an equal-size force from Whiskey-3. Anxious and unsure about what they'd find, or even if other outside forces had gone into the Chowkay since the start of the war, Jesse knew that the Soviets had tried to penetrate deep into the chasm that Alexander the Great had passed by during his march up the Kunar Valley. He'd also heard the reports of those Soviets—entire armored columns, in fact—who were never seen or heard from again, earning the Chowkay the name "Valley of Death."

Narrow, dizzyingly steep in places, and violently washed out along much of its route, the road into the Chowkay made the worst of the Pech Road seem like a superhighway. Slowly edging up the road, which was etched onto the face of a cliff with a four-hundred-foot sheer drop, the Marines finally reached a point through which their Humvees could no longer pass. Jesse and his Marines dismounted and continued on foot. After two and a half days, they'd seen no sign of enemy activity, or that of any outsider, at least since the Soviets. They returned to JAF with stories and photographs and reported that the locals seemed friendly, even offering watermelon at one village.

With Chizmadia's mission successfully completed, the battalion finalized *Whalers'* specifics. On the night of 7 August, platoons of Echo Company would simultaneously enter the Korangal and Shuryek valleys from the Pech River Valley on the north side of Sawtalo Sar. Twelve hours later, Marines of Golf Company would enter the Narang Valley on the mountain's south side, and twelve hours after that, Marines of Fox Company would push into the Chowkay, one valley west of the Narang. Wood, Donnellan, Westerfield, and Rob Scott felt that the final showdown between the Marines and Shah's small but growing army would take place in the upper Korangal, possibly by Chichal, once the extremist determined that all of his escape routes had been blocked, as Fox and Echo met at the planned rendezvous point at the tiny village of Qalaygal, about five kilometers to the southeast of Chichal at the very upper reaches of the Korangal. Jim Donnellan and Tom Wood would head downrange with other key battalion staff and a large contingent of Afghan National Army soldiers, participating in the operation on the north side of Sawtalo Sar. Matt Tracy would perform his roles at A-Bad, and accompanying Matt would be twenty-seven-year-old Captain Zach Rashman, a Marine CH-53D heavy-lift helicopter pilot working with 2/3 as a forward air controller. But while Rashman would pride himself on the large amount of time he spent in the field over the course of the battalion's deployment, during *Whalers*, the FAC would spend his time entrenched in a concrete room with Tracy, maintaining constant contact with all aircraft in the area of operations. Rob Scott would remain at JAF, maintaining continuous communication between Marine commanders, Task Force Devil, and CJTF-76. During *Whalers,* Rob would continue doing what he did best— and had been doing since he checked into the battalion—keeping the 2/3 machine rolling forward toward their mission goal, which for *Whalers* was to "disrupt ACM activity, providing stability and security in support of the upcoming September elections."

Wood and other senior 2/3 staff would lean on time-tested USMC tactics and techniques, literally taking pages from the *Small Wars Manual* in their development of *Whalers*. Indigenous forces would not just accompany Donnellan and his staff during the op, but travel in trace of all units, learning and honing their combat skills under the guidance of the Marines in the vein of O'Bannon during the Barbary Wars of 1805. All communication would be tightly integrated—tested and retested—

with redundant backup, before *Whalers* kicked off. Although aerial re-supply drops might be available from high-flying C-130s, the grunts would portage their gear deep into hidden corners of the region on their own backs and on the backs of scrawny local mules. The plan of action tightly integrated all available indirect fire assets, from 81 mm mortars, to Doghouse's 105 mm howitzers, to close air support assets including AH-64 Apaches and A-10s—planned just as they had during the predeployment training exercises they'd done at Twentynine Palms. This would be no surgical, highly specialized strike triggered by technology-dependent SIGINT hits; instead, *Whalers* would unfurl on the land, progressing upward step by thrusting step, funneling the enemy through the Hindu Kush's labyrinthine topography into the Marines' grasp to crush Shah and his force.

Although tasked with undertaking one of the key roles in *Whalers*—that of driving deep into the Chowkay as the final piece of the op's master plan—Marines of Fox Company hadn't yet operated in the Sawtalo Sar region. Upon arriving at their forward operating base at Laghman province's Mehtar Lam, the Fox Marines immediately em-barked on missions targeting an extremist operating in the area, a man who called himself Pashtun. Pashtun had been responsible for killing two of 3/3's Marines in May of 2005, and had proved an elusive enemy. Led by the stalwart Captain Kelly Grissom, who first served as an en-listed combat engineer before graduating magna cum laude from North Carolina State and commissioning as a second lieutenant as an infantry officer, individual platoons of Fox embarked on grueling multiday op-erations that brought them deep into the Hindu Kush, and drove Ma-rines to their physical breaking points.

Not just surviving the gravity-fighting ordeals, but growing increas-ingly stronger, the grunts of Fox Company quickly acclimatized to their new environment. Rotating the company's three platoons in a regular pattern—an outside-the-wire mission tracking Pashtun, then a rest cy-cle, then a stint at base security before embarking on another foray into the heights—Grissom drove his Marines to hone their mountain-fighting skills and prepare their lungs and legs for the high altitude and steep terrain. By August, the grunts of Fox were ready for the combination of heat, steep earth, and seemingly endless days of hauling their 80- to 110-pound combat loads in chafing packs encased in suffocating body armor in the Chowkay.

Faced with determining just what size force he should send into *Whalers,* Grissom looked to base a maneuver element around a single platoon, reinforcing them with 81 mm mortars. And the platoon Grissom chose for the critical role in *Whalers* was Fox-3. Commanded by twenty-three-year-old Second Lieutenant J. J. "Konnie" Konstant, Fox-3 had seen its share of foot-pounding, back-galling movements into the cruel Hindu Kush. During one such operation, the platoon had actually pushed into Nuristan, through the Alingar Valley, where they took mortar fire from a series of caves. Charging ahead, sensing that Pashtun must be close because of the intensity of the attack, Konnie radioed Grissom, pleading for clearance to assault the cave complex. But Fox-3 had pushed outside of 2/3's area of operation; and their patrol fell on 28 June—when all available air assets had been put on standby for the rescue of the SEALs, so Fox-3 returned to base. A high school basketball star from the south side of Chicago who attended St. Ambrose University as a business and finance major on an athletic scholarship, Konnie seemed to have his entire life planned in his very early twenties. Then, like so many in the current crop of young Marines, he woke on the morning of September 11, 2001, to the infamous al-Qaeda attacks, attacks planned in the very mountainous part of the globe through which he would lead troops in 2005. He shelved his plans to become a businessman and aimed for USMC infantry.

Konnie, along with Fox-3's fear-inspiring thirty-two-year-old platoon sergeant, Lee Crisp III, a staff sergeant from Laurel, Mississippi, aggressively challenged every one of the grunts of his platoon, both physically and mentally. "Where we going and when we goin' to get there?" was a question often uttered by Konnie's Marines early in their deployment during long foot-mobile ops.

"We'll tell you when we get there. Now keep movin', and keep lovin' life," was the inevitable answer from either Crisp or Konnie. Konnie saw

Crisp as the ideal hard-ass, unfaltering in his projection of rigidity and toughness, and Crisp fondly regarded Konnie, whose cool, cigarette-smoking manner and calm drawl reminded him of John Wayne, as a "crazy-ass motherfucker." Grissom, who on more than one occasion pulled both Konnie and Crisp aside to discuss what the captain felt to be their overextending of Fox-3's grunts, ultimately viewed the duo as uncannily in phase with his own outlook on leadership through fire.

"I really don't think you can go in with just a single platoon rein-forced, Grissom," Donnellan told Kelly during the latter part of the *Whalers* planning process. Based on the after-action report of Jesse Chizmadia's brief mission into the Chowkay, Grissom surmised that the terrain would likely pose the toughest challenges to the grunts of Fox-3 and that the threat of enemy contact in the local villages seemed small. "You really should strongly consider taking two platoons," Donnellan insisted, knowing that while Shah would most likely retreat to Chichal for a fight, as that was the village in which he had the strongest ties, he and his men could lash out anywhere in the four valleys surrounding Sawtalo Sar. Grissom agreed, ultimately planning to take a second platoon—Fox-1—and attach a full 81 mm mortar section (four 81 mm mortar tubes and full crew) and a sniper team, in addition to forty-five Afghan National Army soldiers.

Konnie, looking to learn as much as possible about this part of the Hindu Kush that he and his Marines had never before ventured into, sought the most recent after-action reports from operations in the Saw-talo Sar area both to glean general insight into the region and to learn Shah's tactics. The report he thought to be most relevant, of course, had been that of the Navy SEAL Marcus Luttrell. Konnie studied the two-and-a-half-page after-action and attempted to visualize the team's final moments. Shortly after Luttrell's team had been soft-compromised by a couple of local goat herders, Shah and his men had opened up on them. The SEALs moved into the gulch below them, attempting to establish comms with friendly forces. But Shah's group, which Luttrell estimated to number between twenty and thirty, killed all but the corpsman, then landed an RPG round next to Luttrell, knocking him behind a rock.

Attending to his own extensive wounds after regaining consciousness, Luttrell evaded the ACM fighters by hiding deep in the recesses of the gulch, even submerging himself at one point in a pool of water as Shah and his men passed just feet by him. Konnie, like others in the battalion, also studied the footage from the two Shah videos, noting the extensive amount of gear now in the hands of the extremist and his group. While most of the stolen gear showed up on the video, Lieutenant Konstant, after reviewing the recon team's equipment manifest, wondered what had happened to the sniper rifle. Just like the night-vision equipment, the M4s, the spotting scopes, the laser rangefinders, and the grenade launchers, he had to assume that Shah and his men had in their possession, and would possibly use, the powerful, long-range sniper rifle against the Marines of 2/3 in any engagement during *Whalers*.

But just as Shah had "adopted" the SEALs' equipment, the Marines would adapt their operational tactics and gear roster to determine if Shah and his men had American forces in the sights of any of those M4s, grenade launchers, or even the sniper rifle as well as their own weaponry. "You need the ICOMs. That is how they communicate," a confidant known as "Cousin-O" informed Rob Scott during the planning of *Whalers*. "If the terps can listen to the conversations of Shah and his men, you'll know exactly what is about to happen." Cousin-O, who'd been imprisoned by the Soviets in western Afghanistan in the eighties, then escaped after killing two of his prison guards to flee to the United States by way of Iran and Germany, ultimately worked for the Defense Language Institute in Monterey, California, before directly aiding American forces inside Afghanistan. But the standard military-gear acquisition process could take months, leaving the Marines without a potentially critical piece of gear. "Don't worry. Just get me the money and I'll get someone to go into Peshawar and buy the ICOMs for you there. I'll have them for you in just a few days," Cousin-O confidently reassured Rob. In his typical fashion, Rob got Cousin-O the cash, reminding himself that it was his job to keep the battalion progressing forward in its mission, however unorthodox the means.

9

WHALERS
UNLEASHED

Deep into the night of 7 August, with brilliant starlight hanging in the sky above the Hindu Kush, Echo Company's First Platoon slipped into the Shuryek, and Second and Third platoons entered the Korangal. Twelve hours later, the operation was declared a victory—without a shot fired, or a single sighting of Shah or any of his men. "CJTF-76 decided that we've met the end state of the op," Rob Scott incredulously reported to Tom Wood. "Over before it even began." With the operative words of *Whalers'* objective being "disruption of ACM activity," senior CJTF-76 staff, to whom Wood had briefed the mission just days earlier, decided that the mere presence of coalition forces in such numbers in the Korangal and Shuryek had constituted sufficient "disruption."

"Sounds to me like they're nervous. Gun-shy after *Red Wings*," Wood opined about CJTF-76's stance. "We came. We didn't really see anything. They figured we conquered—just because we went in there. Now we're out."

Rob Scott, wedged squarely between keeping 2/3's mission objectives on track and the in-country higher command's restrictions, once again set about developing a work-around solution. After consulting with Wood and Donnellan, he had 2/3's operational fix: as CJTF-76 continuously monitored 2/3's progress, Task Force Devil would control the battalion's movements by phase line, meaning that individual units—Fox Company in the Chowkay, Golf in the Narang, etc.—could only move to a predetermined latitude within a given time span, with approval required to continue beyond each line. The operation also had a concrete time limit as a result of the upcoming elections: *Whalers* needed to be completed by the nineteenth of August. While the parameters restricted the fluidity of the op in what would certainly prove to be an evolving battle, at least the grunts of 2/3 would have their second crack at *Whalers*.

CJTF-76 command, however, worried about another dramatic helicopter shoot-down, held strong reservations about the op. The only air assets, other than close air support and high-flying C-130s for cargo drops, they'd grant the battalion were Air Ambulance medevac birds, absolutely crucial for the long-distance movements 2/3's Marines would be undertaking. CJTF-76 mandated, however, that if medevac missions were to be flown, then the battalion would follow every textbook procedure to the last written letter. 2/3 Command knew that if so much as a single enemy round came anywhere near an American aviation asset in the post-Chinook-shootdown operational atmosphere, then air assets, other than close air support, would be almost impossible to procure in the Kunar for any subsequent operations. *Whalers* would prove decisive not only in the battalion's fight to break the enemy's back before the elections, but in allowing 2/3 to continue to conduct operations for the remainder of their deployment.

Nearing midnight on 11 August, Second and Third platoons of Echo Company with attached Afghan National Army soldiers swarmed into the Korangal as First Platoon, under Kinser, pushed into the Shuryek with their contingent of ANA. Donnellan, Tom Wood, and Scott Westerfield—the "Jump CP" (a term referencing a forward command post consisting of the battalion commander and some, but not all, of his staff, and in Donnellan's case during *Whalers,* two squads of Marines)— accompanied by fifteen Afghan troops, some in senior leadership roles, headed toward the base of Sawtalo Sar's north ridge. Matt Tracy stood ready at A-Bad to coordinate indirect fire assets with the array of individual units participating in the op, and of course, Rob Scott held the fort at the JAF COC. Keeping the battalion sustained with food, water, ammunition, and other supplies, Captain Jeremy Whitlock, the battalion's logistics officer, would keep hours as long as Rob's as *Whalers,* a truly "distributed op," marched forward.

At roughly noon on the twelfth, twelve hours after Echo's troops entered Sawtalo Sar's northern valleys, Golf Company's contingent stormed into the Narang, including First Platoon, under Kyle Corcoran, and Second Platoon, under Lieutenant Clif Kennedy, and a platoon of ANA. Grissom, ever conscious of the importance of his Marines' role in plugging Shah's final outlet, pored over intel, maps, and after-actions throughout the day. Sleep-deprived but never fatigued, Grissom churned the variables of the tactical calculus lying before him as the Marines of Fox Company rested and prepared to enter the Chowkay. Having studied Chizmadia's after-action, the captain knew that the locals had been receptive to the Marines during their probing mission—but he also knew that one foray into a remote valley couldn't come close to determining the true character of the populace, or the threat level they posed. Grissom couldn't discount even the slightest risk, as just a small handful of well-placed fighters with PK machine guns and RPGs could ruin the day.

Grissom, wanting to move as fast as possible toward Objective-4—the village of Qalaygal near the juncture of the upper Chowkay and Korangal—chose as Fox's route the relatively navigable valley floor rather than the more "tactical" (more positions behind which to take cover and move covertly) ridges above the Chowkay. Logistically, however, the captain knew that the valley's steep topography wouldn't stand as the only factor limiting Fox's rate of ascent into the Chowkay. In addition to Fox-3, his force consisted of a section of 81 mm mortars (four mortar tubes with three Marines per tube to operate the weapons); Fox Company's First Platoon was to act as a security element for this vital mortar section, a company of forty-five Afghan National Army soldiers, and to aid in the portaging of gear for the Marines, Afghan soldiers, and interpreters in the absence of helicopters for troop insert and resupply, Fox Company enlisted the aid of thirty-six donkeys. Thirty-six very fickle, very stubborn donkeys. This was the other factor Grissom had to consider.

Referencing Chizmadia's report and photographs as he traced his index finger along his map's densely packed contour lines from the Chowkay's opening at the Kunar River into the valley's heights, Grissom reaffirmed a decision he'd made earlier: he would have the 81 mm mortar section, commanded by Lieutenant Ben Middendorf, along with Fox-1, the Afghan soldiers, and the cargo-laden donkeys, move in trace of Fox-3, providing crucial indirect fire coverage with the 81s, if needed—a plan devised in part by Middendorf. Grissom, ever impressed by Konnie and Crisp's motivational and leadership synergy, would travel with Fox-3, pushing as fast as possible toward their objective, ahead of the more heavily laden Fox-1 and mortar team. Since their route into the Chowkay would take them just outside of the effective range of Doghouse's 105s at Asadabad (even with RAP rounds), Grissom planned to have Fox-3 stay within the "umbrella" of Middendorf's 81s once deep into the valley—of course maintaining radio contact with the mortar team at all times. Also traveling with Fox-3, Casmer "Pigeon" Ratkowiak, the onetime battalion air officer, had sought a closer perspective of the fight and attached to Fox for *Whalers* as a forward air controller. Known by his radio call sign "Venom-11" to pilots working in the area, Pigeon would prove a crucial member of the contingent. With Pigeon—and his ability to guide Army AH-64 Apaches, Air Force A-10 Warthogs, and other available platforms onto any of Shah's men should they engage the Marines—and Middendorf's 81 mm mortar team, Grissom would essentially be leading a small, ad hoc MAGTF-like element, on foot, into the unknown Chowkay. And with the addition of the forty-five Afghan soldiers, Fox Company was also embarking on a unique counterinsurgency training mission, giving the Afghans a firsthand look into classic U.S. Marine Corps combined arms tactics. Completing the forward component of Fox's push into the Chowkay, which totaled forty-nine, were two Navy Corpsmen, two combat engineers, two attached scout/snipers, and two interpreters, "Jimmy" and "The Rock"—each armed with AK-47s and brand-new ICOM scanners courtesy of Rob Scott and Cousin-O.

The night before their departure, on the eleventh, after arriving at Jalalabad Airfield from their forward operating base at Mehtar Lam by convoy, Konnie and Grissom discussed the upcoming op, a Marlboro dangling from the mouth of each during the conversation. "In a way, sir, I want there to be continuous contact with the enemy. That'll keep all of us on our toes—no one will ever get complacent," Konnie said. "Them constantly trying to kill us in the end will keep us from getting killed."

"Be careful what you wish for, there, Lieutenant," the stocky captain began with a laugh. "Don't get me wrong. I see what you mean. Just watch what you wish for." The two hadn't spent much time together before that evening's cigarette break. To that point, Konnie had regarded Grissom primarily as the boss who rode his ass for running the Fox-3 Marines too hard; Grissom saw Konnie not so much as overly enthused or zealous, but just ultradriven, albeit in a very controlled manner, someone who might need to be reined in from time to time.

In the big picture, Grissom just wanted to ensure that the young lieutenant and the acerbic Crisp operated aggressively, yet in a balanced way, to ensure combat-readiness. He wanted to storm onto Objective-4 as quickly as possible, but knew that he'd be walking a delicate line. "Based on Westerfield's work—he's really gotten into the mind of this Shah guy, he knows the rat lines, the hideouts, the tactics, pretty much everything relevant—we know that when Shah sees Marines in the Korangal and Shuryek, and then in the Narang, he'll head down the Chowkay. And once he sees us, he'll make a run back into the Korangal. It's unlikely that he'll engage us, not when he can hightail it back to more familiar ground in the Korangal," Grissom explained to Konnie. "I just hope that he doesn't get a jump on us moving into the Chowkay and escape. That's why I want to really move—move fast. I'm really gonna tap you and Crisp to keep things together up there." Grissom again pondered the balance of speed versus efficacy for Fox-3. The heat, even in the middle of the night, would remain in the nineties, the terrain would present backbreaking obstacles, and a host of other variables— 2/3's higher command, supplies, weather, not to mention Shah and his army—would undoubtedly present confounding hurdles as well. The only solution, in the minds of both Grissom and Konnie, was to embrace the struggle ahead, to love the challenge of leadership under adversity. And having familiarized themselves with the land, the conditions, and most importantly, Shah and his army through Westerfield's briefs and *Red Wings'* after-action reports, Grissom and Konnie knew that adversity could reach extreme levels.

At 7:00 P.M. on the twelfth, as the last of the sun's glowing orange rays split into the sky above the peaks to the west of Jalalabad and the temperature clung to low triple digits, the Fox Marines gathered for a brief on their upcoming mission. With platoons of Echo and Golf already deeply entrenched in the valleys surrounding Sawtalo Sar, Kelly Grissom disclosed part of the *what,* but not specifically the *where* or the *how long* of the upcoming op. "We're going to start walking—up. And we're gonna keep walking—up, and walking, and walking—up, until someone tells us to stop. Don't ask where we're walking up to. Don't ask how long we'll be walking. We just keep walking."

"Hey, Lieutenant." Crisp turned to Konnie as Grissom wrapped up *Whalers'* very general overview. "How come you neva' give no pep speeches?"

"Because, Crisp"—the lieutenant turned to the staff sergeant— "speeches are about as cool as a boner in sweatpants." Crisp erupted into laughter. "You want a pep talk? How 'bout this: don't puss out." The two of them geared up for the convoy about to take them up the Kunar Valley to the opening of the Chowkay.

Fox-3's *Whalers* journey began at 10:45 P.M. on the twelfth of August as the convoy of hulking, three-axle 7-Ton troop transports rumbled off the Asadabad–Jalalabad road at the village of Chowkay, on the shores of the Kunar River. "I hear we're goin' where Osama bin Laden himself used to run training camps," Crisp overheard one of the platoon's grunts remark as they dismounted and prepared to stage for their penetration into the secretive valley. "We're goin' after the guys who took down the SEALs."

"Osama bin *my ass*," the staff sergeant interjected. "You best be preservin' all yo' energy for yo' feet—not fo' runnin' yo' mouth," Crisp boomed.

By eleven, Fox Company's lead element, consisting of Fox-3 and attachments, Grissom, Pigeon, and Jimmy and the Rock, had loaded into a convoy of Whiskey Company's highback and hardback Humvees at the V-cleft opening of the Chowkay to begin their insertion into the valley. Running blacked out along the narrow roadway notched into the sheer eastern wall of the chasm, the Marines let their eyes adjust to the pallid greenish light shed onto the landscape by the half-moon hanging in the sky above them. Forty-five minutes after Fox-3 pressed through the rocky gates of the Chowkay, Fox-1 and the Afghan National Army contingent arrived at the mouth of the valley and linked up with Middendorf and his Marines of the 81s section. As Fox-1 staged to move into the valley, Whiskey's Humvees continued to push Grissom and Fox-3 farther north; as soon as the road narrowed to a point where the vehicles could move no farther, the grunts would jump out and continue on foot. *Whalers'* success hinged on Fox-3 penetrating deep into the Chowkay at just the right time, to deny Shah's force an escape route, necessitating constant movement deep into the heart of the treacherous mountain landscape.

At 2:00 A.M. on the thirteenth of August, Whiskey's Humvees reached their limit, ten kilometers into the valley, at the village of Amrey. As the empty convoy headed down the steep terrain toward lower ground, the grunts set about the last of their preparations for the journey ahead, stuffing their packs with enough water and MREs to last a full three

days, as well as checking their combat gear, and even basics like tooth-
paste and shoelaces. Amrey village lies at the convergence of two main
arms of the Chowkay, one that strikes to the northwest, and one branch
that heads to the northeast. The Fox Marines would move up the northeast valley—the upper Chowkay—along the Amrey Creek bed, toward
the base of a mountain named Cheshane Tupay, a 9,528-foot-high peak
about eight kilometers southwest of Sawtalo Sar. While their route
would traverse roughly six kilometers of horizontal distance, those six
kilometers would take the Fox-3 Marines from an elevation of just over
3,000 feet at Amrey, almost a vertical mile higher, to roughly 8,000 feet
at the base of Cheshane Tupay, the latitude of *Phase Line White*, from
which the Marines would then re-embark on their journey toward
Objective-4—once approved by higher, of course.

Fox-3 wasted no time hurling their packs onto their shoulders and
pushing off on their pump into the upper Chowkay. Their eyes attuned
to the muted glow of the half-moon, the Marines dug into their task,
moving single file up a narrow trail into the darkness. The pitch-black
of the bottom of the steep valley virtually blinded them, while the walls
looming above them glowed eerily under the wan light, the rock faces
so coarse that even the moon's muted light cast harsh shadows off bare
slabs, boulders, and cobbles. They couldn't be certain if they walked on
the trail itself, or if their route simply meandered near the pathway—
and they certainly wouldn't use lights, of any kind, to help them stay on
track. Konnie, traveling with his platoon's First Squad at the lead end of
the movement, at first used a small compass and a GPS unit for guidance, but then resorted to raw tactile navigation, relying on the soles of
his boots and the strain in his legs against gravity to "feel" his way into
the heights of the Chowkay. As Grissom had said in his talk just a few
hours prior, "Just keep walking—up." Guided by the deep recess of the
valley itself, the grunts closed on their destination, by doing just that.

The glow of dawn's approach revealed the landscape the Marines
had known only as tightly packed contour lines on their maps as some
of the steepest, most daunting topography any of them had ever witnessed. Never stopping for more than five minutes at a time, the grunts

inhaled their water throughout the grueling nighttime haul, their legs burning under the struggle to inch ever higher over smooth boulders, around narrow ledges, over tree stumps, and sometimes along terraced hillsides. By sunup, just a few hours into the mission, many had killed half their three-day supply. As soon as Crisp's eyes detected the light of dawn, his skin felt the first inrush of the heat he knew would soon wallop the grunts like a tsunami. By the time the sun rose above Cheshane Tupay to their northeast—a mountain so steep that many of the grunts couldn't see its summit because their helmets bunched into the tops of their backpacks as they tried to look up—the heat had topped 110 degrees.

"Fucking donkeys!" Lieutenant Stuart Geise, Fox-1's commander, blared to one of the lance corporals in his platoon midmorning on the thirteenth from his disembarking point near Amrey, when a call came over the radio from Grissom on the status of their movement.

"You guys movin' yet?" Grissom asked, staring at ever-steepening terrain above him.

"Fuckin' donkeys!" Geise roared aloud, then jumped on the radio in response to Grissom's request. "We're moving, but it's the damn donkeys." He paused. "They're . . . delaying us." *They're fuckin' donkeys!* he screamed in his head.

"All right already. You need to push hard, Geise," Grissom barked, peeved at the delay.

"Those donkeys, you got 'em loaded up, right? They moving with you guys?"

"No, sir!" *The fuckin' donkeys are fuckin' fuckin' each other,* the exasperated lieutenant bellowed in his head, not able to state the case over the radio—then explained it in more sanitized terms.

"What? Each other?" the bewildered captain asked.

"Yeah. They're mounting up on one another. And some committed suicide—they just jumped off the cliffs! It's a circus. None of us can control these—" *Little bastards,* he thought. *Fuckin' jumpin' off cliffs! Loaded with our chow and water. Runnin' around!* "—donkeys!" Geise responded.

But Ben Middendorf already had the solution; he'd ordered his Marines to unload the supplies off the backs of the donkeys, then divvy up the cargo among the grunts, "spread-loading" the gear. With their four-legged logistical means no longer an option, Ben got on the line with battalion's assistant logistics officer, Lieutenant Hal Everheart, and let him know that the element would need resupply by CDS drop—and due to the heat, they might start needing those drops soon. "Get all the gear and supplies off the donkeys and spread load everything. Your packs are gonna weigh a ton, but we can't have you delayed any longer. Just get moving!" Middendorf ordered his Marines.

"Damn, Lieutenant, the hell with those bad guys, it's this valley and this heat that's gonna do us all in," Crisp said to Konnie during a noon rest outside a tiny village under the looming Cheshane Ghar ridgeline. "Ain't neva' been so hot in my life!"

"It's just gonna keep getting more fun. I can't wait for more of it," Konnie coolly responded. "Just think about all the fun we'll have once the bad guys start shootin' at us. It's all about smokin' cigarettes and slingin' guns, Crisp." The lieutenant feigned a wistful tone as he cracked a grin.

"Commander Konstant!" Jimmy the translator approached Konnie with a shy local villager in tow. "The man is confused about you and the Marines. He thinks that you may be the Russians."

"The Russians?" Konnie responded, taken aback for a moment. Then the lieutenant realized just how deep into the valley that Fox-3 had penetrated, so deep that they'd run into a villager who probably hadn't seen an outsider since the Soviet occupation, decades earlier. "Jimmy"—Konstant turned toward the villager—"tell him that in fact we are the Russians—and that it is 1987, and we're about to defeat the Americans in the Cold War." Jimmy translated as ordered, then the villager stared blankly at Jimmy and Konnie, and after a brief moment of silence, the Marines threw on their packs and continued higher. "Come on, comrades," Konnie quipped, "onward for Mother Russia."

By midafternoon, the grunts had put approximately four kilometers—and thousands of feet of elevation—to their rear. While the high sun drove the air temperature into the 120s at ground level, the men found themselves surrounded not only by walls of shattered rock and house-size boulders, but by lush green; with altitude came dense tracts of ferns and large cedars. As they entered the hottest part of the August day, however, they had to fight not just to keep moving, but to keep from collapsing. Crisp, himself struggling in the dangerously torrid conditions, kept a hawk's eye on every one of the Marines in the platoon. Drenched in sweat from the inside out, dehydrated, burning with pain where their pack straps dug into their shoulders, their heads throbbing inside the ovenlike Kevlar helmets, their eyes stinging with sweat pouring off their foreheads, they'd reached their limits.

"Okay, Marines. We're done," Konnie proclaimed, himself feeling shredded by the toughest feat of endurance he'd ever undertaken—and fighting not to show it. Just as the Marines had reached what he and Grissom felt to be the outer edge of combat effectiveness, the lieutenant spied a perch on which they could put down—at least for a few hours, maybe all night. "We're staying here until further notice," he stated. "Here" was a point on a hillside about a half kilometer west of the Amrey Creek bed, a few hundred feet shy of eight thousand feet in elevation. "We just went nearly a mile—" The Fox-3 Marines shot Konnie a look; to them, "nearly a mile" had felt like fifty. "—a mile *up*. Pretty much five thousand feet *vertical* in the last eighteen hours. Good job, Marines," the lieutenant finished in his typical, understated tone.

The patrol base, exactly two kilometers to the southwest of Cheshane Tupay's summit, while just shy of *Phase Line White*, stood in as good a position as the platoon could hope to have, despite being surrounded by high ground from which Shah and his men could attack, Konnie had chosen a location that stood back from the high terrain as much as possible. Additionally, the patrol base lay at the eastern base of a small hill, to which the lieutenant sent the snipers and half of First Squad, to provide overwatch of the encampment and to keep the location secured, and it was an ideal helicopter landing zone, should the grunts need a medevac. Konnie, relying on tried-and-true tactics he learned at the Basic School and at Infantry Officers' Course, set a perimeter defense around the patrol base, established a casualty collection point behind some large boulders, then set himself at the east end of the camp facing Cheshane Tupay, what he felt to be the most probable location from which Shah would launch an ambush.

"Nobody does anything but keep an eye out for the enemy," Konnie instructed. "Nobody takes their eyes off the surrounding terrain. Nobody sleeps, nobody eats," he finished, with a glaring Crisp at his side. Grissom and Pigeon established a command post in the cover of some large downed trees a good distance from Konnie's position to ensure that if Shah attacked with overwhelming opening salvos aimed at the CP, the Marines wouldn't be left without leadership. For the remainder of daylight on the thirteenth, everyone at the base stood watch, scanning every trail, rock, ridgeline, peak for any trace of Shah.

As Fox Company battled the elements and the terrain to reach their position, the platoons of Echo in the Korangal and the Shuryek pushed southward, and Golf moved up the Narang. Donnellan and the Jump CP moved along the north ridge of Sawtalo Sar, intending to link up with Second and Third platoons in the Korangal Valley, and meet with locals and leaders in a number of the valley's villages. Everything had been timed and choreographed perfectly so that Shah and his small army would fall right into 2/3's hands—but just where would the showdown happen? That, nobody knew. ICOM chatter, intercepted by Golf Company's interpreters in the Narang, indicated that some of the extremist's force was on the run out of the Korangal and had tried to move into the Narang—until they spied the grunts, and turned around. Blocked in the Shuryek as well, Shah's force had to move toward the Chowkay, but coalesced in strength as they did so. Intel revealed that Shah had elements of his force located at different villages throughout the upper Korangal, and that once he was on the run, he was merging these elements into a force of between sixty and eighty fighters, all moving toward the grunts of Fox Company.

Stymied by the intractable donkeys, but determined to position his mortars to ensure that Fox-3 was safely within the weapons' umbrella of indirect fire, Middendorf led his mortar team, along with Fox-1 and the Afghan soldiers, into the upper Chowkay during the very worst of the day's heat. Each Marine carried at least one mortar round, twenty bottles of water, six MREs, and his own weapons and ammunition; without the donkeys, they also carried the four 81 mm mortar tubes, each weighing a total of over 93 pounds (able to be broken into three components, the gun tube weighs 35 pounds, the mount 27 pounds, the base plate 29 pounds, and the sighting unit weighs 3 pounds). Thus many grunts carried over 130 pounds of gear—on a movement with temperatures in the deep, bare-rock valley of over 120 degrees.

By nine o'clock that evening, as the last of twilight faded, Middendorf set up a patrol base within a draw on the steep western face of the Chowkay Valley. Despite the heat, the terrain, and the weight on their backs, his grunts had traveled over two kilometers, covering an incredible 3,500 vertical feet. But their movement, like Fox-3's, didn't come easy. Some Marines were suffering from acute dehydration, which required corpsmen to rehydrate them not with bottles of water, but with IVs. Others bent over, vomiting, during the hellacious march. But perched at their night's camp, high on the slope above the Amrey Creek bed, Middendorf's all-important mortar tubes stood at the ready to support Fox-3; at just two and a half kilometers north of the mortar team, they sat well within the effective range of the weapons.

"Sir!" Jimmy the translator ran to Konnie's position at the Fox-3 patrol base around seven in the evening. "Sir, Ahmad Shah and his men are looking for you. We have heard them talking over their ICOMs!"

"What are they saying, Jimmy?" Konnie asked.

"They have a lot of fighters. I don't know how many. But a lot. And they are looking for the Marines. They are coming into the Chowkay Valley!" Kelly Grissom, who had also been apprised of the ICOM chatter, wondered if an attack was imminent, or if the messages had been sent solely to get intercepted, for psychological purposes. Every last

grunt continued to stand watch that evening, glaring at the landscape
as the shadows of dusk swept across the Chowkay. At nine o'clock,
with the grunts not having had a wink of sleep in over thirty hours,
Grissom moved the patrol base from 100 percent on watch to 50 percent, thereby mandating some sleep for the unit's Marines.

The pitch-darkness of the night drove home the insularity of the
Fox company's situation. Amrey village, the closest point with vehicle
access, was hours and hours away by foot. Medevac support was iffy at
best. And Middendorf's 81s were their sole organic indirect fire support
assets, while close air support was as much as a full hour away. Knowing as well that they were surrounded by Shah's force, the Marines of
Fox Company dug in for one of the longest nights of their lives.

Back at the mortar team's position, the intermittent beeps of Middendorf's radios split the otherwise silent night. With all four mortar
tubes ready to fire at a moment's notice, the lieutenant knew that the
Marines were ready to push through the very worst of Shah's onslaught.
Although confident, the lieutenant also knew that the Marines of Fox
Company were very, very alone in the austere high Chowkay that night;
but they would forge ahead in the operation with the utmost focus, un-
deterred by the heat, dehydration, lack of water and food, and pure
exhaustion, but even the slightest mistake could avalanche into disaster.

10

ARMAGEDDON, DENIED

After eighteen hours of movement, the Marines of Fox-3 were completely wasted. "Eighteen hours straight," a lance corporal muttered on the morning of the fourteenth, gazing at the shattered rock at his feet, "all that pain, to get to . . . to *this* place." The young Marine craned his neck and squinted at a distant ridge to the east, but could see nothing more than an outline of the jagged buttress under the blinding light of the rising sun. He shook his head and leaned back against a tree stump, not wanting to think about anything but a few more hours of sleep.

Just over two kilometers due south of Fox-3's camp, Middendorf's mortar section, accompanied by Fox-1 and the Afghan soldiers, had been on the move since five-fifteen that morning, well before the sun crested the eastern peaks. The temperature slammed the grunts—even during the predawn hours—and conditions would only worsen with each passing hour. The Marines and Afghan soldiers arduously trekked up the

Chowkay, pushing ever higher under their crushing loads. Some felt like they were teetering at the very edge of sanity as the movement taxed them to the very limit of their strength. But the mortar tubes needed—*absolutely needed*—to be kept well within range of Fox-3, even if higher command, based on up-to-the-minute intel, ordered Third Platoon to keep moving even farther north. The Marines, isolated in the Chowkay that August day, could count solely on one another, as they strained into the heat and heights, each grunt resolving to keep the chain that was Fox Company uniformly strong.

As the sun launched into the heights that morning, drowning the eastern Afghan mountains in life-sapping heat, Staff Sergeant Crisp stared hard at his Marines, feeling in his gut that something wasn't right, that the stillness of the morning would soon be shattered by a vicious enemy. It wasn't that he knew something that the others didn't; he just had an instinct. And the thought of any of his Marines not being absolutely prepared for any eventuality made his blood boil. *Complacency kills, complacency kills!* he thought. *Don't ever fucking forget it. Complacency kills!* "You hear me?" he roared a moment later. "I said get ya gear on NOW!" The staff sergeant glared at those Marines who'd removed their flak jackets and Kevlar helmets. Konnie seconded Crisp's motion, albeit less vociferously.

"No. Let them rest—*without* their flaks and Kevlars," Captain Grissom ordered as he approached Crisp and Konnie. The captain was determined to afford the Marines every possible comfort in order to rejuvenate their enervated bodies; he knew that in just a few hours they'd be embarking on yet another grueling march, higher and deeper into the strange and forlorn mountains on their journey toward Objective-4. "Just got off the hook with battalion. We're moving again at twelve hundred and I want half the Marines resting at any one time while the other half stands to. And when I say rest, I mean *rest*, not just laying there gettin' their heads cooked inside their helmets and having body armor jamming into their ribs. It's gonna be a bitch again today and I want to minimize heat casualties." With their water supply quickly dwindling, and many in the platoon exhausted from the hellish first movement, Grissom wanted everyone as strong as possible. Conditions would only get worse in the coming days.

"Roger that," Crisp responded before turning toward his Marines, "Okay, Devil Dogs! Rest up—*without* your gear on—but keep the *fuck* in a covered position." Pondering the troops' upcoming noon movement into the unknown terrain looming above, he glanced at his watch: a few seconds past 9:00 A.M. The staff sergeant peered through the morning quiet, visualizing fighters lurking in the terrain above, watching his platoon through binoculars, readying RPGs, PK machine guns, AK-47s—fighters who knew how to melt into this raw, unforgiving landscape, who were motivated and skilled, who had experience organizing and executing complex and well-coordinated ambushes. He didn't care that intel had suggested that the Korangal was the likeliest location for a showdown. They could attack from anywhere. Like the others, Crisp had been worn down—but his flak and Kevlar would never come off. He couldn't see any immediate threat, but that didn't mean the enemy wasn't out there, somewhere.

"Konnie! Get over here!" Captain Grissom ordered the young lieutenant—who, like his Marines had been told, had dropped his body armor and Kevlar helmet—to see him for a face-to-face discussion. Konnie knew that he'd be grilled about having the Marines keep their gear donned; he could tell by Grissom's stare that he was pissed. But the discussion would have to wait for another time. As the lieutenant took his first step toward the peeved captain, the very worst of Crisp's premonitions exploded into reality: the ridgelines surrounding Fox-3 erupted in a maelstrom of machine-gun and RPG fire, focused expertly on Fox-3's position. *So it would be the Chowkay,* Konnie realized.

Rounds began to split tree branches and ping off rocks. Konnie could hear the heavy 7.62×54 mm PKM machine-gun rounds whizzing just feet above him; then came the frightful *crack* that rounds passing just inches from one's head leave in their wake. RPG explosions encircled the Marines. Blasts of impacting 82 mm mortar shells came next, bursting in massive yellow-and-black-smoke fireballs, turning rocks into dust, splintering trees, smashing the morning air with earsplitting concussions.

Konnie might not have had his body armor on, but he, like all Marines, was never without his weapon. *Overwhelming fire superiority. Rounds downrange!* The muzzle of Konnie's M16A4 sprang to his right eye's level with a flick of his wrist as he dropped to the ground in the "Marine Corps sitting position." *Does anyone really shoot from this position?* he wondered, laughing to himself. He'd been taught to assume this position in TBS, but he'd never heard of anyone in a firefight really shooting from it. *Holy shit! I'm in a fucking firefight, and doing it sitting Indian style—with no flak or Kevlar!* he thought. His ass hit the ground as his thumb flicked the selector to semi on his condition-1 weapon. *Well-placed shots!* But where to shoot? *Wherever those rounds are coming from, that's where,* Konnie thought. *Everywhere. They're coming from everywhere atop the surrounding ridges!*

Put-sheeew . . . boom! As the distinctive, bloodcurdling screech of a launched RPG connecting with a target rocked Konnie's eardrums and sent a flash of heat to his right cheek and head, he spotted the point of origin of the launcher, a puff of rising white smoke. The lieutenant quickly realized that Shah's force had set up an L-shaped attack, with a line of men to the east, on the southwest side of Cheshane Tupay, and another to the Marines' north, from a ridge on a mountain named Lamkandah Sar, which defined the very upper limits of the Chowkay. Crisp, too, immediately oriented himself to the enemy's fire: plunging, interlocking machine guns and coordinated mortars and RPGs, launched from superior positions; this was exactly the way Shah had attacked the NAVSOF recon team a few weeks prior, just a few miles to the northeast. *Combined arms!* Crisp muttered in his head. *These motherfuckers are doin' it just like the Marine Corps does it!*

The buttstock of his M16 planted against his right shoulder, Konnie locked onto one of Shah's men high on a ridge to his east who was scrambling to reload another RPG round below the dissipating smoke of his last shot. The lieutenant judged the shooter to be about 650 meters distant, out of point-target range of his M16, but nevertheless, if he put enough rounds downrange, something might hit. *Right? Get some!* Elevating his gun to adjust for range, Konnie aimed through the M16's iron sights and loosed round after round. *Crack! Crack! Crack!* Streaks of red marked the trajectory of Konnie's bullets; like many U.S. Marine Corps platoon commanders, he used a magazine of tracer rounds in the opening shots of a firefight in order to help others orient themselves and get rounds on target. The gun weighed a little less with each burst, until the bolt locked open, indicating his thirty-round magazine was spent. Without looking—without even thinking, for that matter—the lieutenant slapped the ejector button and popped out the empty mag, then slammed another one packed with tracers into the gun's well, releasing the bolt catch with a flick of his right thumb. The bolt thrust forward, locking another 5.56 mm round into place, and Konnie immediately began firing, alternating between "semi" and three-shot "burst." *The M16 has to be one of the greatest creations humanity has ever developed,* he thought, bracing the perfectly balanced weapon against his shoulder. *It's just damned functional art.*

Put-sheeew . . . boom! Another RPG exploded, and another—then yet another. Mortars rained down, closer each time. A forward observer for Shah's mortar team "walked on" the high explosive rounds by relaying fire-adjustment instructions after each impact, zeroing in on the Marines. Shah had clearly added a large number of highly trained, seasoned fighters to his cadre, no doubt the extremists that intel had identified as funneling through Pakistan from throughout the globe. Ahmad Shah's small army couldn't have done a better job. That intel had stated that Shah's band now ranked among the world's fiercest, best organized, and capable. Now the Marines were experiencing this proficiency firsthand.

But despite their entrenched positions, their skills, their multiple weapons platforms, and their knowledge of these mountains, Shah and his men were attacking United States Marines. And within thirty seconds, the extremist's cell would experience the infamous and overwhelming force and fury of a United States Marine Corps unit under attack—giving it right back, in spades. The Marines had proven themselves to be the fiercest, most effective fighting force in the history of warfare.

The Operation *Whalers* chapter of this tradition now opened.

Lance Corporal Dustin Epperly had left his flak jacket, with thirteen full mags of 5.56 mm attached to it, on the ground near the spot onto which Konnie had dropped and started firing. *Convenient,* thought the lieutenant. *Now where the fuck is Epperly?* Konnie called for Lance Corporal Karsten Machado.

"Yes sir!" the lance corporal barked as he finished off another of his magazines.

"Where's your Kevlar?" Konnie asked.

"Uh . . ." Machado gave Konnie the "what you looking at me for?" look. "Where's yours, sir?" he asked back.

"Right here next to Epperly's flak and all his rounds that I'm about to send downrange on these motherfuckers." Konnie picked up his helmet and tossed it the three odd feet to Machado. "Now get back to what you were doin', Machado. And keep up that good work, Marine."

"Oorah! Sir!" Konnie continued to do his part to saturate ridges to the east, north, and southeast with rounds, courtesy of Epperly's well-placed, ammo-adorned flak jacket.

The first few seconds of Shah's ambush proved the most hellacious, having caught Fox-3 by surprise. While Konnie, Machado, and a few other Marines immediately returned fire, other grunts oriented themselves to the fight, including Epperly, who shot to the aid of Lance Corporal Paul Greenfield with his 240. The ambush had literally caught some Marines with their pants down, relieving themselves when the attack started. Once the 240 opened up, however, shocking the ridges with deadly 7.62 mm rounds at the rate of nine hundred per minute, the others in the platoon fell into place.

"I wanna hear those guns talkin' to each other, got that, Devil Dogs? I wanna hear 'em talking to each other. Talkin' guns!" Staff Sergeant Crisp boomed over the explosions of Shah's attack, reminding the grunts behind the SAWs and Epperly and Greenfield on the 240 of the tried-and-true method meant to both accurately and effectively put machine-gun rounds on target while conserving ammunition for the next engagement; one gun would unload for a few seconds, then stop as another started. Crisp relished the loud, clattering symphony.

But Crisp, like Konnie and the other Marines that day, knew that their real return punch would come with the synergy of the classic Marine Corps combined-arms attack—laying everything on Shah at once: M16 rounds, light machine-gun rounds, mortars, and aerial strafing and bombardment. At that point, however, Fox-3 had just their M16s, SAWs, and the 240, while Shah's mortars, RPGs, and machine-gun fire continued to rain down at an ever-more-feverish pace.

"Get battalion on the line! Now!" Grissom told his radio operator. The skilled RO dialed in the SATCOM frequency. "We're in heavy fucking *contact*!" Grissom roared to Captain Perry Waters, the watch officer at the JAF COC. "We're in the fight of our motherfuckin' lives!" Grissom then immediately set out to direct serious pain on Ahmad Shah and his crew. "Get me Middendorf. We need an 81s suppression mission. We need it. We need it RIGHT FUCKING NOW!"

"Corpsman UP! Corpsman UP!" a Marine bellowed over the cacophony of battle for any "doc" within earshot to come help a wounded Marine. Lance Corporal Matt Wilson, dumping blood from his left calf and left ass cheek, writhed in pain, having been shot twice by heavy PK rounds. Hospital Corpsman Third Class Travis "Doc" Beeman and Hospitalman Iram Figueroa lunged through the volleys of machine-gun fire to aid Wilson. Kneeling beside him, his hands clumping with grit, dirt, and congealing blood, Figueroa cut off the left side of Wilson's pants as Doc Beeman readied a tourniquet. The two corpsmen worked furiously to stop the bleeding, ignoring the risk to their own lives, but Wilson continued to lose blood.

"He's gonna go into hypovolemic shock!" Beeman exclaimed, worried that the blood loss would lead to multiple organ failure.

"Can't stop the damn bleeding!" Figueroa responded. "The wraps aren't stopping the bleeding!" Beeman grabbed a flat rock.

"Plug it with this rock!" Beeman ordered.

"Huh?"

"Plug it with the fuckin' rock! Put the rock under the tourniquet, and that'll slow the bleeding!" Figueroa followed Beeman's instructions— and amazingly, Wilson's blood loss slowed, and eventually would stop.

Meanwhile Konnie, emptying Epperly's magazines, wondered when the big guns would start unleashing their destructive furor on Shah's positions. He knew that Fox-3 was out of range of Doghouse's 105 mm howitzers back at Asadabad, and figured that Middendorf's 81s would open up in just seconds.

"Sir! Sir! I've been shot! I've been shot. Oh God! I've been shot! I think I'm gonna die!" Konnie looked down to see Corporal Tyler Einarson, clutching his bleeding right wrist. Einarson crawled up to Konnie and leaned on the lieutenant's right shoulder.

"You're gonna be okay, Einarson. You'll be just fine." *Crack! Crack! Crack!* Konnie continued to send rounds downrange.

"Sir, do you think I can get the Silver Star for this?" *Put-sheeew . . . boom!* Another RPG launched; another impact far too close. *Put-sheeew . . . boom!* Then another.

"You'll get the Purple Heart, for sure. Not too certain about the Silver Star, though." *Crack! Crack!* Konnie killed one more mag, then quickly slammed in another.

"Okay. Sounds good . . ." Einarson responded. *Thud!* "Ugh!" Einarson gasped as one of Shah's rounds slammed into his right rib cage, exiting his chest—narrowly missing his heart—but shredding a good chunk of his lung. As Einarson reached up to Konnie, he fell to the ground.

"Einarson! Crawl back behind cover! Get COVER! NOW!" Konnie boomed. *Crack! Crack! Crack!* The situation became dire within the first salvos of the attack. RPGs and mortars exploded throughout their position, a roar of machine-gun fire deluged them, and now a Marine lay dying. *Crack! Crack! Crack!* More rounds downrange. "Vargas! Greenfield!" Konnie bellowed. The two Marines had been firing shredding volleys of 7.62 onto Shah's positions, but the lieutenant needed them to get Einarson into a covered position. "Get your asses over here and take care of Einarson!"

"Roger that, sir!" Sergeant Carlos Vargas responded. *Put-sheeew . . . boom!* Yet another in an endless shower of RPGs rocketed toward them.

From a large rock about fifteen meters behind Konnie, Vargas and Greenfield emerged, grabbed Einarson, and dragged him to safety.

Crack! Crack! Crack! "We need to get on that 240! It's fuckin' sittin' there not doing anything but gettin' shot at!" Konnie yelled. He had been so wrapped up in scanning the ridges, then making sure that Einarson got to a safe position—and then firing on those ridgelines—that he forgot that he was on the receiving end of machine-gun fire himself. *Man . . . I don't see any clouds, but it's raining . . . raining all around. Big-ass raindrops, but where are the puddles of water?* he wondered.

Crack! Crack! Crack!

Oh . . . yeah, I'm getting shot at, not just shooting. Pretty intense now, too. Lots of rounds impacting all around me . . .

"Sir! *Sir! SIR!*" Vargas screamed at Konnie. "How the fuck you not gettin' your ass shot off, sir?"

"I don't know." Konnie paused for a minute. "I have no idea. Thought for a minute it was raining!" He and Vargas started laughing hysterically.

"You're fucking crazy, Lieutenant. I mean, damned motherfucking crazy!"

Crack! Crack! Crack!

"You CRAZY MOTHERFUCKER!" Crisp shouted at Konnie, amazed that the lieutenant was still alive, sitting within a hale of impacting rounds, wearing a flopping "boonie cover" in place of his Kevlar helmet. "Git ya ass back behind some cover, Lieutenant! Can't be getting the commander shot the fuck up!" Crisp then saw Einarson lying in a growing pool of his own blood. Turning to aid the wounded grunt, the staff sergeant slipped and accidentally kneed Einarson in the head. "Damn! You dead? I think I killed you!"

"Am I gonna get the Silver Star?" the lance corporal asked Crisp, shaking off the jolt to his face.

"You ignored my ass this mornin' when I was tryin' to keep y'all at least in covered positions without your gear on. You be lucky you don't get a silver bullet!" Crisp yelled, and Einarson laughed. "Quit ya laughing—and here . . ." Crisp grabbed the lance corporal's hand and pulled on his index finger. "Shut ya mouth and plug your suckin' chest wound with ya finger!" Einarson nodded, and did just that. Crisp then saw the Rock, the interpreter, who'd been shot twice in the chest, still standing—open to more of Shah's rounds. "Get down!" he yelled, then grabbed the 'terp and slammed him to the dirt. "What the fuck? Two holes in your chest not enough?" With the Rock safely on the ground, Crisp turned his attention back to Konnie. "Crazy-ass lieutenant! Get the fuck behind some cover." Crisp raised his M16 and loosed rounds into Cheshane Tupay's bulk, which cloaked Shah's fighters—but not their muzzle flashes. *Crack! Crack!* "Whachoo doin', PFC?" Crisp looked down to see one of the platoon's privates first class crawling under his legs. *Crack! Crack! Crack!* The staff sergeant continued to put rounds downrange.

"AAHHH! I'm hit! I'm hit!" the PFC shrieked.

Crisp knelt down next to the teenage Marine. "What the fuck!" he boomed. "You little ass ain't hit!" The staff sergeant started laughing when he saw some of the hot brass casings ejected from his M16 roll out from under the PFC's sleeve—having fallen into his collar, they burned the private from his neck to his armpit. "Get you skinny little ass the fuck up and put some rounds downrange!"

"Oorah, Staff Sergeant," the vastly relieved PFC responded.

"Hey, Vargas!" Konnie thought for a second. "We need to get on that 240. It's quiet. I don't like that. Get on the 240 and shoot the fuck out of that ridge!" *Put*-sheeew . . . *boom!* . . . *How many RPGs were going to rain down?* the lieutenant wondered.

"Okay. But, sir," Vargas began, "I think you'd better get over here with us."

Konnie turned to dash behind the rock where Vargas and the others were positioned—with the 240. He put his hand down to brace himself . . . and slipped on hundreds of spent brass casings. *Boy, I guess I put a lot of rounds downrange,* he thought.

"Hey, Vargas!" Konnie boomed as he began sprinting to the rock. "Make sure that when you start shooting that 240, you don't shoot me!"

"No problem . . . no problem at all, crazy ass lieutenant!" Vargas yelled, part laughing, part gasping from his sprint with Einarson. Then he let the 240 rip. Konnie dove behind the rock just as the machine gun started belching fire. Streaks of red marked the rounds' trajectories, gouging into Shah's men's hides on Cheshane Tupay's shoulders.

"You guys good?" Konnie asked once he got to Vargas and Greenfield. "I wanna make sure you know where you need to shoot." The lieutenant double-checked that they had Shah's positions locked on. They did. And with that, he took off to Crisp, who was with Einarson and Wilson at the casualty collection point. "What's the status, Staff Sergeant?" Konnie asked Crisp.

"Yo' crazy ass is fucking crazy as ever, dat's the status!" Crisp replied.

"Don't make me laugh. I'm afraid I might hurt myself. Now really, what's the status?" Konnie asked.

"Einarson's got it pretty good. But the corpsman says he'll make it. Wilson got shot twice in the leg, once in the ass. He'll make it, too. Stuffed rocks in his arteries to keep him alive—I don't know, some crazy corpsman trick. Three others got shot, but not bad enough that they can't keep fighting."

"Good. I'm off to Grissom and Pigeon."

"Keep yo' crazy ass head down, Lieutenant!" Crisp barked.

Konnie nodded, then bolted to Grissom's position. *Put-sheeew . . . boom!* Halfway there, though, one of Shah's RPGs impacted just a little too close to the lieutenant. Konnie sailed through the air, landing on his side in a wave of smoke, dirt, rocks, and splintered wood. He rolled over and checked to see if he still had his M16. He did. Then he checked to see if he was bleeding. He wasn't (not too badly, at least). *No shrapnel that I can feel. Keep going,* he thought.

Moments later, Konnie lunged behind a rock to see Grissom and Pigeon, staring at their respective radio operators, who were furiously trying to coax uncooperative comm boxes into sending and receiving. "Sir." Konnie snagged Grissom's attention.

"What, Konnie?" the captain replied with an annoyed tone.

"Does battalion know what's going on?"

"No," Grissom shot back.

"We got mortars?" the lieutenant asked.

"No. Not yet," Grissom responded.

"Pigeon?" Konnie turned to the forward air controller.

"What?"

"We got CAS yet?" Konnie was referencing close air support assets—A-10s and AH-64 Apache gunships

"No," Pigeon responded.

"Well then, what do we have?" Konnie asked with a laugh.

"Radios that don't fucking work because this fucking Afghan heat is making them melt down!" Grissom furiously barked. "Mountains are supposed to be damn cold. Not like a hundred and twenty degrees in the shade!"

"Well then, you know what they say? Never go anywhere without at least two captains," the lieutenant retorted sarcastically.

"Not fucking now, Konnie," Grissom roared. "This isn't the time for your smart ass bullshit!" Konnie just laughed to himself.

"Got battalion!" one of the radio operators piped up.

"Get a request in for CAS. Immediately," Pigeon ordered.

"Where's Dorf's 81s?" Konnie threw himself back into the dialogue.

"Almost there—almost got him . . ." the radio operator responded.

Along the eastern wall of the Chowkay, roughly one kilometer south of Fox-3's position, the echoing booms and clatters of the massive ambush had instantly snagged the attention of Ben Middendorf and his Marines. The twenty-six-year-old lieutenant, who graduated from West Point, then "snuck" out of the Army to join the Marines—urged there by his father, who had served in the Marine Corps during the Vietnam War in the venerated First Recon Battalion—instinctively built a plan within seconds as his grunts dove to the ground and stared at the lieutenant with "what now?" expressions. "Go firm! Get into defensive positions!" Dorf commanded. "Get those tubes fire-capped" (fire-capable, meaning that the mortars are ready to fire). The Marines jumped into their heat-of-combat roles, with Middendorf looking to get the vital mortars ready to crush Shah and his force. But the Marines stood on steep ground, and each burly 81 mm mortar tube needed a patch of flat ground roughly two feet by four feet, at the very bare minimum, to get positioned.

Seconds melted into minutes, then Corporal Joshua Plunk, whom Middendorf considered one of the best Marines he'd ever worked with, reported, "We got one up, sir! But just one!" With the tube mounted to the base plate, and standing firm against the bipod, Dorf just needed to get in comms with Fox-3. But Grissom's weren't the only radios with problems that morning. When Middendorf's radio operator dove to the ground, a vital cable from the PSG-5 high-power satellite communication radio tore from the unit, rendering it useless.

"I just happened to bring a spare, sir," the RO revealed.

"Eighty-ones good to go, sir, got Lieutenant Middendorf on the hook." Grissom's radio operator called out moments later.

"Excellent!" Grissom called back.

But just then, *boom!* The Marines looked at one another, then at a smoking crater forty-five meters distant. *Boom!* Again . . . but the next one landed just thirty meters away.

"Get down! They're walking mortars onto our position!" bellowed Grissom.

Boom! Fifteen meters.

"The next one's on top of us. RUN!" yelled Konnie.

Boom! Right on top of the group of them—literally *on fucking top*. The mortar round detonated about twenty-five feet above Pigeon's head, the tail fin actually hitting him in the shoulder after smashing into the ground aside the FAC.

"Thought one of you guys was punching me . . . but it was the ass end of the mortar!" Pigeon nervously laughed. Unlike the Marines, extremists like Shah can't always be sure of the quality or the supply consistency of their munitions; when a cell gets a crate of mortar rounds, only some may detonate as engineered, and often they don't function at all—or some, like number four in the barrage that was launched on the command post that morning, might air-burst safely above the intended target.

"I guess that makes this our really lucky day," Konnie again chimed in with his dry sarcasm. "Somebody get me a lottery ticket."

"Okay, motherfuckers. Now let's get some," seared Grissom, wiping the sweat from his brow—brought on not just from the heat, but from fear of incineration by an exploding mortar round. He contacted Middendorf directly, and passed him a grid reference point for the attackers to their east. Seconds after the gun team received the coordinate, they had the deflection and elevation for the gun from their mortar ballistic computer—and a round downrange. *Whump!*

"You got an FO yet for the fire package?" Konnie asked the captain. Middendorf's forward observer had remained with him; with Grissom, Konnie, and Pigeon able to pass back fire-adjustment instructions to the mortar team, Dorf felt confident.

"No. Wanna be a forward observer, Konnie?" Grissom asked.

"Rog. Let's pass some adjustments to Dorf," the lieutenant responded. Seconds later, more 81mm mortar rounds detonated along the ridgeline—slamming directly on the points of origin of Shah's attacks. "Fire for effect," Konnie annunciated with a grin, and the ridgeline exploded in a series of deafening fireballs. "Dorf, your mission is dead on. The only adjustment I have will be to have you guys walk rounds along the ridge, just to make sure you get all of 'em, especially the fleeing ones." By now, Shah's attack had all but ceased, but Middendorf's crew continued to pummel the ridgelines.

"They're egressing," Grissom called out after scanning the ridges with his binoculars. "Konnie, keep the mortars raining down."

"A-10s rollin' in," Pigeon interjected.

"Good. We need Dustoffs for the wounded. Get 'em in here. But work those A-10s for everything you can. Gun run after gun run on those fuckers running into the mountains," commanded Grissom.

After Dorf's mortar barrage, the enemy quit firing on Fox-3's position, but a small group of Shah's men, positioned just to the west of the mortar team on a small peak known to the grunts as Hill 2510 (for its altitude—in meters—on their maps) took a couple potshots at them. Returning fire immediately, the Marines around the mortars silenced the minuscule ambush. But then, as the Air Force A-10s raced toward the Chowkay, Shah's main effort once again sprang forth, and began firing on Fox-3; not with the furor of the first ambush, but well coordinated and deadly, nonetheless.

"Middendorf, I need a mark for the A-10s." Pigeon radioed the lieutenant with grids of Shah's men's current positions, asking not for high-explosive rounds, but for white phosphorus illumination mortars—to mark the extremists' positions for the high-explosive rounds plugged into the A-10s' seven-barrel high-speed rotary guns, soon to be available for close air support. With two mortar tubes now up and running, Middendorf and his Marines had the targets marked for Pigeon, who then passed a series of preliminary attack instructions to Grip-21 and Grip-11, the call signs for the two A-10s. But Grip-21's inertial navigation guidance system went faulty, preventing the pilot from undertaking attack runs as he'd been accustomed to doing. Pigeon, who graduated at the top of his flight school class at Meridian, Mississippi, had, like all Marine combat aviators, close air support indelibly stamped into the DNA of his very being. He'd chosen the job as FAC—forward air controller—one of the most respected tours a Marine aviator can undertake—in order to be on the ground with those he'd trained for so many years to support. And now he was experiencing the ground side of things at their most intense. Ever concerned about a possible friendly-fire event, particularly with Grip-21's guidance system out of commission, Pigeon made a handshake deal with the Air Force pilots—he would give a detailed "talk-on" to the A-10s of Fox-3's position, then the FAC, once oriented, would talk the attack aircraft onto the enemy's positions based on Fox-3's location. But it took over twenty minutes before the A-10s positively identified Fox-3's location, during which time Pigeon's radio started to lose power and malfunction. But the determined FAC was able to get Grip-21 to launch a five-inch-diameter white phosphorus rocket onto ground in an area where he suspected Shah's men had taken up positions; using that brightly burning mark, Pigeon talked the A-10s onto specific locations where they unleashed bursts of 30mm rounds at a rate of one hundred per second. As Pigeon worked to fix his radio, the two Grip A-10s climbed in altitude and took up a holding pattern far to the west of the activity. But the Chowkay's summer heat once again proved its potency, overheating Pigeon's radio anew after he got it working, keeping the Grips from unleashing their cocked might for another set of runs.

"Venom-11," Grip-21 began, "we're being replaced by Boar-11 and Boar-21. They'll be checking in soon. Good luck." With mortars continuing to rain down on Shah's fleeing men, all of the terrorist's attacks, save for the occasional sniper shot, had ceased. But some of the most difficult work still lay ahead: Pigeon needed to coordinate not only the A-10 attacks against the fleeing enemy, but also the Dustoff Air Ambulance extraction of the wounded.

Soon after the drones of the Grips' turbofans faded into the background of the Hindu Kush, the Boars sped into zone. Meanwhile, Pigeon's radio operator had gotten the FAC's communications up and running once again. Pigeon, who was accustomed to going into battle in the front seat of a Marine Corps F/A-18D Hornet, driving the supersonic aircraft with steel-cold nerves, carried that experience with him on his ground tour, under the press of combat. But it was one thing to be forced to watch fellow Marines thrown into the air by RPG blasts and to witness a mortar-shell burst just meters above his head, not to mention the continuous barrage of machine-gun rounds ripping throughout his position. Having to deal with his failing radio was quite another.

"Come on, Pigeon. Get that shit rollin'!" Konnie wailed. "Get some! Motherfuckers be turnin' tail and runnin'! Clear some shit hot and shred those bastards! Dorf's marks are on the ground!"

Boar-21 jumped on the net, "coaching" Pigeon: "Venom, slow it down, buddy. We know you're in a shit sandwich. Take a second and key the mike *before* you talk. We're here to help you, but if we can't understand what you want to communicate, we can't do anything but fly around way, way above all the action. Talk us on. Get us into the thick of it."

Pigeon sat back and laughed at the irony of his situation. He remembered his time in the cockpit of a Hornet during OIF-I, supporting an FAC near Al Asad, in Iraq's Al Anbar province. *That guy was in a panic,* he thought. Pigeon had told the FAC in Al Asad to slow it down, just as the Boar pilots directed him—but he wasn't in a panic that day in the Hindu Kush, far from it, in fact. His radio was teetering on the edge of frying itself, sending out chopped transmissions. He finally got it working yet again.

"Konnie." Pigeon looked toward the lieutenant. "Listen; these guys can't attack unless they have a confirmed target. I've been too busy working this radio and coordinating the air side of things to get eyes on to confirm anything. Their rules, you know. You got a confirmed target?"

"Abso-fuckin'-lutely I got targets," Konnie piped up. "All along that ridge to the east." He peered through binoculars and passed positive identification of the fighters to Pigeon, noting their positions relative to Dorf's illum marks. "The bad guys are fleeing. Smoke-check their asses. Every last one of 'em!"

Pigeon nodded, "Gotcha. Roger. Will do," the FAC said, then he and Dorf expertly deconflicted the mortar fire, having Middendorf shut down the mortar barrage to ensure that the A-10s wouldn't collide with a high-explosive mortar round meant for one of Ahmad Shah's men. Seconds later, after passing to the A-10 pilot a "nine-line brief"—a standardized set of instructions guiding a pilot onto a ground target—Pigeon uttered the words that Konnie had been waiting so desperately to hear: "Boar-21, you're *cleared-hot* for a thirty mike-mike gun run."

"Roger." Boar-21's voice echoed from the radio. The Marines gazed skyward as the A-10 approached the target ridgeline, made a tight bank turn, then dove into an attack run. Cheers rang out as the target lit up like a massive, high-speed Fourth of July sparkler as the 30 mm rounds detonated in coruscating explosions upon impact. Then the Warthog banked hard, expending flares—standard operating procedure to cloak its path from potential incoming ground-to-air heat-seeking missiles—and pulled into the cobalt sky above. Heartbeats later, the sound of the furious salvo echoed throughout Fox-3's position, a deliciously guttural *brrrrrrrrr!* of loosed high-explosive rounds, punctuated by the whine of the aircraft's twin turbofan engines. Three more cleared-hot gun runs, and Pigeon sent the Boars back to base.

"Thanks for a great job," Pigeon calmly announced.

"No problem. Anytime, Venom," one of the pilots replied.

With that job completed, Pigeon's most difficult task of the day began. The Army UH-60 Air Ambulance Dustoff medevac birds approached, accompanied by Army Shock AH-64 Apache gunships. Einarson and Wilson were hurting, and Pigeon knew it. *Get 'em out of here, back to Bagram, where they'll have the best medical care in the world,* the FAC thought. As Middendorf's mortar barrage and Pigeon's A-10 attacks were going down, Crisp had led Marines carrying the wounded to a designated helicopter landing zone, a high point to the west of their position. There they waited . . . and waited. One of the Marines who helped haul the wounded up the hill, Lance Corporal Mark Perna—one of Wilson's closest friends—watched as Wilson passed out on morphine, and waited for the extract, wondering if his friend would ever see the light of day again.

"Okay. They're close. Approaching our position," Pigeon stated.

"Got a message from battalion," Grissom interrupted. "CJTF-76 is demanding a SEAD package before they'll let *any* Dustoff inbound."

"What!" Konnie shouted. "Let's get those birds on the ground, get the Marines back to Bagram! What the fuck good is a suppression package going to do now? Those guys are in retreat!" Pigeon agreed, knowing that with AH-64 escort—more than capable of not just prepping an LZ, but engaging specific-point targets—starting up a SEAD would just waste precious mortar rounds.

"Check in the box," Grissom replied. "Anything with a helicopter needs to be done to the letter of the rules after the Chinook shootdown, every box needs to be checked. Let's just do what we gotta do to get these guys out."

Although little known to the general public, Dustoffs, a blanket term for Army medevac Air Ambulance units, rank as some of the most selfless, capable aviators in the entire United States military. Flying completely unarmed—only their bright Red Cross symbol distinguishing them from standard UH-60 Blackhawks—the Dustoffs (a name coined in Vietnam because of the dusty rotor wash of the aircraft at

Behind the M-16 in the back of a highback Humvee.
USMC/TASK FORCE KOA

Boyd, after getting shot in the face. A few hours later he'd get shrap-nel to the face.   *USMC/TASK FORCE KOA*

The Commandant of the Marine Corps pins on a purple heart to
Staff Sergeant Lee Crisp. Konnie in background.
USMC/TASK FORCE KOA

Commandant of the Marine Corps awards Joe Roy, sniper, a purple
heart after a gun battle with Shah's men on Sawtalo Sar during
Operation *Whalers*.   *USMC/TASK FORCE KOA*

1st Lieutenant Rob Long shows a spent AK-47 casing.   *USMC/TASK FORCE KOA*

Justin Bradley in the Hindu Kush. A favorite photograph of mine.
© Ed Darack / Darack.com / Science Faction Images

Facing page: One of my favorite images from my time embedded with 2/3 in Afghanistan, silhouette of a U.S. Marine machine-gunner at sunrise, heading into the Hindu Kush. The Marine is Mike Scholl, who would become a good friend. Mike was killed just under a year after this photograph in the Anbar province of Iraq by an IED.
© Ed Darack / Darack.com / Science Faction Images

The Marines of 2/3 at Camp Blessing regularly ate with the local fighters whom they worked with (they lived with them at Camp Blessing).
© *Ed Darack / Darack.com / Science Faction Images*

Memorial service for
Marines of 2/3, Kaneohe Bay,
Hawaii.
*© Ed Darack / Darack.com /
Science Faction Images*

Kunar River from a Chinook   © *Ed Darack / Darack.com / Science Faction Images*

Ronin, sniper team, at Nangalam.
© *Ed Darack / Darack.com / Science Faction Images*

Justin Bradley scans the distance toward Sawtalo Sar and the Korangal Valley.
© *Ed Darack / Darack.com / Science Faction Images*

Afghan logistical method.   © Ed Darack / Darack.com / Science Faction Images

155mm artillery at Asadabad.
© Ed Darack / Darack.com / Science Faction Images

1st Lieutenant Matt Bartels and his interpreter, Sultan, at Tantil Now, a small village across the Pech River Valley from Sawtalo Sar.
© *Ed Darack / Darack.com / Science Faction Images*

Roe Lemons, artillery forward observer.
© *Ed Darack / Darack.com / Science Faction Images*

A member of the ASF.   © *Ed Darack / Darack.com / Science Faction Images*

1st Lieutenant Patrick Kinser and Sergeant Keith Eggers, Ronin sniper team leader. © *Ed Darack / Darack.com / Science Faction Images*

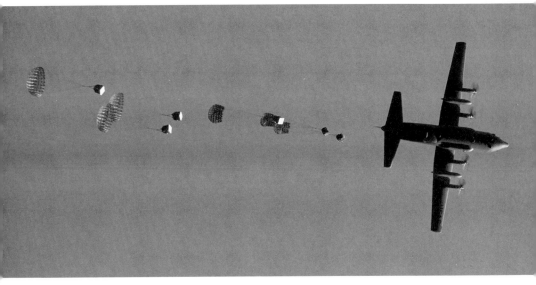

An Air Force CDS drop.   © Ed Darack / Darack.com / Science Faction Images

Houses built of stone into stone, Nangalam.
© Ed Darack / Darack.com / Science Faction Images

Helicopter assault on a ridge across from Sawtalo Sar and Korangal Valley.
© *Ed Darack / Darack.com / Science Faction Images*

landing zones, and today an acronym for Dedicated Unhesitating Self-less Service to our Fighting Forces), the Dustoffs have earned a reputation of flying not only into hot landing zones, but *any* landing zone, regardless of threat level.

"Okay," Grissom said after conferring with Middendorf. "Let's get this SEAD under way." The captain laughed. But while fast inbound, the two Dustoff UH-60s, commanded by Army Chief Warrant Officer Jim Gisclair, and accompanied by two Shock AH-64 Apaches, didn't have direct communications with Pigeon. And with the mortar barrage running for the suppression package, Middendorf needed to know just when the birds would arrive so he could work with Pigeon to deconflict the lobbed mortars with the inbound Dustoffs.

"Sir, I think you should know that four Army helicopters just entered the Chowkay Valley," came the nervous message from a Whiskey Company Marine at a vehicle checkpoint at the opening of the Chowkay to Rob Scott.

"What! They're there already! The SEAD is under way!" Without deconflicting the mortars with the Dustoffs, a friendly-fire disaster was imminent. Rob immediately got on the hook with Grissom, who passed the information to Pigeon, who contacted Middendorf. Middendorf, although not formally trained as a fire support team leader, had taken on the job for the mission, drawing on skills he'd learned at Infantry Officers' Course as well as from technical publications he'd read dealing with the complex art. With direct comms finally established with the Dustoffs, Middendorf arranged for a "lateral offset" deconfliction, allowing the 81s' barrage to continue as the birds slipped by to the west of the mortars' trajectories; as well, the 105s at Asadabad, under the watch of Matt Tracy, had been able to range to a ridge to the north of the Chowkay and suppress any enemy activity there.

"Dustoffs are here," Pigeon stated. "They're ready to extract the wounded." The FAC grabbed his radio and sprinted to the top of the hill where the Dustoffs would land.

"Okay. Let's get these Marines the fuck out of here," Grissom declared as he folded his arms. "Okay. SEAD complete, bring the Dustoffs in."

Minutes later, the escort gunships arrived. AH-64 Apaches, driven by Shock Army aviators who wanted nothing more than to smoke bad guys and help the Dustoffs get the wounded out, roared overhead, energizing the grunts' spirits with their menacing head-on profiles and the growling drone of their engines. *Heavily armed, rotary-wing CAS—delicious,* Konnie thought to himself. The unarmed Blackhawk Dustoffs orbited in the safe distance.

Pigeon, talking the Apaches onto their position, then built the situational awareness of the Shock aviators to the greater battlefield. Although forged from different air-ground combat doctrine (the Army considers helicopter gunships to be "maneuver" platforms, used to attack ground targets without ground control, a mission called "close-combat attack"), Pigeon and the Shock aviators seemed to read one another's minds. His hair practically standing on end at the sight of the raw skill and professionalism of the Apache aviators as they coursed up the valley, Pigeon knew that the tide of the morning battle had decisively shifted to the side of the Marines. The FAC passed his plan to the Shock aviators: scan the ridgelines first for enemy, engage them if found, then the FAC would bring the Dustoffs in to land.

"We're taking small-arms fire," the lead Apache coolly informed Pigeon as the craft passed over one of Cheshane Tupay's ridges to the east of Fox-3. Pigeon radioed a quick six-line brief, a set of instructions, similar to a nine-line, first developed by the 160th SOAR(A) aviators for autonomous aerial fire missions.

"Cleared to engage." Pigeon gave the call for the Shocks to attack the targets. The two Apaches lit up the ridgeline with their 30 mm guns and 2.75-inch Hydra rockets. They made a second pass—and then a third. The grunts of Fox-3 stood in awe as the Shock pilots maneuvered their aircraft in ways the Marines didn't even think possible—at one time one of the Apaches hung vertical, facing directly onto a ridge, while firing, then rotated ninety degrees, then another ninety on another axis, as the pilots continued the attack. One of the most amazing displays of combat aviation he'd ever seen, the performance of the

Topographic map of the upper Chowkay Valley

Shock aviators that morning caused Pigeon to wonder if he should have flown helicopters instead of Hornets.

"Cherry ice," the lead Shock AH-64 called, indicating that the landing zone was cold, that is, ready to safely accept the unarmed Dustoffs. The AH-64s continued to reconnoiter throughout other parts of the valley. But Shah's skilled, motivated men were still feeling bolstered by their successful ambush of the Navy special operations team and subsequent shoot-down of the MH-47 just weeks before. As the aviators of the lead Dustoff approached the designated landing zone, they hoped for a quick extraction. The Marines had chosen a good location—good cover from the ground troops, a relatively flat top to the hill, and no tall vegetation to threaten the spinning rotor blades. Pigeon ordered a green smoke flare popped to indicate the exact location on which to put down, as well as the direction and speed of any wind. The pilots rolled in hard, as usual for the Dustoffs, and pulled back steeply. The aviators could feel the ground effect cushioning their craft's close approach to the deck. Instinctively, they scanned right, then left . . . okay. *Wait . . . What was that?* One of Shah's men popped up from behind a refrigerator-size rock, toting a loaded RPG, high on the slopes of Hill 2510. Somehow, he'd hidden his position from the Marines, the Shocks, and the A-10s. Somehow, he knew that the wounded would be extracted from the hill to his north. But the Dustoff pilots already had their craft flaring hard. They couldn't pull out; they'd fully committed. *Would this be a repeat of the special operations disaster?* the crew wondered, icy chills zipping up and down their spines. The Dustoffs had no choice but to continue on their path; they had no weapons onboard to defend themselves, and the Apaches were too far off to provide cover. They could only hope that the RPG gunner would miss.

But he probably wouldn't. In fact, he was probably the same terrorist who had downed the MH-47, killing all on board. He, like others in Shah's group, was probably one of the world's most proficient, most determined extremist fighters. And after having sent the MH-47 to the ground in flames, he was confident that he could blow the Dustoff bird out of the sky. He rested the RPG launcher on his shoulder, dropped his right index finger onto the trigger, and buttressed his stance, preparing for the sharp blowback of the RPG launch to which he'd become so accustomed.

Seven hundred meters away, near Middendorf's mortar line, Lance Corporal Lavon Pennington, a combat engineer attached to Fox-1, saw the terrorist spring forth, holding the RPG launcher. An image of a fiery explosion and senseless death flooded Pennington's mind. He lifted his standard-issue M16, squeezed his eyes shut—knowing that he'd have only one chance, one shot. Pennington opened his eyes and positioned the insurgent in his iron sights. Then he squeezed the trigger. *Crack!*

The eyes of the Dustoff aviator on the right seat of the Blackhawk were transfixed on the RPG gunner. He could have thought of his home, his family, his dog . . . his car. He knew he could do nothing, so he just continued to do his job. Life before him continued in real time—no slow motion; he didn't even pray for survival. He just worked the tough machine through the wispy air, readying for a landing and to get wounded troops to safety. He ignored the fact that he was about to be blown out of the sky, that he was about to be incinerated on top of some forlorn peak deep in the hinterlands of Afghanistan, that he would never see his home again.

Puff! And that was it. The end. The men in the second Dustoff saw it all: as the lead bird was in final flare, Shah's RPG gunner locked onto the Blackhawk, clasped the trigger of the launcher, just as had been done before the MH-47 shoot-down . . . and then the RPG gunner's head disappeared in a cloud of pink mist. Pennington's 5.56mm round had connected with his scalp just a neuron's response time before he could squeeze the RPG trigger. The lead Dustoff swooshed down, cushioned by the craft's ground effect, and landed on the small flat spot amid the steep terrain.

As Pigeon knelt under the rotors, barking orders into his radio, Konnie had his two "horses"—twenty-year-old Lance Corporal Albert Mendiola and twenty-three-year-old Lance Corporal Justin Monk—race down the hill to carry the casualties and their gear up to the aircraft. "So, sir," the interpreter known as the Rock began before he was loaded into the medevac, "I am leaving. I will see you soon. Try to kill all of these Taliban fucks."

"Will do, Rock," Konnie replied.

"I wish I could stay and watch them all die!" the big terp finished.

"I think most of 'em are dead, after all that." The lieutenant smiled.

"Look, sir." Lance Corporal Jason Dunaway grabbed Konnie's

attention by holding up a carbon-scored piece of melded lead and copper. "The 7.62 round—we pulled it out of my SAPI."

Konnie laughed at the sight, the round having gone through Dunaway's left biceps before lodging into the front ceramic-plate insert on his flak jacket. "Now get on the bird with Einarson, Wilson, and the rest of 'em," he ordered. All told, five Marines and the Rock had to be evacuated that morning, including Lance Corporal Anthony Adams, with shrapnel to his arms and legs, and Lance Corporal Dustin Epperly—one of Fox-3's most proficient Marines—with shrapnel to one of his arms from an RPG burst.

Waving off the second Dustoff—the LZ didn't have enough space for two birds at the same time—Konnie and Pigeon huddled as the pilots spun up the first Blackhawk's engines, lifting the bird into the sky. The second craft landed, and Konnie and his Marines loaded it with gear from the wounded—which would get the lieutenant in a bit of trouble later on, as Air Ambulances adhere to strict rules forbidding the carrying of anything but wounded personnel.

The Marines had thwarted what Ahmad Shah surely felt was his destiny for that day. They dashed his goals through skill, through perseverance, through sheer will—and though some classic USMC improvisation as well. The grunts relied not just on their instincts, but on the lessons the Marine Corps had ingrained into them. Armageddon had descended upon the grunts. They fought hard. They fought harder than anyone could imagine. And they won. Armageddon had been denied.

But to what extent had they won? Had Ahmad Shah survived? Would he continue in his campaign of terror? Was he mortally wounded? Or dead? And what of his die-hard adherents? How many of them had fallen to the Marines' trigger pulls, to the mortar teams' 81s, to the A-10s' 30 mm guns and the Apaches' rockets? Only time would tell. And that time would come soon.

11

ONE RIDGE
DISTANT, A
WORLD APART

know the SEAD was a little rough. But the Dustoffs got everyone out—" Rob Scott was explaining to a senior member of Task Force Devil's command, a very irate senior member, who cut the XO off mid-sentence. Shah's force had come too close to downing another helicopter, and with Marines still operating deep in the Chowkay and other surrounding valleys, another Dustoff extraction might be necessary if the extremists attacked again. As he'd done through the entire operation, Major Scott continued to battle to keep the grunts of 2/3 fighting the enemy, and the critical date of 19 August, when CJTF-76 mandated that *Whalers* draw to a close, loomed larger with each passing hour. As much heat the XO took from the Devil staff, however, Devil took tenfold from CJTF-76, who, after the battle on the morning of the fourteenth, wanted to pull the Marines out entirely. And while tensions flared between Rob Scott and TF Devil, Rob knew that the task force had fought just as hard as he and other senior members of 2/3 to keep the Marines on track—the way they'd vowed upon arriving in Afghanistan—regardless of vexing Army-Marine Corps cultural differences.

With Shah's force in tatters and on the run, with untold numbers of dead and wounded, Fox Company worked to hold security of the area after the Dustoffs lifted the injured to the safety of Bagram. "Konnie, find me an LZ large enough for Chinooks to come in and extract us," Grissom instructed the lieutenant.

"Roger that, sir," responded Konnie, who assumed from these words that CH-47s, if not already en route, would soon arrive. After he and some of the Fox-3 Marines found and then secured a plot of level ground large enough to accommodate two Chinooks, however, the bad news arrived.

"I don't think they're comin' to get us," Grissom informed him.

"Sir, I want to be very clear when I tell you that I think we *need* an extract," the lieutenant replied, with a serious, almost solemn tone. "We're red on ammo, water, medical supplies, and with five Marines and the Rock now gone, we have a serious force-strength issue." Konnie explained Fox-3's situation, the term *red* referencing near total depletion of supplies.

"Yeah, Konstant. I understand what's goin' on," the captain replied, frustrated. "But from what I'm hearin' on the net, we're not gettin' outta here—not by helicopter, at least. They just now almost lost another helicopter. They're gonna do everything they can to avoid another shoot-down, meaning that when we leave this place, we leave it on foot." Although Shah's army, what was left of it, had scattered, solid intel on the enemy's strength at that point, or about whether Shah was regrouping, had yet to roll in. With the area's greatest threat diminished, and the clock loudly ticking toward the nineteenth, the grunts would continue to press onward with *Whalers*.

As their conversation continued, Konstant and Grissom each killed a Marlboro. "So then we consolidate—Middendorf and his mortars moving to our position?" Konnie asked.

"Everything's evolving, every minute," Grissom responded as he took a drag off his cigarette. "But that's what I'd prefer at this point."

"You know, sir," Konnie told him, "we're also red on cigarettes."

"I know. We're smokin' like champs up here. Be bad if we ran out."

"Well, don't worry. Middendorf's got more. We'll consolidate forces, and then we'll raid Dorf's smokes." Konnie shot the captain a wry, conspiratorial grin.

Grissom just shook his head, trying to hide his laughter. "I guess this is what they mean when they say 'alone and unafraid,'" he stated.

"Sir . . ." Konnie paused, holding back laughter. "At least we have each other."

"Go lead Marines, Konstant."

With that, Konnie set about reinforcing the camp's defense, sending the two scout/snipers attached to Fox-3 and five other Marines to an observation point to the west of the patrol base. Pigeon, wanting to know how things in the area looked from up high, kept radio contact with two A-10s flying above the Chowkay. With a variety of targeting sensors, the A-10s would be able to pass information to the FAC while he directed them to sweep the area. When the seven Marines Konnie had sent out established a firm position, a sergeant in the group radioed a grid of their exact location, which Konnie passed on to Pigeon. But the seven were looking to find an even better location, so they set out to reconnoiter ground a few hundred yards to their north. Realizing that their initial location gave them a better view of the surrounding area, they turned back.

"Konnie," Pigeon said, "A-10s reporting personnel moving toward the snipers' grid they just occupied."

"Movers, huh?" Pigeon gave Konnie the location at which the A-10 pilots had reported seeing the suspected bad guys; they'd approached from north of the snipers' grid. "If they're heading south to the snipers' grid, then there's about to be an ambush." Konnie paused for a moment. "Tell the A-10s to take them out, sir. Tell them to take them out now!" he exclaimed.

"Okay. That'll be danger-close" (a situation where friendlies lie close enough to a target to risk getting hit). But Pigeon, studying his map and the terrain before him, had doubts about the accuracy of the grid. "I want you to do a show-of-force run. I *repeat*—show-of-force run." Pigeon directed the A-10 to essentially perform just a flyby, without releasing any ordnance—showing, but not applying, force. He then contacted the sniper team; "One of the A-10s will be coming in—if he's aimed at you, let me know. Let me know *immediately*." The burly Warthog banked hard and put its nose toward the ground, the barrel assembly of the 30mm rotary gun protruding from the craft like a blunt stinger.

"He's pointed right at us. *Right at us!*" came the call from the snipers as they eyed the fast-approaching bulk of a huge gun framed by a gray fuselage, wings, engines, and tail fins.

"ABORT—ABORT—ABORT," Pigeon boomed over the radio to the A-10, instinctively calling for the aircraft to break off its attack vector, even though the pilot had no clearance—or intention—to release ordnance. The pilot rolled out of the dry run, spewing flares on his egress.

"Holy shit, Pigeon. I almost smoke-checked seven of our own guys," Konnie remarked as his face turned ashen. "Man. You saved eight lives just now." He paused. "Those seven—and me . . . from drinking myself to death before I reached thirty."

"Just doin' my job, Konnie," the FAC calmly replied.

And with Fox-3 red on everything essential, Pigeon would continue to work his job at a feverish pace that morning—Jeremy Whitlock and his staff already had Fox's vital supplies roaring toward the Chowkay. Cruising at more than a mile above the Hindu Kush, the crew of an Air Force C-130E Hercules gently pushed the big craft lower in altitude as they equalized the pressure inside the airplane with that of the outside air. On cue from the pilot, one of the Hercules' loadmasters released the rear doors on the craft at ten thousand feet above sea level. The upper door hydraulically tucked inside the bird as the lower ramp folded and locked flat, revealing a roughly ten-by-seven-foot open-air "window" to eastern Afghanistan. The four powerful turboprops echoed throughout the Chowkay in a dull hum, announcing the approach of the Marines' resupply. "Eyes on!" a parched, exhausted lance corporal announced as he thrust his index finger into the sky at the fast-approaching bird.

"Pop smoke!" Pigeon ordered. Two Marines each yanked the pins out of purple smoke grenades and tossed them onto a drop zone Pigeon had designated.

"Hope they kick that shit out at just the right moment," Konnie mumbled under his breath.

"Here it comes." Pigeon craned his neck back as the Hercules swooped overhead. On board the craft, the loadmasters watched six large crates careen on rollers out of the open cargo hold and into space, drogue chutes deploying just seconds later. Banking hard after the drop, the Hercules disappeared behind a high ridge, leaving only the supply crates, swaying below their green chutes, in the sky above the Marines. The men were always on guard during CDS drops, since the heavy cargo could easily squash an unknowing grunt, but the parachutes' trajectory quickly showed there to be no danger of a crushing death. In fact, the drop missed the area completely.

"Off. *Way off*. It'll take two *fuckin'* days to recover that stuff," Konnie muttered in a pissed-off tone. "Guess we're stayin' red for now."

Just over a kilometer to the southeast of Fox-3's camp, Ben Middendorf, having decided to co-locate his mortar team with Fox-3 after conferring with Grissom, began moving toward Hill 2510. Not wanting to cover the same ground that Fox-3 had traversed during their push up the Chowkay for fear of walking into an ambush, the lieutenant felt it best to move by way of the terrain to their west. But Middendorf and his Marines were also red on supplies; the one-kilometer movement, down the steep ground to the Amrey Creek bed, then back up even steeper slopes on the base of Hill 2510—portaging the heavy mortar tubes—further weakened the already-enervated grunts. Arriving at dusk at an isolated village not shown on any maps, Middendorf noticed the chilling sight of a white flag waving above one of the village buildings—a sign of solidarity with the Taliban. Under the dying glow of twilight, the Marines greeted the standoffish villagers, then bedded down for a few hours just outside the tiny enclave—maintaining very tight security.

While Middendorf and the mortar team were closing on the village on the slopes of Hill 2510 that evening, Pigeon worked with another C-130 on a second CDS resupply attempt. This time, through a number of low passes, the trajectories of which he computed with his map and his instincts, the FAC guided all six loads perfectly on target, one by one. "Pigeon," Konnie commented, "you just continue to dominate awesomeness." Completely green on supplies, Fox-3 would be able to fully stock Dorf's mortar team—once they arrived. The next morning, with Fox-1 and the Afghan soldiers still providing security for them, the mortar team broke camp before dawn and pushed north toward Fox-3 and their much-needed food, water, and ammunition. Middendorf first led his team to the top of Hill 2510, to get a commanding view of the route ahead for the grunts. Scanning the distance, the lieutenant noticed two men watching the Marines—no weapons, no ICOMs, just two men observing them. Unsure if they belonged to Shah's cell, if they had been employed by the terrorist as lookouts, or if they were just villagers walking the area's trails, Middendorf decided to press onward. With the mortar team weak from exhaustion, dehydration, and now near starvation, he split the team in two to move by leapfrogging, keeping two mortars always ready to fire as the grunts with the other two tubes pushed northward. By noon, the Marines had drunk every drop of their water and their corpsmen had administered their last rehydration IV. With their destination just a half kilometer away, a lance corporal collapsed in the heat.

"Unless you get up and fuckin' walk," Middendorf acerbically began, "you *will die*." Each Marine in the team had deteriorated to a level Middendorf had never before seen; they stared at the lieutenant vacuously from sunken eyes—many having bent over with jabbing abdominal cramps and vomited. "I can't explain the reason, but you will die, and possibly cause other Marines around you to fuckin' die as well. *Now get the fuck up!* Let's go!" Pressured by the lieutenant's forceful command, the lance corporal staggered to his feet and fought onward with the group, which finally arrived at Fox-3's camp a few hours later.

"Hey, man. How you doin'?" Konnie asked Middendorf upon his arrival.

"I'm doin' a lot better than you guys. I'm glad you're still alive. So what happened?" Dorf asked back.

"I think we killed a lot of bad guys," Konnie told him. "Is that bad?"

"I don't think its bad," Middendorf replied. "I think it's great. How'd you not get your ass shot off?"

"I'm good at a lot of things, Ben," Konnie said, "but I'm best at bein' lucky, I guess."

The Chowkay wasn't the only corner of 2/3's area of operation during *Whalers* to witness bullets flying and sweat-drenched toil. Golf Company Marines continued to push northwest in the Narang Valley, and Kinser's Echo-1 had penetrated deep into the Shuryek, moving up its eastern wall to Golayshal, the southernmost village in the valley, lying at the same latitude as the summit of Sawtalo Sar. The Jump CP, with senior leaders of the area's Afghan National Army in trace, moved along Sawtalo Sar's spine, then dropped into the Korangal, meeting with villagers during *shura* meetings. Donnellan, who sought to have the ANA capable of undertaking security in the critical valley as soon as possible, worked to establish amicable relations between the Afghan Army brass and the village elders. Through an interpreter, Donnellan learned that the inhabitants of Korangal village—throughout the valley, for that matter—had wanted a heightened presence of Afghan government personnel, be they police or ANA soldiers. But those villagers who spoke up—about a dozen of them in the past year—had been killed by anticoalition militia types such as Shah.

"How many times have you been to the Korangal?" an elder asked

Colonel Nasir, the highest-ranking officer in the Afghan National Army traveling with the Jump CP.

"Never," Nasir replied, after a long pause.

"Why?" the elder asked as he sipped chai tea.

"Because . . ." Nasir paused again. "Because *I'm afraid of the Korangal.*" This attitude was one the Marines would work to completely reverse.

Also moving through the Korangal and along Sawtalo Sar during *Whalers*, Keith Eggers and two other members of Team Ronin, Corporal Joe Roy—Eggers's twenty-one-year-old spotter—and twenty-one-year-old Navy Hospital Corpsman Third Class Jamie "Doc" Pigman, had been tasked with providing forward observation and bounding overwatch of Echo-3, who would be pushing south into the Korangal Valley. Long before sunrise on the twelfth of August, after a previous night's meeting with Echo-3's platoon commander, Nick Guyton, Ronin started up the steep Bakaro Ghar, a spine of gray, shattered rock connecting the opening of the Korangal Valley with the north ridge of Sawtalo Sar. Climbing along loose talus, around teetering boulders, and up small cliffs—avoiding trails to maintain concealment from any unfriendly eyes—the trio gained the north ridge by midmorning, as Echo-3 made strong headway into the Korangal below them. Then Keith received a call from Echo Company's commander, Captain John McShane, who stated that fresh intel had revealed a sizable force of foreign fighters massed in Salar Ban, just on the other side of Sawtalo Sar's north ridge from Ronin's position.

"Want us to check it out?" Keith asked. McShane felt uneasy; the report stated that upward of eighty fighters had gathered in the village. "We'll be going right by an ideal overwatch spot anyway; we might as well," the sergeant continued. Furthermore, in addition to Echo-3, Echo Company's Second Platoon had been working their way into the Korangal. As well, the Marines of Camp Blessing had forward-deployed two 120mm mortar tubes at the mouth of the Korangal, capable of providing instant indirect fire support, and Doghouse's 105s stood at the ready at Asadabad, able to range to Ronin's position with RAP rounds. McShane reluctantly authorized the observation—but for only one hour.

After donning their ghillie suits (camouflage composed of densely packed, long strands of green and brown fabric for concealment in densely vegetated areas) and striping their faces in olive-drab and black camo paint, the trio moved into position and "glassed" Salar Ban with a powerful Leupold spotting scope. "Nothing. No fighters whatsoever," Eggers reported to McShane after sighting just villagers—including women and children, who typically leave once extremist fighters arrive. Ronin would continue their overwatch mission for Echo-3 during the following days, preparing to link up with the platoon at Sawtalo Sar's summit on 16 August. Those intervening days, however, wouldn't pass easily. The amount of specialized equipment they carried—optics and radios, not to mention the sniper rifle itself and its support gear and rounds—meant that they portaged over one hundred pounds each, spread between their packs and gear harnesses, and like the other Marines of 2/3 during *Whalers*, they fought to stay hydrated in the intense heat. Searching for small streams while maintaining cover and providing overwatch proved exhausting. But the risks of their mission meant that they'd get few chances to truly rest and rehydrate—and they had to maintain the very sharpest of focus.

"So, we're gonna get overrun by Shah's guys, huh?" Joe Roy skeptically asked on the evening of the fifteenth at their hide above Echo-3's patrol base just outside of Chichal.

"That's what they say—based off the ICOM hits the terps are picking up," Eggers responded. "*Apparently* they've seen us. But I don't care how many times I've heard it and it turned out to be bullshit, we're not taking any chances." The three of them set claymore antipersonnel mines around a solid, densely treed "harbor site" at the top of steep ground above Chichal in which they'd remain concealed for the night, downed some caffeine pills, and waited—silently scanning the surroundings through their night-vision equipment, and most importantly, listening intently for the approach of anyone in the dead-still air. *It's so densely vegetated you'd have to be superhuman to get to us without us hearing,* Eggers thought.

The night passed without incident—and without sleep, and at dawn, Ronin got word that Echo-3 was fast en route to Sawtalo Sar's summit to investigate some suspicious smoldering fires, possibly left by Shah's men during their movement into the Korangal from the Chowkay after the firefight with Fox-3. The three scout/snipers of Ronin stealthily moved out of their hide and vectored up the north ridge to observe and then meet Guyton's platoon at the summit. With a mission spectrum far broader than targeted hits against individual personnel, Marine scout/sniper teams are often tasked by commanders to undertake the type of "bounding overwatch" missions that Ronin performed throughout *Whalers.* Acting as the "eyes forward"—not just watching out for, and then using their precision rifles to interdict, ambushes against other Marine elements on the move, but acting as observers for forward air controllers and mortar and artillery teams—Eggers and Team Ronin combined their knowledge of the area's terrain with their specialized training to virtually guarantee that units whom they overwatched could safely move through an area. As stealthy, fit, and well trained as they were, however, three men—completely unsupported—stood little chance of survival should an enemy force of greater number descend upon them. Thus, as he had always on such missions, Eggers kept constant watch over his radios—the team's lifelines of support.

"Hides," Pigman noted near the summit of Sawtalo Sar later that morning. "Damn, this is where they probably concealed themselves during the ambush of the SEALs." Eggers, Roy, and Pigman studied the positions Shah's men had made—nothing dug in, but rather walled up with large, felled trees, concealing their locations within the surroundings. Topping out on the mountain's summit at the same time as Ronin, Echo-3 planned to head back down Sawtalo Sar, descending first to Chichal then regaining the north ridge, along which Ronin would ply from the summit downward, providing overwatch as the platoon navigated the steep terrain. They departed around noon.

Moving quickly yet remaining well concealed, and staying to the west of the Super Highway, Ronin did all they could to stay invisible and keep eyes on Echo-3. But as each man in the team knew all too well, avoiding soft compromise on Sawtalo Sar after traveling the mountain's slopes for over five days—especially after linking up with an entire platoon at the mountain's summit—was virtually impossible. And so, a little over an hour into their descent, a lone elderly Afghan man appeared "out of nowhere," as typically occurred in the region. The trio approached him—he was unarmed, carried no ICOM, and looked unkempt and extremely unhealthy. Pigman immediately locked onto the man's milky-white eyeballs. *Trachoma,* the corpsman thought. *Eerie as hell.* The team attempted to ask him some questions in basic Pashto, but the man, whose clothes were torn and soiled, didn't cooperate. Following their rules of engagement, they photographed him, then sent him in the opposite direction of their travel.

"I got a real bad feeling about that guy," Pigman said to Eggers and Roy as the figure disappeared into the trees above them. All three, having read Marcus Luttrell's after-action report, felt the encounter was a bad omen. "First we see Shah's hides, then this guy," the corpsman continued.

"All right. Let's keep moving, gotta maintain eyes on Echo-3," Eggers stated. In addition to their training as scout/snipers, each of the three had grown up with a love of outdoor pursuits. Pigman couldn't get enough of hiking, camping, and hunting in his home state of New Jersey; Roy, from Michigan's Upper Peninsula, lived for hunting season; and Eggers's activities ran the gamut from kite surfing in his hometown of Santa Cruz, California, to multipitch alpine rock climbing in the high Sierra Nevada. The trio might have been far from their stomping grounds, but they felt right at home in the wild environment of the Hindu Kush. Quickly and silently, Ronin flowed down the north ridge.

Soon they reached an open area, surrounded on all sides by high ground—a perfect setting for an ambush. They had no choice, however, but to cross through it; they needed to keep visual contact with Echo-3. Roy scanned the area repeatedly with his spotting scope, but could find nothing. "Stay low," Eggers reminded his teammates. "I got a bad feeling about this." He moved out in front of the team, "on point," with Pigman behind him and Roy acting as "tail-end Charlie," in the rear. Sweating from the noontime heat, each of the snipers sensed every crunch of their feet on the dirt and every whisk past a shrub's branch loudly echoing in their heads as they moved through low vegetation in the steep bowl.

They reached the bottom of the bowl quickly, crouching through the waist-high vegetation and maintaining solid dispersion from one another. Without breaking their gait, the three began to course up the rise in front of them—toward the safety of the forest above. Then, out of the breezy, thin air, they heard a *brrrrrrrrrrrrrr!* The first shots of the ambush rang out. The hillsides to their left and right exploded in machine-gun and RPG fire. Pigman, turning to his left, flung his M16 into firing position, threw the selector onto burst, and plugged three shots downrange—then saw nothing but sky and some distant clouds as his leg buckled under the weight of his pack and he fell backward. A PK light machine-gun round had driven into his left knee, shattering his lower femur before lodging under his kneecap. Rounds cracked over his head, but he continued to fire. He dropped his pack, then felt a round impact his left gut, and rolled over and continued to fire, his knee locked in an L-shape as he struggled to keep putting rounds accurately downrange. Moments later, three more rounds impacted his chest, directly on his SAPI plate holder, throwing him into the dirt. Instinctively following the scout/sniper standard operating procedure under such an attack, the corpsman began to "bound back," moving toward Roy.

"Roy!" he yelled as the intense gunfire ramped up in fervor. "ROY!" Pigman had been hit at least seven times. RPGs burst around him as he clawed his way through the low bushes. The gunfire ceased for a moment, allowing the corpsman to grab a pressure dressing and wrap it tightly around his leg above the wound. Intense pain shot throughout his body—but he was still alive. *Keep moving, keep firing!* he thought.

"Motherfuckers!" *Crack! Crack! Crack!* Joe Roy loosed three-shot bursts at the well-covered positions of Shah's men, revealed only by bright yellow muzzle flashes, about four hundred meters to either side of him. *Thud! Thud!* Two rounds knocked Roy face-first to the ground. "Shit! You motherfuckers!" The bullets struck his rucksack, but not Roy himself. He sprang to his knees, thrown off balance by his heavy pack— which he dumped onto the ground, freeing him to move faster. *Crack! Crack! Crack!* He continued to fire at multiple targets. *Thud!* Another round hit him, hurling him into the dirt. The bullet impacted him squarely on his rear SAPI plate, the shot feeling as if someone had landed a hard-swung sledgehammer between his shoulder blades. Steadily moving back up the hill, Roy repositioned himself to fire and calmly sent yet more volleys of well-placed rounds into the attackers' positions, alternating targets on his left and right as he tried to maintain suppression of the enemy. But the rate of fire from the attackers, whom Roy figured to be between eight- and twelve-men strong, became overwhelming, saturating the air and ground around him. After low-crawling over thirty meters as he inhaled dirt kicked up by rounds impacting just inches from his head, Roy lurched to his knees again. *Crack! Crack! Crack!* He shot repeated volleys, each burst skillfully aligned on an enemy position, emptying magazine after magazine. *Crack! Crack! Crack!* Then, after another low-crawl, he rose up, shooting, and *thud!* Another of the rounds whizzing through the air struck his rear SAPI—again hurling him face-first into the dirt. *This is gettin' old,* he thought. *Where's Pigman and Eggers?*

Below the snipers, near Chichal, the Marines of Echo-3 could hear every burst of the firefight. Guyton immediately grabbed a PRC-117 radio, and accompanied by his strongest Marines, began a sprint up the steep slope. Hearing the overwhelming volume of PK and AK fire, punctuated by the distinctively bloodcurdling sound of launched RPGs, the Echo-3 Marines assumed the three-man team had been killed. Then, out of the cacophony of enemy 7.62 mm weapons, came the *crack! crack! crack!* of the Snipers' 5.56 mm bursts. The Marines, holding firm below, began to cheer.

"Roy!" Pigman yelled again.

"Pigman!" Roy called back, now in range of each other. "You all right?"

"Forget about me. I'm good enough to yell. Where's Eggers?"

"Shit, I thought he was with you . . . EGGERS!" Roy roared into the cruel air during a brief lull in the firefight. "EGGERS!"

"Shit, man. I think he might be dead," Pigman stated in a horrified tone. "He better not be dead. EGGERS!"

But Eggers wasn't dead. He wasn't even hit. After returning fire and dumping his pack—standard operating procedure for scout/snipers under intense attack—the ever-calm sniper leader jumped on one of his radios and contacted First Lieutenant Roe Lemons, an artillery forward observer traveling with Echo-3, and put in an urgent request for both 120mm mortars and Doghouse's 105s. The strike would be danger-close, but given the odds against Ronin already, Eggers had no other choice.

"EGGERS!" both Roy and Pigman continued to call out as they low-crawled and plugged rounds into the enemy's positions. "EGGERS!"

As the two yelled, Shah's men, likely suspecting that their overwhelming ambush had at least injured the three, broke from their cover and moved toward Eggers. Flat on the dirt, his legs splayed out, holding his M4 in his right hand with his straight index finger just barely touching the side of the trigger—his arms and face pressed against the ground as he controlled his breathing in anticipation of at least one carefully placed shot—the sniper rolled his eyes up to see the silhouettes of three of Shah's men pass within fifteen feet of him. He could hear them speaking to one another, he could hear their footsteps, he could even hear their breathing. Timing his breaths—a steadying technique he'd mastered during precision shooting—he menacingly rose from his flat cover and lifted his M4's ACOG sight to his right eye, the only sound he made being the *click* of the selector as he rotated it from safe to semi. *Red arrow on the head—crack! Shift to the next. Crack! The next— more difficult, he's now turning. Crack!* Having loosed three closely aimed rounds—and revealed his location to the men in Shah's team— Eggers flipped the selector to burst. As he quickly built his situational awareness, gauging the possible locations of Pigman and Roy by the sounds of their weapons and identifying locations of the enemy as well, he unloaded three magazines' worth of 5.56 mm.

"EGGERS!" He heard Roy's voice. As he continued to send suppressive fire onto enemy positions—and while they continued to shoot back, but in a now far less organized and coordinated manner—the team leader rejoined Pigman and Roy, and the three of them continued to keep the enemy confused and suppressed with an evenly timed cadence of bursts.

"Thought you were dead—you're not even shot!" Pigman excitedly stated.

"I was busy calling in arty and mortars. That show will start any second now. We'd better find some good cover. Gonna be loud. Are you hit anywhere else besides your knee?"

"Man, I got hit all over the place—but only my knee is fucked up. I thought I took one in my abdomen, but my NVGs stopped the round. Had 'em in a bag hanging off my gear harness. Roy got hit twice in the rear SAPI."

"You want morphine?" Eggers asked. "You look like you're in some serious pain."

"Hell no," Pigman responded. "They're probably regrouping, gonna come back and attack us again. I wanna be absolutely coherent if and when they do move on us, so I can pop 'em. I don't care how much pain I'm in."

"Yeah, they sure are gonna come and get us," Eggers agreed. *Crack! Crack! Crack!* He tore through another few bursts. Then his mind flashed to the Luttrell after-action report, and the Shah videos of the SEAL recon ambush, showing all the gear the enemy had pillaged. "They're gonna go for our packs!" Eggers paused for a second, then gazed at Pigman. "You don't have an IV, do you?" The wounded corpsman just stared blankly at him. The team leader, knowing that the corpsman could soon slip into shock, turned and sprinted back into the "kill box" below them.

"Where the fuck did he go?" asked Roy. Moments later, Eggers bounded through the scrub, Pigman's ruck—stuffed with vital medical supplies, including IVs—slung on his back. Ronin's leader, still fixated on the enemy pilfering their gear, and panting from the sprint, turned, and weighed his actionable options before him. In an instant, Eggers mentally scanned the list of equipment in his and Roy's packs. At the top of that list sat his M40A3 bolt-action sniper rifle, custom-made in Quantico, Virginia, at Marine Corps Headquarters.

Roaring, "I'm not going to let those fuckers get my rifle!" Eggers sprang forth, knowing that the 120s and 105s would be raining down any second, and raced to his pack, dispatching bursts of fire along the way. He dove atop his ruck, digging his fingers into its roughly textured nylon face, and lurched it onto his back. Then he reached for Roy's pack, which held the majority of the team's precision optics. On the move with two big packs—a total of over 150 pounds—Eggers sprinted back toward Pigman and Roy as he unleashed burst after burst from his M4.

"You're just in time. They've regrouped," Roy said. *Crack! Crack! Crack!* The three of them got into a covered position and continued to fend off their attackers, who now advanced on the three from just over four hundred meters.

"Yeah, I did get here just in time. Get your head DOWN!" Eggers responded after a few more bursts as a wavering hiss announced the first of a volley of football-size 120 mm mortars sailing over their heads. *Boom!* Trees splintered and rocks shattered as a mushroom cloud of earth clumped into the sky, knocking the wind out of the three members of Ronin with a pummeling concussive blast. Eggers radioed Lemons, who was on the hook with both the mortar team and Doghouse, and adjusted fires. The scout/sniper team leader told the mortar team to "walk" a swath of destruction along the north ridge throughout Shah's men's positions and along what he felt to be their most likely egress routes. Within a minute, Lemons had Doghouse cleared to fire, but he also had a problem: the members of Ronin that day sat at the very, very outer edge of the 105 mm howitzers' range; when rounds are fired onto such complex terrain, at a target over eight thousand feet above sea level, their trajectories, if off by just a few tens of meters horizontally, could result in a much-greater vertical offset, thereby sending the shells down onto Ronin's position.

Hearing the distinctive sound of an incoming artillery round, Eggers, Roy, and Pigman prepared for the explosion . . . but heard instead a deafening roar echoing throughout the mountains.

"What the"—*boom!*—"hell!" Roy wondered out loud. "Did someone just fire a rocket at us?" Then another round descended, it, too, followed by a thunderous roar and a huge explosion.

"That must be the *rocket assist* portion of the round's flight," Eggers said.

"Man, that's close," Roy began as yet more 105 mm RAP rounds impacted the north ridge, just a few hundred meters from Ronin's position, directly on target. Soon the barrage stopped . . . as did the enemy's ambush.

"Hopefully we got some of them, and then the 120s and 105s finished 'em off," Pigman observed.

"Well, we probably won't ever know. They're good about dragging off their dead, and we're in no position to go and do a battle damage assessment," Eggers replied. "Now we gotta get you out of here," the team leader continued. "Will you take some morphine *now*?"

"Hell no." The corpsman stubbornly held firm in his resolve. "It's still just three of us—and if they somehow survived that barrage, I wanna shoot as many as possible if they come back!" Pigman said as he grimaced in pain. "They almost had us like the SEALs—same number of guys, same positioning, everything!"

Eggers agreed—Shah's men had ambushed Ronin in virtually the same manner as they had attacked the NAVSOF recon team, using plunging, interlocking superior fires from extremely well-covered—virtually invisible—positions with eight to twelve men broken into a few positions.

Eggers radioed Captain Zach Rashman requesting a Dustoff extract. Then the sniper team waited. As Rashman worked furiously to coordinate the extract, which would require Echo-3's Marines to secure an LZ, Pigman slowly began to drift into shock from blood loss. Within an hour after the first shots of the ambush, Guyton and his Echo-3 Marines had sprinted up to the snipers. As they desperately searched for an LZ amid terrain that was inaccessible even for a nimble helicopter like a UH-60, the pilots and crew of two Dustoff Blackhawks raced into their craft at Jalalabad Airfield and spun up the birds' engines. Escorted by two Shock Apaches, the aviators could feel their helicopters struggling at altitude in the afternoon air; although they rocketed up the Pech River Valley at around seven thousand feet above sea level, the intense August afternoon heat pushed the density altitude much, much higher. And once they were close to the mountain itself, that heat would cause all types of convectional turbulence for the pilots.

The lead Dustoff, piloted by Army Chief Warrant Officer Rob Henninger, followed the Apaches up the Shuryek Valley, intending to arrive at the snipers' location by passing over the north ridge, a route the Apache pilots felt to be less of a threat than the Korangal Valley. Their ears popping from the altitude, the Dustoff pilots slowed their craft's forward progress as they quickly approached the high terrain of the upper Shuryek. Henninger, noticing that the four aircraft were literally boxed in by the valley, maneuvered his Blackhawk to allow the lead Apache a quick escape route should the Shock pilots run out of air on their climb over the ridge. With their Blackhawks at max climb and max power, and a wall of Hindu Kush dominating their forward view, the lead Apache radioed back, "We need to back off. We're not gonna make it over." The skilled pilots worked their craft to draw every ounce of lift power out of their engines and rotors. Henninger, looking to his left and right, however, quickly realized that they'd flown into such constricted terrain that to turn around they'd have to carve steep banks in the air, and as they approached the mountain, the amount of vertical airspace between the helicopters and Sawtalo Sar shrank. And since helicopters require increased power to maintain elevation during a bank— and the Blackhawks and Apaches already were running at maximum power—their only choice was to press on as the dark mountain drew ever larger and more menacing in their field of view. Turning with no more power to add literally meant falling from the sky, "knifing down" onto Sawtalo Sar.

Flying at only sixty-five knots of airspeed, and with about one thousand vertical feet to go to surmount the north ridge, Henninger heard the last sound he wanted to hear through his headset—a warning alarm, signaling him to check the bird's diagnostics. The helicopter's master caution light and his number-two engine "chip light" flickered on, meaning that sensors had detected metal chips in the turbofan's oil, which could possibly shut the engine down and send the Dustoff crashing onto the mountain below. Unable to turn, Henninger gazed at the lead Apache as it approached the crest of the north ridge—then disappeared. Buffeted by strong thermals spinning off the steep ground below, the aviators could make out details in individual branches of high cedar—virtually at their eyes' level. At the very crest of the north ridge, with less than fifty feet to spare, the Dustoff pilots pitched the noses of their Blackhawks up and they passed under Sawtalo Sar's summit, then torqued the craft down like a roller coaster, into the Korangal—regaining airspeed and visual on the Apaches.

Letting out a huge sigh of relief, Henninger could hear Rashman talking to the Apaches about the LZ. The Shocks had pushed ahead, in order to scout the area for any RPG-wielding bad guys. When Henninger approached the tiny, sloping landing zone, marked by a purple smoke grenade, he thought for sure that it would be a hoist mission, where they'd drop a litter on a winch. But closer still, he and the aircraft's crew dogs realized that they had just enough space to nestle the craft onto the ground. Henninger circled the craft and hovered high above the slope, with the helicopter's nose facing the Korangal Valley. Constantly monitoring the aircraft's systems, particularly that chip light, Henninger began the slow descent. As a group of Echo-3 Marines hauled Pigman on a tarp toward the inbound bird, the Dustoff crew poked their heads out the side doors of the Blackhawk and called out distances while Henninger—who'd never undertaken a closed-confines landing before—placed the tail of the craft between two small trees, just eight feet apart. With the bird's gear on the ground, the crew chief casually stepped onto Sawtalo Sar as the Marines, carrying Pigman, stormed toward the craft. But the helicopter barely sat on the ground—Henninger couldn't completely let off the collective, which controls the pitch of the rotor blades, as he had to keep the rotor tips from drooping and striking surrounding trees. With their heads hung low to avoid running into the rotors, the grunts loaded Pigman, now doped up on morphine, into the Dustoff. Roy, although not seriously injured, was also ordered to get on the medevac so that a doctor could check his back for any injuries.

With the crew chief signaling that all patients had been secured, Henninger expertly lifted the Blackhawk into the sky. As the dust cleared, Eggers could see Roy smiling at him, waving, as if to say, "Have fun on your hike down. I'll be eating ice cream at an air-conditioned hospital—thinkin' about you!"

12

STAR WARS

While the Marines of Echo and Golf companies continued to squeeze Shah's remaining forces into the upper recesses of the Narang, Shuryek, and Korangal valleys, Battalion Command sought to have Fox Company continue their march toward Objective-4 on the sixteenth. But with 19 August looming ever closer, Command realized that the Fox Marines wouldn't have enough time to egress before the deadline if they moved farther north. So, as of the morning of the sixteenth, Fox-3 and Middendorf's mortar team would stay put, and First Platoon and the Afghan National Army soldiers would travel back to Hill 2510. Then the call came ordering all of Fox-3 to begin their movement out of the Chowkay beginning on the morning of the seventeenth.

"Crisp," Konnie said to the staff sergeant. "I told everyone yesterday to 'shave away a new day' . . . yet I see some guys with stubble." The lieutenant was referencing his order that all the Marines in the platoon shave the day after the firefight. He'd learned about this from an instructor at Infantry Officers' Course who believed that the simple act of shaving could dramatically change one's outlook and boost his morale. "'Get those bristly faces nice and smooth,' I told them."

"Some of these grunts, you know, Lieutenant, they had hairy armpits when they were like eleven years old. Shit grows fast, even up here," Crisp responded. Both knew that, joking aside, the fresh supply of food, water, and ammo, not to mention some rest—and a clean shave—would go a long way toward lifting the spirits of the grunts.

"So we're not goin' any higher, huh?" Konnie asked Grissom, disappointed.

"As of now, no. We're headed back. Task Force Devil figures that what took us sixteen hours to climb up will take forty-eight hours to get out of," the captain explained.

"Sir, that's funny to me," Konnie began, wondering just how much of Shah's force remained. "I wish we could stay up here for weeks, sir, at least until we get every last of Ahmad Shah's little—now littler—army."

"I'm with you, Lieutenant. Really, I think we should set up a combat outpost right up here, permanently man the place. That's the only way to do it."

"Or just take care of 'em all right now—I mean, I guess we have less than, what, twenty-four hours to do it?"

"Well, yeah. If they attack again."

"Come and get some . . . *bitches*." Konnie stretched out his arms and wagged his hands, then slowly spun around and gazed up at all aspects of the high valley, as if he knew that one of Shah's men had him pegged within the reticle of a high-powered spotting scope.

As Fox-1 moved south that morning, the platoon's interpreters picked up ICOM chatter indicating that some of Shah's men had sighted them and were setting an ambush. As First Platoon surmounted Hill 2510, the radio traffic exploded in volume and intensity. Lieutenant Geise, preparing for a possible maelstrom similar to the one Fox-3 had endured, dispatched some Marines and Afghan soldiers to probe the area to the hill's south and had the bulk of the platoon assume a strong defensive posture. Shots rang out—signaling a possible massive onslaught—but then the valley fell silent. The ANA had detected a small band of Shah's men approaching them with AK-47s; the soldiers engaged—and the attackers turned tail and ran.

The activity throughout the Sawtalo Sar region following the attack on the fourteenth seemed to paint a picture of a fractured force—but as fractured as that picture may have been, it was brushed with strokes of ever-determined fighters. Back at Fox-3's patrol base, Pigeon worked with two A-10s, trying to utilize their targeting systems to scan the area around their encampment. But the infamously fickle weather of the Hindu Kush proved the undoing of that plan. Mushrooming cumulus dotted the skies above the Chowkay and other valleys on the sixteenth, granting only fleeting windows through which the Warthogs could glimpse the landscape during their day's mission, preventing them from providing Pigeon with much information.

Enemy indicators abounded, however, on the ground surrounding Fox-3. Peering through a spotting scope, Konnie noted a bizarre sight that afternoon. "Looks like we got a donkey train—goin' up that ridge to the east of us," he said to a lance corporal who was lying next to him. "But no donkey-train tenders. Those guys are loaded down, and on donkey autopilot." A line of the small, scrawny beasts, each about the size of a large German shepherd, weighed down with boxes slung over their backs with colorful rope, wandered up a trail on the shoulder of Cheshane Tupay. A few hours later, the "convoy" came galloping down, empty. ICOM traffic continued to increase through the sixteenth, but the most telling moments of enemy determination and presence came by foot. Two men, from the village of Jubagay, just to the east of the crest of Cheshane Tupay's south ridge, strolled to the outskirts of camp early in the afternoon.

"They are asking that the Marines just leave," Jimmy translated. "They say that there is no reason for you to be in the valley."

"Well, we got six reasons recovering at Bagram," Konnie immediately shot back. While Jubagay had been one of the villages to which Donnellan, Wood, and Rob Scott had wanted the Marines to venture during *Whalers,* the time limit wouldn't allow it. Not knowing the true nature of the village—and who actually lived there—the Marines sent the duo back. But they were replaced by yet another villager claiming to be from Jubagay a few hours later; this time, the village elder.

"Sir," Jimmy told Grissom, "the man wants to know who you are; where are you from."

"Just tell him that we're Marines from the United States. We're here to get rid of any of those who want to bring back the Taliban," the captain calmly answered, but he was suspicious of the man. The elder left, but long after his departure, Konnie and Grissom learned that he'd asked a number of other probing questions, very specific questions— and had gotten answers, not from any of the Marines, but from the interpreters.

"You told them *what*?!" Konnie exploded when he learned that the elder had inquired about the size of the force of Marines at the camp, how much food they had, how much ammunition, what types of supplies landed during the CDS drop, how the Marines had been positioned throughout the camp—and other important tactical details. "Well," the lieutenant concluded, "we can be sure that they know where we are, and what our capabilities are." The security breach emphasized the difficulty the Marines faced in Afghanistan. Their COIN campaign required that they work side by side with locals, in part to prove their intentions. But in a corner of the Hindu Kush as remote as the Chowkay, one where many of the locals had never even seen a Westerner, those locals could be easily co-opted by forces such as Shah's—and used, as had happened that afternoon, as spies. Jubagay represented an extreme example, as the battalion had no record of any coalition forces ever having visited the place, as one of the most remote in all of Afghanistan.

"We need to move our camp around—not by much—but displace everyone. You can bet that by now, Shah knows exactly where our command post is located," Konnie seethed. "He probably also knows the position of our machine guns and our perimeter defenses." Grissom agreed. Konnie made plans to offset the various positions of the platoon's elements, some by just a few tens of meters, others by a few hundred—Grissom's only requirement being that the command post be situated such that a radio operator could aim an antenna to get SAT-COM. Only the mortar team, which Middendorf and his Marines had emplaced and fire-capped within a small fortress of stout boulders, would stay put.

At dusk, cloaked by the darkness of the deep valley, Konstant told his Marines about the planned rearrangement, and he and Crisp helped to establish new positions for the grunts. With utmost stealth, and moving quickly, the Marines got the repositioning under way. Konnie located the command post—which he, Grissom, Pigeon, and Middendorf would occupy—about three hundred meters to the southwest of the old post, where Shah, Konnie figured, would have what was left of his men aim their weapons should they attack. With a CDS drop planned for early the next morning, after which Fox Company would begin their descent out of the Chowkay, Grissom, Konnie, and Middendorf all felt that half the Marines should sleep while the other half stood watch, once they'd completed the position shift.

"Sir, ICOM traffic!" Jimmy the interpreter interrupted the officers' discussion.

"Oh, great, Jimmy. More ICOM traffic. Let me guess, there's nine thousand of them, and they all got flamethrowers," Konnie sarcastically responded.

"Listen, Konstant, we need to take every transmission seriously," Grissom snapped. "What are you hearing, Jimmy?"

"There are two groups, and they are talking to each other. The man from the first group said, 'We are all in position, are you there yet?' And then a voice from the other group said, 'Yes, we are all here,' and then the first guy asked, 'How many men do you have?' And that man responded that he had forty," Jimmy summarized.

"Well, if we've heard that they're massing between forty and sixty guys to come get us, we've heard it a million times," Grissom responded. "But let's stand to anyway," the captain finished, ordering that all Marines stand security.

"And then, Commander Grissom . . ." Jimmy chimed in.

"What is it, Jimmy?"

"And then they said one more thing. The commander man said, 'Good, we're all set, do everything we talked about—but no more talking on the radio or on the phones.' And that was it, Commander Grissom. The ICOM talk went dead."

"Now that's somethin' we don't hear them do very often. Mouthy motherfuckers always tryin' to scare us with their ICOM chatter. They never give the order to shut up like that," Konnie interjected as Konstant, Middendorf, Grissom, and Pigeon stared at one another pensively, each revealing genuine concern over Jimmy's last bit of intel.

"Okay. Everybody stay sharp—as usual," Grissom ordered. "Sounds like somethin's imminent—real imminent, *like within minutes*." The officers spread the word for all the Marines to keep extra focused, on heightened readiness.

But minutes drifted into hours, and the attack never came. The grunts, scanning the surrounding peaks with their NVGs, found nothing even slightly out of place. No unusual lights, no sounds, nothing. With a big movement on the near horizon, and with the Marines slammed with fatigue from the past days, Grissom okayed the return to 50 percent security, allowing half of the grunts to get some much-needed sleep. Jimmy's translated message had caused just another false alarm; in the silence of the dark, cloud-raked night, Konnie, Middendorf, and Pigeon slipped into an almost comalike sleep—along with half of the other Marines of the element—for the first truly rejuvenating rest they'd had in days.

"Lieutenant! Lieutenant! LIEUTENANT!" Staff Sergeant Crisp roared, shaking Konnie, who was sleeping on the dirt wearing just a T-shirt, underwear, and his laced-up boots. "Lieutenant Konstant! How you sleepin' through this! How the fuck you sleepin' through this?!" Konnie woke up to Crisp slamming his shoulders against the dirt, the staff sergeant's face and Kevlar helmet flashing white, yellow, and red.

"Wha—" The disoriented Konstant opened his eyes, clutching at the dirt below him as the most coordinated, most intense of Shah's attacks yet pummeled the encampment.

"Man, get yo' crazy ass the fuck up—sir!"

Konstant awoke to the hisses of incoming RPGs, the earsplitting booms of exploding 82 mm mortars, and the greenish white streaks of PK machine-gun tracer rounds cracking and whizzing above Crisp's head. He grabbed his M16 and dashed for cover. *Boom!* A mortar connected with a large log next to which Konnie and Middendorf had been sleeping, obliterating it and blowing Pigeon and Dorf—both fully geared up—fifteen feet down the steep hillside.

The lieutenant clawed his way to the top of an embankment to get eyes on the attackers' positions. Rounds were pinging off rocks around him and punching into the dirt just feet in front of him; he could hear the distinctive fizzle of glowing tracer rounds' burning pyro—and smell the combusting material's stinging odor. The tracers converged on the camp from a semicircle of positions emplaced on the surrounding mountains, their streaks appearing like spokes on a wheel. Then the RPG storm began; from three different positions, over ten rocket-propelled grenades tore onto the old command post, the crude ballistic weapons seemingly in a competition with the raining mortars to completely obliterate the position. Had they not shifted locations just hours earlier, Grissom, Pigeon, Middendorf, and Konnie would undoubtedly have been killed. Completely pinned down, and with only the one magazine already in his M16's well, Konnie could only unload thirty rounds into the machine-gun position, and that machine-gun position was a long way off, far outside the max-effective range of his M16.

Middendorf, blown awake by the mortar blast just meters from him, immediately linked up with Grissom and Pigeon, and put a call to Corporal Daniel Shelton, his on-site "fire direction center," who would ensure that the targeting data the lieutenant passed to him got relayed accurately to the individual gun operators. Middendorf, however, relied on his PRR—Personal Role Radio—a standard two-way comm set used to communicate with others in close proximity—to speak with the gun team. But in the covered position that he, Grissom, and Pigeon had taken, Dorf couldn't get the required line of sight with Shelton's PRR. Having studied the terrain over the past day while he developed his fire-support plan—anticipating the most likely locations from which Shah's force would attack—Middendorf already knew the exact spot he needed to hit. He just had to give Shelton a four-digit number, referencing an already-plotted grid, and within seconds, the very worst of the incoming fire would cease—violently cease. But he couldn't establish comms with Shelton; so the tubes stood silent. As the seconds ticked away, the barrage grew even worse, with mortar rounds now "walking" onto the new command post's position and RPGs crashing down throughout the grunts' camp. As Pigeon worked furiously to get air on station, Dorf repeated in his head that the only way to avert certain disaster was to get mortar rounds downrange. "I'm leaving," the lieutenant said as he slapped Grissom on his rear SAPI.

"Are you fucking crazy?" the captain shot back. Rounds peppered the dirt around their covered position; the Marines choked on a low-hanging fog of dust and vapor from detonated explosives and burned cordite. The RPGs and machine-gun fire kept coming—and coming, ever more accurate. The professionalism of the attackers struck Middendorf; he couldn't believe they could hit their marks from such distances. He had to get his mortars on target. The lieutenant jumped over the small berm before him and sprinted up the terrain. "What the fuck, Middendorf? You're gonna get yourself KILLED!" Grissom howled.

"You, too? You crazy, too, like Lieutenant Konstant?" Crisp shouted as he unleashed bursts from his M16. "You been drinkin' out of the same—the same *whateva-tha-fuck*—water hole as Konstant!"

Married since 2002—and looking to have kids so that maybe one day he too could talk his son into joining the Marine Corps after graduating West Point—Middendorf thought of his wife and then said goodbye forever to her in his head as he tore a path toward Shelton under the press of copper-jacketed lead hurling through the Afghan night at supersonic speeds, shock waves slapping his eardrums with loud *cracks! Eyes on,* he thought, after seventy-five meters, *eyes on the tubes,* then dove flat onto the ground and pressed the microphone to his dirt-encrusted mouth. "Corporal Shelton!"

"Copy!" came Shelton's response.

"Fire Alpha Oscar 3303! Fire Alpha Oscar 3303!" The lieutenant commanded his Marines to unleash what he'd planned to be a crushing barrage from all tubes simultaneously at the target, three times total.

"Roger." Each of the four gun teams adjusted the elevation and deflection of their mortar tube, snapped a C-shaped charge onto the neck of a round just above its fins, then dropped it into the tube. *Thunk-thunk-thunk-thunk* followed by a stentorian *crack! crack! crack! crack!* Four 81 mm mortar rounds accelerated away from the team's position at hundreds of meters per second, hurling in unison toward their apogees, then sailed down toward the same mark. But before the parabolic arcs of those first rounds had crested, the team had four more en route—then four more after that. *Whump whump whump whump!* Seconds later, Alpha Oscar 3303 erupted in a mass of concussive fireballs, the mortars completely laying waste to the enemy position.

But more of those positions remained, and the mortar team's barrage left them with just seven 81 mm rounds. Not knowing if Pigeon had aircraft inbound—and conscious of the necessity of deconflicting his mortar fire with flight paths—Middendorf again tore across the open field of fire to get line of sight with Grissom and Pigeon. A quick back-and-forth revealed that airpower hadn't yet arrived. But then another of Shah's positions opened up—more mortars, RPGs, and machine-gun fire rained down, loosed by roughly fifteen extremists. Middendorf dove back toward his team. But the new enemy position wasn't one on the list of the lieutenant's predesignated grids.

Unknown to Middendorf, Corporal Joshua Plunk, working in an uncovered position with rounds splitting through the air around him, already had the group of fifteen in the crosshairs of gun number four's sight. Carefully adjusting the deflection for a "direct lay" mortar attack by keeping the crosshairs squarely on the group as he leveled the gun, the corporal then grabbed the mortar team's "Vector" laser rangefinder. *1,775,* the red digital readout flashed after Plunk depressed a small button on the top of the precision optic. Plunk laughed at the irony of the range—the year the Marine Corps was born—and pulled out his "whiz wheel," a circular plastic "mechanical computer" used to determine gun elevation and round charge based on a target's range. As Shah's men belched out machine-gun and mortar fire from their position, Plunk grasped one of the team's last rounds and hung it over the flared mouth of the gun, then with a flick of his wrist, sank the mortar into the guts of the tube. *Crack!* Then he sank another. *Crack!* Seconds later, as Plunk pressed his head into the coarse ground to keep well below the enemy's low-flying rounds, his two mortars plowed into the mountain. *Whump! Whump!* The last of the tracers from the position fizzled into the night as Plunk's two rounds impacted dead on target.

With the mortar team's four-gun barrage and Plunk's direct lay onto the fifteen-man position, the Marines gained decisive control of the battle, shredding the two most concentrated of Shah's strongholds. With those machine guns pinning Konnie down now silenced, the lieutenant grabbed his flak, Kevlar helmet, and ten more magazines of rounds, and Pigeon continued to work to get close air support on station.

But still, some of Shah's men remained. At the Marines' most lonely position in the Chowkay that night, an observation post stood up on some high ground to the west of the main force, seven Marines—two snipers and members of the platoon's Second Squad, led by Corporal Chris Smith—had been on the receiving end of an intense barrage of machine-gun and RPG fire from a position just over two hundred meters away. Taking well-aimed shots at the attackers' muzzle flashes in the night, Lance Corporal Mark Perna heard so many rounds impacting throughout the small position—but without the enemy scoring any hits— that he likened the moment to running through a summer thunderstorm yet emerging completely dry. While the small group immediately returned fire, the enemy shot from stoutly dug-in positions, and their fire seemed to focus ever more tightly and intensely with each passing second. Just as Shah's force seemed to be on the cusp of achieving one victory in the night's battle—with screaming RPGs exploding around the seven Marines and machine-gun rounds peppering their hillside—Lance Corporal Ernest Padilla grabbed an AT4 rocket, loaded with an HEDP (High Explosive Dual Purpose) warhead, and steadied it on his shoulders, released its safety levers, and cocked its firing pin. As another volley of RPGs swooshed toward the Marines, Padilla shouted, "Is the backblast clear?" to make sure that none of the other Marines stood within the cone of superheated gasses about to roar out of the tail end of the launch tube.

"You're good!" a Marine yelled. Lining up the aiming sights on the bright flashes of enemy fire before him, Padilla squeezed the trigger. *Click—Boom!* Reddish-orange fireballs popped out of both ends of the launcher. Padilla tossed the spent tube as the warhead accelerated toward the insurgents—then struck their position, dead-on. The grunts continued firing, then the enemy fell completely silent.

"This is Fox-1, I think everyone in Fox-3 is dead—the entire platoon!" On Hill 2510, Geise pondered how he'd make the call to battalion higher as he watched the attack that night unfurl before his eyes. *There's no way they can survive that,* he thought. *It looks like a scene from* Star Wars, *with all those green and red tracers and exploding balls of yellow flame.* Then a small number of Shah's men attacked Hill 2510. Geise directed his Marines to return fire—and as happened a few hours earlier, the aggressors turned and ran. Fox-1 would continue to hold firm as *Star Wars* raged on.

"Come on, Konnie, now's not the time," Middendorf began as he reached into his pocket and pulled out a pack of cigarettes, assuming that Konstant had run to his position—which was still taking sporadic fire—to bum a Marlboro.

"No. I'm not here for a smoke," Konnie responded as Dorf tried not to laugh at him. Konstant was wearing just his flak, Kevlar helmet, boots, and underwear—no pants. "Pigeon needs us to work up targeting grids. He's got air on the way. But they need ten-digit grids for a JDAM drop."

"What's with your hand, Konnie?" Middendorf asked. Blood, from a shrapnel gash, was oozing from the top of Konstant's right hand. "Guess your luck ran out tonight." Middendorf laughed.

Konnie looked at his watch—a minute past midnight on the seventeenth of August. "Hey, I just realized that it's my birthday. I just turned twenty-four this minute."

"What a birthday party you have here," Middendorf observed drily, then jumped into the job of finding targets for Pigeon. But a ten-digit grid, required for Pigeon to clear a JDAM GPS-guided bomb drop, was far too small a plot of land—one square meter—to resolve on Middendorf's map. He and Konnie, doing a quick map recon, determined the most likely routes of egress for whatever of Shah's force had survived. But the highest resolution Middendorf could discern was an area represented by an eight-digit grid (ten meters by ten meters). So he just added a zero to the northing and a zero to the easting, then passed the now-ten-digit grid to the FAC.

Cruising at over thirty-five thousand feet, a B-52H Stratofortress of the Air Force's Fifth Bomb Wing based out of Minot Air Base in North Dakota, tracked toward the Hindu Kush and the Chowkay Valley, packed with two-thousand-pound GBU-31 JDAMs. With the survivors of Shah's force now on the run, Pigeon worked up a final attack plan for the bomber, based on the grids identified by Middendorf and Konstant, as Grissom, Konnie, and Middendorf looked on.

"What's takin' so long, Pigeon?" Konnie asked.

"A B-52 doesn't turn on a dime, Lieutenant," the FAC shot back. "Not like those A-10s that can just fly around in tight circles all day long *inside* the valley." With direct comms established with the B-52, Pigeon began to pass a nine-line brief to the bomber. Their detailed instructions received, the pilots began to position their massive craft for the attack, taking them out of range of Pigeon's radio. Waiting for a read-back, a confirmation that the aircraft had received all information in the nine-line correctly, Pigeon, realizing that the B-52 couldn't hear his transmissions, jumped on SATCOM to Rob Scott. "Comms are down between me and the B-52," he told the XO. With the huge bomber carving a broad turn into its final attack heading, Rob, in yet another example of his acting as the glue to keep the battalion's operations moving forward, immediately contacted the Air Force's ASOC, or Air Support Operations Center, in Bagram, which contacted the B-52. With a tenuous connection established, Rashman once again stepped up to the plate—using Pigeon's coordinates, Zach got a read-back sent to Rob Scott and Ratkowiak and gave the cleared-hot call down the channel. As clouds began to roll in over the valley, the bomber released one GBU-31, its destination grid having been programmed into its guidance system by the bomber's crew. As the B-52 then turned off its attack run, Pigeon prepared to call in a second strike as the bomb's fins clacked back and forth, deflecting at computer-adjusted intervals, sending the huge munition inside an invisible cone of ingress with the tip of that trajectory field pricking the one-square-meter patch of earth Middendorf and Konnie reckoned to be where the last of Shah's men would most likely be grouping. Just over forty seconds after the B-52's crew released the bomb, night flashed to dawn and the JDAM erupted in a blinding fireball on the ridge to the north of the platoon.

"What about the second grid, Pigeon?" Konnie asked excitedly as Marines in the distance cheered at the billowing fireball, followed seconds later by the rumbling *whump!* of the distant impact. "Let's finish 'em off."

"I'm Rolexing TOTs, Konnie. With the comms the way they are, things are taking more time than normal," Pigeon explained to the lieutenant—in aviator lingo—that he had to push back the time on target for the second JDAM.

"Come on, Pigeon," Konnie goaded. "Smoke check—"

"Okay, Konstant. Shut the fuck up!" Grissom began. "And why don't you go and put some fucking pants on, Lieutenant. You look absolutely ridiculous standing there. A real model officer, aren't you? And what's with your hand?"

"RPG, sir. Hit by shrapnel," Konnie explained as he exhaled a long banner of cigarette smoke.

"Great. We were *almost* able to say that we got in that huge contact with the enemy and got out of it completely unscathed. But you had to go and get hit by RPG shrapnel—the only one of all the Marines out here tonight to get injured."

"But it's my birthday, Captain," Konnie said, oozing sarcasm, before leaving to don his proper uniform.

"Cleared-hot," Rashman called, working with Pigeon, the pilots, Rob Scott, and the ASOC after he received the read-back.

"Roger, bomb on target within the minute," Rob Scott passed to Pigeon. After the night's second "rumbling sunrise," this time over a ridge to the northeast of the camp, the valley fell silent.

"Think we got 'em all, sir?" Konnie asked Grissom.

"We'll know soon enough."

13

KINETIC EXFIL

Up to sixty enemy killed in action over the past three days out of a force of eighty to one hundred—BREAK—enemy command and control now virtually nonexistent—BREAK—" Kelly Grissom earnestly listened to Rob Scott's intel dump early in the morning of 17 August, the XO's breaks giving him time to transcribe the information gleaned from numerous HUMINT and SIGINT sources. "Demeanor of survivors extremely hostile—BREAK—small bands of survivors staging to ambush coalition forces in both the Chowkay and Korangal valleys and possibly along the Jalalabad–Asadabad road—BREAK—these bands are possibly on suicide missions—BREAK—Ahmad Shah severely wounded—BREAK—possibly shot or possibly hit from shrapnel—BREAK—escaped to Pakistan and now seeking medical care." The second-to-last line in the transmission put a grin on Grissom's face. The insurgent leader, gravely wounded during the fighting, had been "medevaced" by way of his men carrying him on their backs and then on the backs of donkeys, down from Cheshane Tupay, out to the Kunar Valley on the ridges between the Chowkay and Narang Valleys at night—then stashed away in a car's trunk driven into the Peshawar region of Pakistan. 2/3 had crushed the force that had posed the greatest threat to the region's upcoming elections—the small army that had brought tragedy to the SEAL recon team and their rescuers, and caused untold chaos and destruction throughout the region.

But, as Rob Scott summarized that morning to Grissom, small pockets of Shah's paid force lived on, and sought to inflict as much destruction on 2/3 as possible—through ambushes, possibly suicidal in nature. Shah had ordered his remaining men to fight to the death in a sort of ad hoc jihad, to engage the Marines wherever they could as 2/3 egressed from the high valleys surrounding Sawtalo Sar.

Fox-3 prepared to break camp well before dusk on the seventeenth of August in anticipation of a final CDS resupply drop and a strong push to move back to Amrey village. Once at Amrey, Whiskey Company's Humvees would transport them to the mouth of the Chowkay, where they'd head back to their forward operating base at Mehtar Lam. Having gotten no sleep after the *Star Wars* firefight, the Marines just wanted to get moving that morning—the sooner they made headway down the valley, the sooner they'd finally get some sleep.

"Work your magic again, Pigeon," Konnie said as he heard the first wavering drone of an approaching C-130. "We can't be wasting time and energy chasing all over the place for off-target CDS drops."

Using the technique he'd devised a couple of days earlier, the FAC controlled the C-130 for the resupply drop just as he'd control an A-10 dropping a laser-guided bomb—*he'd* make the drop call, and instead of having all containers dropped at once, he'd have the Hercules crew make a number of runs, "clearing-hot" just one package during each pass. Once again, Konnie and the other Marines of Fox-3 stood in awe of the Hornet aviator's almost uncanny ability to integrate air platforms with the ground element—be those air-assets attack aircraft dropping deadly munitions on enemy targets or cargo birds delivering much-needed supplies to friendly positions.

But while their supply problem of just a few days prior had been scarcity, after the big parachuted containers swooshed into the drop zone that morning, the Fox-3 Marines realized that they'd been resupplied with enough food, water, and ammunition to last them another full week. And since speed ranked as the highest priority at that point in *Whalers,* portaging all those additional supplies would only serve to slow the already-beleaguered Marines, further exposing them to the few of Shah's determined men who remained. "We should just take what we need, and then have the engineers blow this stuff," Grissom thought out loud. But after conferring with the engineers, who told him that they didn't have enough demo to blow the overflow items to a point at which they'd be worthless to the enemy, the captain gave the command to spread-load the gear—days-upon-days' worth of food and machine-gun rounds.

But the mortar rounds would see a different fate. As Fox-3 worked to distribute the overload items, distant explosions rang out. Lieutenant Geise contacted Grissom: "Sir, they're trying to adjust fires to your position, but they're off by eight hundred meters!" Middendorf immediately had his team prep the gun tubes for a powerful barrage—using the excess mortars just delivered by the Hercules.

"Commander Grissom! Commander Grissom!" Jimmy the terp sprinted toward the captain. "They're shooting at us!"

"Thanks, Jimmy, but I don't need you to interpret explosions for me—just Pashto."

"No, sir. Yes—" the flustered Jimmy began. "I *know* that you can hear the *booms,* but I am hearing them talk about trying to find you, they can't see where we are at."

"Hold tight, Jimmy. We're in the process of taking care of these guys right now." Within minutes, Middendorf's four 81s stood as a canted phalanx, ready to unleash the just-delivered high-explosive rounds. With known enemy positions already plotted, Middendorf first had his gun teams send volleys at those targets farthest south, where the enemy could possibly get direct eyes on Fox-3's position.

"Sir," Jimmy interjected, grabbing Grissom's attention. "They are now saying that they see the explosions from the Americans—and that they are nowhere near where they are sitting!"

"Hit the northern targets, Dorf." Grissom passed to Middendorf what amounted to the enemy's own fire adjustments—on themselves. The gun team realigned their tubes and within seconds had rounds directly on target; Middendorf then ordered a fire for effect, catapulting rock, earth, and Shah's men skyward.

"What are they sayin' now, Jimmy?" Grissom asked with a sarcastic smile.

"Nothing—nothing at all, actually." Jimmy gave the captain a stunned look. After a few minutes, the terp finally had some news: "Sir, others are saying that you just killed all of them and destroyed their mortars. They're very mad at you and the Marines for this." Grissom laughed. "Now they really, really want to kill you all for this."

The captain just shook his head. With yet more of Shah's remnants obliterated, Middendorf had his team pack up the gun tubes and then the grunts pushed south, linking up with First Platoon and the Afghan soldiers at Hill 2510. Grissom now faced a tough decision: push south by heading into the depths of the valley—their route *up* the Chowkay—or take the more tactical, but more difficult-to-traverse route on the high ground of the western wall of the valley. Weighing expediency and ease of terrain against the remaining enemy's determination, Grissom had only one choice—run the high ground, despite it challenges. After a brief rest on the southern shoulder of Hill 2510, Fox-3, Fox-1, the mortar team, and the Afghan soldiers began the trek southward.

"You've been using ICOM scanners! Monitoring enemy transmissions! That's SIGINT! You're not authorized to do SIGINT work! We have specially trained teams for that. You need to have those scanners turned off—turned off right now!" came the voice from one of CJTF-76's senior intel officers at Bagram, roaring at Rob Scott for 2/3's use of ICOMs in adjusting fires on the morning of the seventeenth. "You'll be interfering with sensitive SIGINT work we already have under way!"

"Those ICOM scanners have saved countless lives at this point— just in *Whalers* alone," the XO responded.

"Turn those ICOMs off. Turn them off now!" the irate officer blared—as Jimmy continued to feed translated intercepted ICOM traffic to Grissom.

"Commander Grissom! More ICOM traffic." Jimmy grabbed the captain's attention once again that morning. "They're hurting bad, and still want to kill you—but they can't find you!" The ICOM use confirmed that taking the high ground had kept the Marines and Afghan soldiers out of the gunsights of the last of Shah's men. Jimmy's information also indicated to the captain that they might not have been detected because Shah—if he were even still alive—simply had so few remaining troops under him.

Back at JAF: "I'm not turning those ICOMs off. I'd be crazy to do that. They're saving lives as we speak! I don't care how it's seen by higher command—*anyone*—if we have something that's keeping our Marines functioning—keeping them safe and alive—they're gonna keep using it. Period." The line went dead. Rob Scott never heard another word from the intel officer.

As it had during their march up, the Chowkay's terrain proved to be a near killer—even more so on the Marines' egress, as they'd chosen a route that traversed ground that was severely lacking in trails and brought them along the edges of dangerously steep, often vertical rock faces. At times, their movement bordered on rock climbing. Sensing the hesitation of the Marines, Crisp continued to prove himself a moving orator in the heights, ensuring that the line of grunts progressed southward at an even clip. "Osama bin Laden himself gonna be out here soon and git yo' asses, y'all movin' so slow!"

With so many exhausted, battle-weary troops moving through such extreme terrain in the summer heat, the environment was destined to claim a victim. "Marine down!" one of the grunts yelled in the middle of the afternoon as a lance corporal slipped off a cliff edge and landed on his back after falling over thirty feet—his pack absorbing much of the force of the fall. With sharp jabbing pains in his spine, the Marine nevertheless continued to press on—but after an hour he couldn't take any more. A corpsman who took a look at his condition surmised that he'd probably fractured a vertebra. The Dustoffs once again jumped into action, pulling him off to Bagram, where doctors determined that indeed, he had broken his back.

The southward movement proved to be the most difficult yet for the Fox Marines during *Whalers*. By early in the evening on the seventeenth, exhaustion and heat-induced dehydration actually caused many of the grunts to begin hallucinating. Even the stalwart Crisp felt as if his feet were shredding and joints grinding during the push. And despite moving toward the opening of the Chowkay, the Marines didn't descend in altitude much as they pushed along the high ridge. By four o'clock in the morning of the eighteenth, as an AC-130 gunship orbited overhead scanning the area for enemy activity, the grunts bedded down for a few hours.

"We're never gonna make it outta here, man!" Konnie overheard one of his Marines breaking down as the column moved into a steep draw above Amrey village, their conduit between the high ridge they'd traversed and their extract point. "Nobody knows where we're goin'— no sleep in days—hot as hell itself, even at night!"

"We're making it out of here just fine. So shut the fuck up," Konnie said. "We know right where we're going."

"Roger . . . sir." In fact, during the brief rest early that morning, Grissom scouted ahead, locating a direct line into Amrey and the extract point—a very direct line. Often sliding down rock slabs and clinging to tree limbs as they choked on dust and the heat of the day, the grunts walked and skidded down a steep draw, funneling them into Amrey. But as their rate of descent picked up, so did the ICOM chatter. By the time they reached the extract point—just before noon—the ICOMs were blaring constantly with enemy voices trying to coordinate yet another attack. And when the grunts stepped off the steep slope of the rocky draw onto the level ground of the village, they couldn't find a soul: the town was deserted, an ominous sign.

"We made it," Grissom stated to Crisp and Konstant. "Whiskey's highbacks and hardbacks will be here shortly."

"We got a lot of awards to write up," Konnie remarked as he gazed at the completely spent grunts—too exhausted even to express relief. Out of water, they sliced off the tops of their water bottles and scooped water from muddy puddles left from recent rainfall, then collapsed against their backpacks. The sheer physical challenges posed by the Chowkay and the grip of combat would leave indelible marks on every one of them.

"We ain't out yet," Crisp remarked to the resting grunts. "Stay alert. Don't get yo' asses killed!"

"Sir." Jimmy approached Konnie. "Now they're saying that they want to organize the people of the villages below Amrey to fight you. They are going to a mosque in the lower valley to announce it to everyone."

"Great. Just what I wanted to hear, Jimmy."

Just then a convoy of Whiskey Company's Humvees rolled up to the village. Fox-3 and half of Middendorf's mortar team were loaded into five highbacks, with Whiskey's command element in the lead vehicle. As the sound of engines faded, Konnie and Grissom spotted two enemy, each with an AK-47 and one with an ICOM, on a ridgeline high above them. Both officers immediately fired, causing the two to flee. Regardless of their exhaustion, the brief encounter reminded all the Marines to stay alert. As that first convoy rolled out of the village, every one of the grunts kept his eyes on the ridges above and surrounding them, and their weapons at the ready. A small caravan of Toyota Hiluxes had also arrived, and carted away the Afghan soldiers, leaving just Fox-1, with Pigeon, Middendorf, and Grissom, whom Whiskey would pick up on their next turn. High above the Chowkay, two A-10s arrived and checked in with Pigeon. Also showing up for the extract, an RQ-1 Predator UAV—rare in that area of operation—buzzed above the grunts with feed beamed via satellite to a host of commands, including CENTCOM, Task Force Devil, CJTF-76, and the JAF COC, where Rob Scott watched "from above" as the Marines coursed down the steep road to lower ground.

Riding in the first highback directly behind the lead vehicle in the convoy, Konnie kept a sharp eye out for activity on the ridgelines as Amrey disappeared behind a bend in the road. But while the Marines had been descending to the village, some of Shah's last surviving men had worked to collect a handful of local men in the lower Chowkay, non-fighters to whom the militants gave AK-47s and instructed them to shoot at the infidel outsiders; their intention was to inflict whatever damage they could in a final act of desperation. Staring at the black-and-white "pred feed" flickering before him, Rob Scott noticed movement about one hundred meters from the opposite side of a blind turn the convoy was about to round. "Guy's got an RPG!" the XO yelled at the sight of one of the enemy preparing to strike at the convoy. Rob furiously tried to raise the convoy—but the lead vehicle's radio had gone down. The XO, completely helpless to stop what he was sure would turn into a bloodbath, stared in horror as the terrorist rose from behind a rock and aimed the launcher in the direction of the blind turn.

The fighter tracked the lead Humvee as it rounded the bend, preparing to shoot, but then the next Humvee, the highback carrying Konnie, Crisp, and eight other Fox-3 Marines, emerged, presenting a much bigger target. *Put-sheeew!* "MISS, YOU BASTARD!" the XO roared at the video screen. By the time the Marines in the highback heard the echoing boom of the launch, the high-explosive round—capable of penetrating almost a foot of solid steel armor with a stream of molten metal—had self-armed and was just a few tens of meters from the hardback. Konnie saw the round just before it hit his window—about eight inches from the lieutenant's helmet—his head spinning toward it out of surprise. Then the round connected with the plate glass with a deafening *clack!* Rob Scott lunged toward the screen—it had hit the Humvee dead-on. "It didn't go off. It didn't go off!" he uttered in relief as the dud round bounced off the truck into the mountainside. Now alerted to the opening of an ambush, the Marines in the highbacks immediately locked onto the shooter, as other attackers emerged from hides above the road, and put a barrage of rounds into him, instantly killing yet another of Shah's men.

The ensuing ambush sounded as if hundreds of fighters had opened up on the convoy at once, every burst of gunfire echoing repeatedly throughout the canyon walls. Only a few rounds actually impacted the highbacks of the convoy; however, one of them ricocheted off the vehicle's steel plate armor and chipped the tooth and tore the lip of one of the combat engineers, Lance Corporal Ken Boyd; in addition, a nearby RPG explosion sent shrapnel into the right shoulder of Sergeant Andres Torres, one of the scout/snipers. But the enemy, disorganized and inaccurate in their shooting skills, probably numbered no more than twenty, with actual members of Shah's cell manning the RPGs. One of the latter had already been taken out, and another, quickly spotted by an A-10 pilot working with Pigeon, saw his career as a terrorist end in a blaze of high-explosive 30 mm rounds at the top of a nearby ridge. But before he'd taken his last breaths, his RPG knocked out a narrow, precariously built-up portion of the Amrey Road, thereby effectively sealing off Grissom, Pigeon, Middendorf, and the Marines of Fox-1 from Humvee extract.

As the voice of one of Shah's men boomed from a nearby mosque, attempting to incite the locals to take up arms against the Marines—and as Shah lay in a dirty, makeshift "hospital" somewhere outside of Peshawar, the once up-and-coming 'Taliban commander' not even able to stand on his own feet—the convoy carrying Fox-3 emerged from the Chowkay Valley into the Kunar Valley, occasionally taking sporadic AK-47 fire along the way, to which the Marines immediately replied with a tsunami of M240 as well as M16 and SAW bursts. Meanwhile, back at Amrey, Grissom, Pigeon, Middendorf, and Fox-1 awaited their convoy. But learning of the destroyed road—impassable to Humvees—and hearing an increasing volume of ICOM chatter, the four reasoned that they should just stack their nonessential gear on the side of the road, throw thermite incendiary grenades on the pile, then sprint to the awaiting Humvees at the RPG-created roadblock—a recourse to be taken only in the most dire of situations. As they pondered their options, though, a Toyota Hilux, stuffed with fifteen men, suddenly rounded the corner before them. Reasoning that they were locals the last of Shah's men had incited to attack the Marines, Grissom fired a warning shot their way. They immediately turned tail and ran—

prompting a torrid rage of ICOM chatter, the new on-site "commander" furious that the locals didn't proceed with an attack on the infidels.

Isolated by a long stretch of roadway and out of food and water, the Marines realized that their only option was to hightail it down the road—for five kilometers—and meet up with Whiskey Company's second convoy when they arrived. The situation seemed so dire, with ICOM chatter indicating that the enemy was massing, that at one point they considered resorting to hand-to-hand combat. Then four Hiluxes appeared from down valley, speeding toward the Marines.

"Another attack?" Geise wondered aloud.

"They're empty—just drivers," Middendorf responded.

"Suicide car bombs?" Grissom speculated as he raised his M16 and prepared to fire.

Suddenly the lead Hilux stopped, its driver hopping onto the dirt of the road, holding a piece of paper in his upraised arms. Middendorf approached the fearful man—he clearly felt the gravity of the situation—then grabbed the paper. On it was written: *Sir, you can use these to carry your gear as you walk out, signed—Todd Lohstreter.* The battalion's assistant logistics officer had saved the day.

"Forget using them to carry our gear while we walk—they'll carry our gear and us, and get us out of here." The Marines piled into the trucks—completely overloading them, with some grunts clinging to the vehicles' bumpers as others, including Middendorf, locked arms with the hangers-on to keep them from flying off—which then began to move. But the second vehicle, with Lieutenant Geise in the front passenger seat, slowed to a crawl, as the driver worried about damaging the truck's suspension.

"Tell him to fuckin' haul ass, Geise!" Middendorf barked over the radio.

"He won't move!"

"Then *you* drive. Or better yet, make him think that you're gonna shoot him if he doesn't drive." Geise, pointing to the upper ridges, mimicked an explosion with his hands, took a deep breath, and roared, "VROOOM!" Then he pointed to the gas pedal and slapped the side of his M16. The driver got the message and gunned the accelerator, racing down the road. After slowly navigating the very narrow strip of the road that remained after the RPG hit, the Hiluxes delivered the grunts and their gear to Whiskey's awaiting Humvees. With every last Marine on the second convoy very well aware of the attack on the first caravan that left the Chowkay that day, they readied their weapons for an intense firefight—when a couple of shots rang out. As Whiskey's Humvees navigated the sinuous road, an overwhelming return volley slammed into the bare ridge from where the enemy shots had split into the air. There were a few more potshots from above, then the enemy's barrels went cold. It looked like Shah's belatedly enlisted soldiers just didn't have the conviction, or the hate, to carry on the fight against the Marines.

The entire company consolidated in the village of Chowkay on the shores of the Kunar River, just outside of the valley's opening. By nightfall, they were en route back to JAF in large 7-Tons. So utterly drained from the previous days' intense travails, most nodded off, even if for just seconds at a time—a rare minute's worth of actual sleep seeming like a full night along the bumpy, rutted road. Soon, however, the jolts and jars of the dirt road gave way to the smooth hum of asphalt, and the convoy was motoring onto the Jalalabad Bridge, crossing the Kunar River when . . . *put-sheeew!* The hiss of an incoming RPG round shocked the grunts awake. The night lit up above them with the grenade's explosion, sending shrapnel into the large troop carrier. Crisp, his hand hit with burning metal, stood up—to have a PK machine-gun round drive into the side of his helmet, throwing him onto the floor of the 7-Ton. The Marines once again returned fire—at a small house from which the small attack had burst forth—silencing what would be the very last of their aggressors during *Whalers*.

His "bell rung" from taking a round that missed punching through his Kevlar and instantly killing him by only an inch, Crisp wiped the blood from his right hand, and asked, "Anybody hit . . . besides me?" Staff Sergeant Kevin Walker had also been mildly injured on his hand by flying shrapnel. "You, too, Boyd?" Crisp glared at Lance Corporal Boyd, already hit once in the mouth by a bullet earlier in the day. "Where'd they get you this time?"

"My mouth," Boyd responded.

"No. I said where'd you get hit *this* time. Your ass already got shot in the mouth earlier."

"My *mouth*," Boyd replied.

Crisp leaned into the lance corporal—and started laughing hysterically at the sight of the lance corporal's bleeding lips. "Man, they shot you twice in the mouth in the same day!" Boyd laughed along with the staff sergeant—at a wound that would heal with little if any scarring. "I tell you what, probably did your ass some good. You kinda ugly anyway, so you should be happy you had your face rearranged!" Crisp joked.

Earlier in the day, however, in the Korangal Valley, the remnants of Shah's cell inflicted a harsh and unforgettable blow to the battalion. In the afternoon hours of the eighteenth, as Echo Company's Second Platoon pushed out of the Korangal, a group of the cell's men covertly set up positions above a transect of the valley about two kilometers south of its juncture with the Pech. Corporal Salvatore Cirencione, a fire-team leader in the platoon's Third Squad, felt an ominous chill run down his spine as he spotted two young girls playing in the middle of the dirt road—completely by themselves; he couldn't see anyone else. Then he noticed a freshly stacked pile of rocks on the side of the dirt road, and thought he eyed another about twenty-five meters in front of him . . .

Justin Bradley, who was at an overwatch position with Echo-1's First Squad on the steep terrain above the mouth of the Korangal, kept a close eye on the slopes looming over that spot, figuring that if an ambush were to occur, it would go down at dusk, when the combination of still-bright sky and shadowed valley gave the enemy the advantage of confusing lighting, a common tactic in the region. But Shah's men, spotting Echo-2 passing directly beneath them from their perches about two kilometers to the south of Bradley and First Squad, didn't wait for dusk. The breezy afternoon was shattered by the roar of the most intense ambush Bradley had ever heard just as Cirencione locked his eyes onto the second set of stacked rocks—they were ambush marks. At the focus of the ambush, twenty-two-year-old Lance Corporal Phillip George, from Pasadena, Texas, also a fire-team leader in the platoon's Third Squad, immediately locked onto the points of origin of the fire—detecting the puffs of dust kicked up by muzzle blasts. Sending rounds directly back at the attackers, George immediately got his fire team's eyes on the attackers' positions from the side of the dirt road. Second Platoon's 240 gunners, SAW gunners, and M16-laden riflemen immediately began laying down suppressive and point-target fire onto Shah's men, perched hundreds of feet above them in the steep chasm.

"George is hit! George is hit!" a Marine shouted. In the heat of the ambush, George disappeared from the side of the road, having been thrown five feet to a field below by the shattering impact of a PK round. But the fire grew so intense that none of the Marines near him could jump to his aid. Cirencione, however, hearing that his close friend—they'd known each other since George checked into the battalion two years prior—had been hit, tore through the field of fire to find the lance corporal. As he sprinted toward George's last known position, he fired his M16 at the attackers above—but he could find no sign of George anywhere.

"Bradley!" Kinser called. "Can you see the point of origin of the fire?" The lieutenant was located at the village of Kandagal, directly below the finger of rock on which Bradley and First Squad stood.

"No, sir, I can't. Too far into the valley. But I can see our guys' tracers tracking to a number of points on the east side of the valley," Bradley replied.

"Bradley. Listen," Kinser replied sharply—even more sharply than usual. "The next thing I want to hear out of you is a fire mission for these 120 tubes."

"Roger." The corporal and Corporal Burgos dove into studying their map of the valley, deriving a grid for an initial volley within a minute. Two deafening *cracks!* echoed throughout the area as the rounds sped toward their targets. *Whump! Whump!* The corporal could feel the reverberations of the explosions in his chest—and could see that the first salvo had missed the target by about a hundred meters. After readjusting, the two tubes once again explosively hurled rounds toward the attackers, and this time they hit dead-on. The ambush ceased, the fighters turning their attention from assailing the Marines to saving their asses—they grabbed their weapons and began to egress. "Fire for effect," Bradley transmitted.

Over the next few minutes, the two 120 tubes hurled another thirty rounds onto the ambush position. The gun team would have sent more, but two A-10s checked in on station, screaming into the depths of the valley, and quickly identified the fleeing attackers. With multiple cleared-hot calls by Rashman, the Warthogs finished off the last of the ambush team, flying so low at times that the grunts of Second Platoon could see details on the pilots' helmets as they roared through the Korangal. Meanwhile Cirencione, jumping down the side of the road where George had last been seen, found his friend. He and three corpsmen tried repeatedly to revive him, as Second Platoon commander, Lieutenant Chris Hagan, called for a Dustoff extract. But the lance corporal had died. *Whalers* drew to a close early in the morning hours of the nineteenth on an exhausted, somber note.

14

VICTORY POINT

With Shah's flight to Pakistan and the decimation of most of his small army, the battalion had crushed the extremist's force by the time *Whalers* drew to a close. Through detailed, thoughtful planning, well-coordinated integration of all assets availed to them by Task Force Devil—not to mention some classic USMC war-fighting improvisation, perseverance through fire, and some remarkable battlefield valor—2/3 had defeated a determined and vicious enemy intent on destroying a fledgling democratic government and reinstating a draconian tyranny. But while the victory was far from Pyrrhic, bringing Shah's cell to its knees had come at great cost. With injuries ranging from shrapnel wounds that would heal completely in a matter of weeks, to deep-tissue trauma that would haunt the injured for the rest of their lives, 2/3 proved unfailing in their commitment to mission. Of course, Phillip George, having sacrificed his life as he directed his fire team during the furious, last-ditch attacks of Shah's men, would never be forgotten by any in the battalion. His death, like that of Joyce just before the kickoff of *Red Wings*—as well as those of the NAVSOF recon team and the crew of the downed MH-47—illustrates the kind of selfless, indefatigable fidelity that is essential in effecting dramatic, broad-based change. In the case of Afghanistan in the summer of 2005, the magnitude of that change would reveal itself on the eighteenth of September, the day of Afghanistan's national parliamentary elections. Ahmad Shah had been silenced, but the battalion couldn't be sure that he wouldn't pounce again.

With some precincts throughout the Kunar, Nangarhar, and Laghman provinces reporting an incredible 100 percent voter turnout rate and the average for the region no less than 70 percent—without a single ballot box being compromised—the Second Battalion of the Third Marine Regiment, continuing the work of their sister battalion, 3/3, and those before them, realized a true moment of victory. Shah didn't strike; he couldn't strike. The Marines had quashed him and his operation.

Following the successful elections, 2/3 continued to build the region's security, maintaining a presence in the Korangal and other hot spots. Subsequent to 2/3's time in the area of operation, the First Battalion of the Third Marine Regiment would oversee the construction of the first permanent base in the Korangal Valley. The Chowkay, too, where Grissom had wanted to build an outpost, would eventually see the construction of a small base.

Shortly after the election, General Michael Hagee, the commandant of the Marine Corps, and Marine Corps Sergeant Major John Estrada, paid a visit to 2/3, venturing to the forward operating base at Mehtar Lam, where they pinned on nearly a dozen Purple Heart medals. The Commandant and Sergeant Major then journeyed to Asadabad and to Camp Blessing, where a grinning Joe Roy received his Purple Heart. Numerous members of 2/3 were also nominated for combat awards, including the Bronze and Silver Stars for their incredible bravery.

Once recovered, Shah again attempted to wield influence over the Kunar and Nangarhar provinces, but he was never able to reinvigorate his campaign to the status he achieved after the *Red Wings* ambush and

MH-47 shoot-down. Spending more time in Pakistan than in Afghanistan after his crushing defeat during *Whalers,* Ahmad Shah died the death not of a vaunted warrior, but of a petty criminal, at the age of thirty-eight, near Peshawar, Pakistan. He had attempted to raise money by kidnapping the son of a wealthy Afghan cement magnate, but the authorities interdicted him, killing him and one of his minions near the Afghan border on April 11, 2008.

But the real measure of victory for the Marines would be the continuing push for security and stabilization throughout the Kunar, Laghman, and Nangarhar provinces. While the Korangal would continue to be a vexing pocket of insurgent activity, the region in general saw a steady, rising tide of development. Roads are slowly being paved; even cellular telephone towers have migrated into the depths of the Pech. The Afghan government, with the help of coalition forces, continues to build schools, drill wells, and develop infrastructure throughout the populated sections of the Hindu Kush.

The first order of business in the process of nation building is the stamping out of violent insurgencies, effectively laying the groundwork for stability; schools and roads can't be built in an area where 82 mm mortars and 107 mm rockets rain down regularly. Ahmad Shah's group—even at its peak—represented not a broad-based resurgent movement but a sharply focused and ardently fired cancer, a threat not of metastasis but of stunting through localized necrosis. That is to say, Shah never really stood a chance of spreading his ideology throughout Afghanistan, but he could have handicapped the process of nation building through his destabilizing acts in the Kunar. To stop him, the Marines had had to go kinetic.

In the long run, though, "the key terrain was people and mind-sets," according to Rob Scott, not geographic features like valleys and ridgelines. Drawing on lessons hard-learned throughout United States Marine Corps history, not just referencing, but living the timeless *Small Wars Manual,* the battalion continued the USMC tradition of working and living with the local populace, training local fighters, always improvising, and of course, laying waste with combined-arms tactics and the legendary doggedness of the Marine Corps grunt in a hard kinetic fight. In the end, numbers of enemy killed didn't matter; stability and nation building did. Shah's group had stood in the way of 2/3's work to continue that progress. So they took him out, quickly and furiously—but their accomplishments went overlooked by world media.

The Marines of 2/3 began heading home from Afghanistan in December of 2005, their area of operation vastly different from when they arrived. Locals, hearing of the grunts' departure, arrived at the gates of forward operating bases, most notably, Camp Blessing, to wish tearful good-byes, a testament to the unquantifiable successes of the Marines during their tour.

Not long after their arrival back at K-Bay, 2/3 began preparing for yet another COIN campaign, this time in the Anbar province of Iraq. Although their minds were focused resolutely on the forthcoming, and very different, area of operation, none of the Marines would ever forget their time in the high, wild, austerely beautiful world of the Hindu Kush.

AFTERWORD

Inaccurate and incomplete media reports often leave important elements of any story missing in their attempt to influence an audience. The reports regarding Afghanistan in the summer of 2005 were implying weakness and incompetence about us, the troops on the ground. A tidal wave of unfortunate circumstances shook America's confidence in the mission overseas. The enemy's propaganda machine saw an opportunity and exploited it. We became portrayed as pathetic and, to a certain degree, doomed. We were said to be victims of policy, climate, heat, and terrain. It was implied that we were at the mercy of a better-prepared, more experienced, and hardened enemy. Some of our own media even seemed to buy into it, forgetting our strength.

My initial reluctance to cooperate with Ed Darack on this project stemmed from my own preconceptions about journalists. I learned quickly that I was wrong. A gentleman's agreement to compose a book focused largely on the actions of my Marines (the Marines of Fox

Company's Third Platoon) throughout a daunting combat operation evolved into an intense and thrilling narrative that never deviates from fact or reality.

No exaggeration is necessary when describing the actions of the Marines of Fox Company throughout Operation *Whalers*. We were uninterested in policy, we routinely beat the heat, overcame the terrain, and sought out the enemy in a place they never imagined we could, or would, ascend to. Inspired by our company commander, forward air controller, platoon sergeant, and the individual efforts of each of the forty-two Marines with Fox-3 on Operation *Whalers*, Third Platoon achieved feats that were almost unbelievable, and entirely unreported. The story runs deep, but best illustrates successes resulting from firm doctrinal approaches to basic warfare. From the genius plan developed at the battalion level through the execution at the company and platoon levels, *Victory Point* tells the tale of Marines performing in exceptional fashion regardless of their given assignment within the battalion, or the adversity they faced.

I'm lucky: the small scars from minor shrapnel wounds to my right hand remind me hourly of the bravery I witnessed from the time the fighting began on August 14, 2005, until it ended in the early morning hours of the nineteenth. I remember all of the selfless contributions my Marines made. I remember the Marines who were hurt, what their faces looked like, and their desire to keep fighting. I remember the immediate and heroic actions of so many even without direction. I remember an entire group of men working together, in the midst of total chaos, to try to save one another's lives, but to ensure the end to those of our enemy. I was proud beyond words as we confronted and pounded an army of insurgents riding a high that was a U.S. armed forces' worst nightmare.

It was refreshing to see the courage and resiliency, determination and initiative, it takes to win such a critical battle in such a major war. You will feel better about the military, about our inevitable victory over terror, and ultimately about America after reading this book. *Victory*

Point is going to remind you that there's an American man still alive and still strong, preserving the democracy we have enjoyed for the past 233 years. His name is the U.S. Marine . . . just in case you forgot.

Semper,
J. J. "Konnie" Konstant

ACKNOWLEDGMENTS

First off, everyone mentioned in the book—and their families and friends.

Justin "JD" Kinser, Stacy, Rick and Christy Crevier and family, the Kinser family, the Konstant family, Kevin Crowe (for the name *Victory Point*), my mother, Kelly Mackey, Scott Miller and the staff at Trident Media, Michelle Vega and Natalee Rosenstein and everyone at Penguin Group, Ellen Liebowitz, Kain "Chewy" Anderson, Doug "Oedi" Glover, everyone at MAWTS-1, Rob Dolan, Danny Ponzo, Gabe Garcia, Doug "2FS" Pasnik, Scott Pierce, Eric Sheline, Mitch Aschinger, Steve Morris, everyone at Bridgeport (MCMWTC), Bart "Pickle" Betik, Robb "Robb-T" MacDonald, Robb Etnyre, Colonel Durrant, Kelsey Smith, Doug and Kathy Stone, Bits—wherever you may be lounging in the dirt, Mike Martley, Ryan Hough, Matt "Shocker" Vought, Rick Scavetta, Michael Swanson, Kerry Knowles and everyone at the *Marine Corps Gazette*, Patrick Mooney, Kevin Digman, Jeff Lee, Joel Schwankl, Dave and

Barbara Arendts and family, Ryan Powell, Matt Sewell, Jill Henes, John Selengo, Ed Ross, Bill and Dorothy Ross, Karina Vesco, Joe Sullivan, Bill Winternitz, Amos Hollar, Cara Zucarelli, Nigel Allan, Richard Strand, Roger Ressmeyer, Ryan Palmer, Lisa Vasquez-Roper, Skip Jacobs, Shasta Jacobs, Bill Murray and everyone at Murray and Young, Linda Shiner, Mark Vogel, Pete Faeth, Robert Timberg and the staff at *Proceedings*, Jasmine Khan, Lynn Elsey, Brian Kelly, Jason Schmus, Tony Powers, Joe Miller, Graham Golden, Drew Reeder, Henry Christle, everyone at the 107th Weather Flight, the family of Michael Scholl, the family of Jeremy Sandvick-Monroe, the family of Terry Elliot, Alex VanSteen, Fred Wasser at Adorama, Tim Walker, Jason Walker, Matt Watt, TTECG, Jamie and Elizabeth Damm, Caroline Sheen, Steve Mraz, Christian Beckwith and Katie Ives and everyone at *Alpinist, Weatherwise* magazine, Ben Early, Jason Tarr, Greg McNamee, Maldo, Scott Kensiger, Tom Doyle, Kathy Joseph, Matt Connors, Steve and Melissa Coumo (and Toby), Tony "Tea" Baggs, Ricco "Guido" Scalise, "Smoke" and all of the Green Knights, the "Gunrunners" of HMLA-269, MAG-11 and Colonel Owens, Dustoffs of 45th Medical Company, VMA-231, VMA-211, HMH-362, VMGR-252, HMM-262, Mike "Sluggo" Farrell, Brian Bracken, Sergeant Major Cowart, Mike Beltran, Sergeant Major Patrick Wilkinson, the family of Max Galeai, Jason Matthews, everyone at the Printer in Davis, Scott Moss, Jeremy Dohl, Joshua Dart, Darrell Carver, Brett Rankin, Dave Moore, Keith Rollin, Noah Hunsacker, Scott Stephan— and everyone from the 2005 Summer MLC course, Sergeant Major Daniel Fierle, Rita Frangie, and Tiffany Estreicher.

PRIMARY
WEAPON
SYSTEMS

Primary Weapon Systems Relevant to Operation *Red Wings* and Operation *Whalers*:

GROUND WEAPONS

M16: The hallmark weapon of the US Marine infantryman, the M16 is a tried-and-true rifle that fires 5.56x45 mm magazine-fed ammunition. The iteration currently fielded by the USMC, the M-16A4, can operate either in semiautomatic or in three-shot burst mode. Each Marine of 2/3 typically carried ten to fifteen thirty-round magazines on combat patrols and large-scale operations in the Kunar, with more available through resupply drops. The modular rail system of the M-16A4 allows Marines to mount a variety of optical and aiming accessories, including the ACOG (Advanced Combat Optical Gunsight), combat flashlights, a variety of laser sight aids (both visible wavelength and infrared), and infrared floodlights.

Marine infantry must be masters of the M16, capable of field-stripping the weapon, cleaning it, repairing it, and most importantly, sending rounds downrange from its muzzle—on target—aiming with either optically enhanced or basic, iron sights. The M16 has a rated maximum effective range of 550 meters for a point target, but in reality, Marines have had confirmed kills (some using just iron sights), at much greater distances, some exceeding 1,000 meters.

An M16 configured with an attached **M203 40 mm Grenade Launcher** represents one of the deadliest weapons in the Marine Corps infantryman's arsenal. Mounted below the frame rail, forward of the magazine well, the launcher adds just three pounds, but can lob a 40 mm grenade as far as four hundred meters during a firefight. Not only can an M203 launch high-explosive rounds, it can send smoke grenades downrange, to "mark" a target for a close air support attack or an artillery or mortar-fire package.

M4 Carbine: "An M16 with a collapsible buttstock and a short barrel" probably best describes the M4. While over 80 percent of the M4's components can be interchanged with the M16, the weapon strongly distinguishes itself as a stand-alone platform because of its size and collapsible buttstock—allowing Marines to "dismount" from a Humvee (jump out of the vehicle) and engage the enemy in one fluid movement, whereas the larger M16 has proven to be cumbersome. Firing a 5.56×45 mm round (like the M16), some versions of the M4 can be operated in either semiautomatic single shot or fully automatic, or semi and three-shot burst, like the M16A4. Like the M16, the M4 can be fitted with a number of accessories, including the M203 40 mm grenade launcher, infrared floodlights, the ACOG, and others. 2/3 brought just a few M4s with them to Afghanistan, where they were issued to unit commanders and the sniper team. The SDVT team also used a version of the M4 known as the SOPMOD (Special Operations Peculiar Modification), which allows a highly customized upfitting of the weapon. Each SDVT member had his SOPMOD fitted with the M203 40 mm grenade launcher, a muzzle suppressor, an ACOG, and a suite of visualization/aiming aids.

M249 Light Machine Gun/Squad Automatic Weapon (SAW): A light-weight machine gun capable of firing up to 725 rounds of 5.56×45 mm belt-fed ammo per minute out to a maximum range of two and a quarter miles (accurately out to one thousand meters, or .6 miles), Marines use the SAW to lay down suppressive fire—keeping the enemies' heads low while other Marines lock their weapons' crosshairs onto specific targets. Marine SAW gunners typically carry one-hundred- or two-hundred-round belt-fed magazines, and can fire the M249 while moving, standing, knee-bracing, or from the prone position.

M240G Medium Machine Gun: Firing up to nine hundred rounds of heavy 7.62x51 mm belt-fed ammunition, the 240 is one of the Marine infantryman's most lethal tools. During 2/3's deployment to the Kunar province, Marine machine gunners used the G, or Golf model almost exclusively; later in the deployment, the battalion issued some gunners the B, or Bravo. Requiring brute force to haul up the side of a steep mountain, and then delicate finesse to fire accurately, once it is emplaced in a covered position, the 240 can lay waste to both enemy as well as many hardened structures behind which they hide. The Marines of 2/3 used the 240 both on foot mobile operations and mounted on the turrets of Humvees and 7-Tons.

M2 Machine Gun: Known as the "Ma Deuce," the M2 is a beast of a weapon, capable of sending up to 550 rounds of heavy .50-caliber (half-inch diameter, or 12.7 mm) rounds into the enemy per minute. The Marines in Afghanistan used the M2 as a fixed-perimeter defense weapon, as well as mounted on the turret of Humvees. With a maximum effective range of 1,830 meters (1.1 miles) and a maximum total range of 6,800 meters (4.2 miles), the M2 is both powerful and capable of accurately knocking out distant targets.

MK19 Grenade Launcher: Arguably the most destructive ground-based automatic-weapon system in the Marine Corps arsenal, the MK19 chews up targets at the rate of 350 per minute—not with standard rounds, but with 40 mm high-explosive grenades. With a maximum effective point-target range of 1,500 meters (nine-tenths of a mile), the weapon can reach out to just over 2,200 meters (1.3 miles). Since the rounds don't just penetrate, but explode, gunners don't have to hit the target directly, just be close—as with horseshoes and hand-lobbed grenades. While the casualty radius of each exploding round is classified, one can easily imagine what a burst of Mark-19 can do to a group of attackers. While effective, the M19 must be diligently maintained, more than any other automatic weapon, as the large linked rounds easily jam the MK19's inner workings. The MK19 is heavy and bulky, like the rounds it fires, restricting it to fixed positions or mounted to turrets of vehicles.

M9: Semiautomatic sidearm firing the 9x19 mm NATO standard round. Not very useful for the long-distance engagements typical in the mountains of Afghanistan due to the weapon's limited range and small round size. Marines were nevertheless required to pack it.

AT4 Rocket: A "fire and forget" antitank rocket; the Marines of 2/3 used the version of the AT4 preloaded with HEDP (High Explosive Dual Purpose) rounds for shots against fortified bunkers.

M40A3: Handcrafted by U.S. Marine Corps gunsmiths at Quantico, Virginia, the M40A3 combines extreme accuracy with extraordinary ruggedness. The M40 is a bolt-action rifle, firing a 7.62x51 mm round. In the hands of a Marine scout/sniper, working closely with his team, the maximum effective range of the weapon exceeds one thousand meters. A scout/sniper team may mount a wide variety of scopes to the M40A3 for various applications.

M82A3 SASR: The SASR, or Special Application Scoped Rifle, is a semiautomatic .50-caliber (12.7 mm) rifle capable of engaging targets up to 1,500 meters distant. While available to the snipers of 2/3 during Operation *Red Wings* and Operation *Whalers,* the SASR was not used;

the Marines utilize this weapon primarily for antivehicle missions. The SASR is considerably heavier than the M40A3, and not as reliably accurate.

M224 60 mm Lightweight Mortar: Referred to as "the 60," the M224 is a packable mortar tube with a maximum effective range of over two miles (3,490 meters) that while technically requiring a crew of three, can be fired by just one in a pinch (using the "direct lay" technique). Marines of 2/3 frequently employed these during combat operations, not only to hurl high-explosive rounds at enemy positions, but to turn night into day above enemies' heads with phosphorus illumination rounds.

M252 81 mm Medium Extended Range Mortar: Referred to as "the 81," the M252 is an extremely accurate—and extremely deadly—weapon, capable of firing up to thirty fifteen-pound rounds per minute out to a range of nearly three and a half miles (5,608 meters). While it is possible to carry the 81 throughout the mountains of the Kunar (in pieces), this mortar system was typically set up at established bases and not used by infantry on the move. Marines use the 81 to fire a variety of mortar types in addition to high explosive, including illumination rounds.

M120 120 mm Heavy Mortar: While not "organic" to Marine Corps units, 2/3 borrowed several 120s from the Army during their tour in the Kunar province. Capable of firing up to sixteen rounds per minute (for the first minute, four rounds per minute sustained) of massive, football-size, thirty-three-pound mortar rounds, the M120 can hit targets as close as 200 meters or as far as 7,200 (4.5 miles), and everything in between. Like the other mortars on the list, the M120 can fire a number of types of rounds.

M119 105 mm Lightweight Towed Howitzer: With the rated ability to lob a thirty-three-pound standard high-explosive round 14.5 kilometers (9 miles), and a Rocket Assisted Projectile (RAP) round 19 kilometers (11.8 miles), the two-gun battery operated by the Army at Asadabad could accurately support troops as far west as the upper Korangal Valley. In early October of 2005, months after the end of Operation *Whalers*, the Army moved the 105s west to Camp Blessing, replacing them with two of the much larger 155mm M198 at Asadabad. Marines of 2/3 called fire missions from the 105 battery, known as "Doghouse," for high-explosive rounds as well as illumination rounds in both *Red Wings* and *Whalers*.

HMMWV: The High Mobility Multipurpose Wheeled Vehicle, aka the Humvee, was used both to transport troops and for CAAT—an acronym for Combined Anti-Armor Team. Although the enemy didn't have any armored *anything* for the CAATs to engage, 2/3 utilized the concept for convoy escort and troop support. 2/3 configured each CAAT Humvee with either an MK19 automatic grenade launcher and an M240G medium machine gun, an M2 .50-caliber machine gun, or an **M220A3 TOW** (Tube Launched, Optically tracked, Wire-guided missile), an antitank weapon that can be used to destroy structures.

MTVR: Officially known as the Medium Tactical Vehicle Replacement; Marines know this vehicle as the 7-Ton (it replaced the 5-Ton, hence the word *replacement* in its official designation). Relatively fast, highly survivable (particularly to IEDs, because at its high clearance), off-road capable, powerful, and able to carry tons of cargo and troops, the 7-Ton was nonetheless limited to a few main routes throughout 2/3's area of operation because of the tortuous and narrow profiles of most secondary roads in the Kunar. 2/3's 7-Tons typically had an M240G mounted on their turret (above the cab of the truck), but Marines could mount MK19s as well as M2s, if the mission required.

AIRCRAFT

A-10 Thunderbolt II: Flown extensively in support of ground troops in Operation *Red Wings* and Operation *Whalers;* pilots of the A-10 (known to most by its nickname, the Warthog) relied primarily on the aircraft's devastatingly powerful GAU-8 30 mm rotary cannon for their close air support attacks. While the GAU-8, the business end of which juts out of the aircraft's nose like a blunt stinger, can fire a variety of projectiles, pilots shot high-explosive incendiary (HEI) rounds during *Red Wings* and *Whalers*. At 3,900 rounds per minute, even the standard one- to two-second burst put the equivalent of 65 to 130 grenade explosions into a tight swath. The A-10 also can carry a large assortment of rocket pods, air-to-ground guided missiles, and an assortment of unguided as well as precision bombs.

AC-130: The infamous Spectre/Spooky gunships of the Air Force Special Operations Squadrons aided Marines on the ground during *Red Wings* and *Whalers* both kinetically (with the onboard 105 mm howitzer and suite of high-speed rotary and Bofors guns) and with the platform's high-precision-imagery capabilities—helping troops locate enemy positions at night.

B-52: A massive, versatile platform, the B-52 Stratofortress delivered GPG-guided JDAM munitions for the Marines during Operation *Whalers*.

C-130 Hercules: Invaluable for providing resupply airdrops to troops on the ground; these drops nonetheless required incredibly detailed coordination to ensure that the cargo, dropped by parachute (called a CDS, or containerized delivery system), didn't land hundreds of meters (or more) distant from the intended target—which in the steep mountains of the Kunar can mean many more hundreds of meters of elevation troops needed to climb or descend to get to their needed supplies.

AH-64 Apache: Crewed by two Army aviators, the Apache gunship provided Marines of 2/3 invaluable close air support during both *Red Wings* and *Whalers*. With a 30 mm M230 cannon—aimed through a reticle mounted to a pilot's helmet—Apaches, controlled by Marine forward air controllers, laid waste to numerous enemy targets in the summer of 2005 in the Kunar. The Apache can be loaded with a wide variety of other weapons systems as well, including 70 mm (2.75 inch) unguided Hydra rockets (employed extensively during *Red Wings* and *Whalers*) and the Hellfire laser-guided missile.

UH-60 Blackhawk: One of the most versatile helicopters ever manufactured (the *U* denotes "Utility"), the Army Blackhawk served two roles during *Red Wings* and *Whalers:* troop transport and the all-important mission of Air Ambulance (with the **UH-60Q MEDEVAC** variant).

CH-47 Chinook: With one of the most recognizable profiles of all the world's helicopters, the twin-rotored Chinook was ideally suited for supporting troops in the mountains of the Kunar province with its powerful engines and thick rotor blades. While other helicopters reach their performance limitations well below the altitudes (as well as summer heat and hence density altitudes) required to fly throughout the Kunar, the Chinook handles such challenges easily—fully loaded.

MH-47 SOA Chinook: The Special Operations Aircraft (SOA) Chinook is a modified (hence the *M* designation) version of the conventional CH-47 designed for special operations applications. Modifications include: more powerful engines, larger fuel tanks, an in-flight refueling probe, enhanced night/adverse conditions imaging systems, armor, and weapons systems. The state-of-the-art night-vision capability of the MH-47, as well as other navigation and guidance systems, allow the Army Aviators (of the 160th SOAR[A]) to maneuver their craft in even the darkest of nights.

MQ-1 Predator: Capable of multihour loiters over an area of operation/area of interest while sending real-time video feed to 2/3's combat operations center, the Predator proved to be a vital link in the command-control-imaging chain, particularly during Operation *Whalers*. Predator imagery was also used extensively to plan both *Red Wings* and

Whalers, identifying possible targets, named areas of interest, and potential egress routes of enemy troops—as well as possible routes of attack for the Marines.

ENEMY WEAPON SYSTEMS

AK-47: The most prolifically manufactured gun in the world, the AK-47 saw production in a variety of countries including China and Pakistan (from where many of the AKs found in Afghanistan today originated). A gas-operated, magazine-fed weapon, the AK-47 (and its many variants) can be fired either on semiautomatic single shot or fully automatic. Although the AK's round (7.62×39 mm) is larger than that of the M16, its effective range is much shorter, and it is less reliably accurate.

SKS: A 7.62×39 mm semiautomatic carbine, originally made in the Soviet Union, but mass produced by other countries, including China and Pakistan. It is not as common as the AK-47.

SVD: The Dragunov Sniper Rifle was produced in the Soviet Union, China, and Iraq. A favorite of the well-trained Chechan snipers, this coveted 7.62×54 mm weapon is rare.

RPK: Best described as an AK-47 with a bipod, the RPK also has a longer muzzle than the AK-47, but fires the same type of ammunition (7.62×39 mm) and has an effective range of up to one thousand meters.

PK: The favored weapon of Ahmad Shah, the PK medium machine gun is a bipod-mounted, belt-fed machine gun that fires 7.62×54 mm rounds. The PK is relatively lightweight, and is fed through metal drums containing anywhere from 100 to 250 rounds.

RPG-7: Initially designed as an unguided, shoulder-launched, anti-tank weapon utilizing an armor-penetrating shaped charge; al-Qaeda fighters often use the RPG-7 as an integral part of a coordinated ambush with other weapons such as the PK and IED strikes. It has a maximum range of just over nine hundred meters, at which point, if it hasn't struck a target, the warhead will self-detonate.

PP87 82 mm Mortar: Used frequently in nighttime ambushes of Camp Blessing, this Chinese-made mortar tube can launch a projectile out to 4,660 meters (2.8 miles). Because it breaks down quickly into three pieces, Ahmad Shah's men used these mortar systems in both *Red Wings* and *Whalers*.

Type 63-2 107 mm Rocket: A North Korean– and Chinese-manufactured unguided rocket containing eighteen pounds of TNT, the Type 63-2 was designed to be launched in twelve-tube multiple-launch vehicles or on single-tube launchers. Throughout the Kunar, however, insurgents and terrorists would simply lean these up against rocks behind the crest of a ridge near the intended target, then launch them. Because the 63-2 utilizes an electric actuator, it could be set on timers, allowing insurgents time to egress back to their safe houses long before an attack began. Inaccurate, these were used as harassment and terror weapons, but nevertheless inflicted causalties.

IED: Most Marines consider the Improvised Explosive Device, or IED (frequently referred to as a "roadside bomb"), to be the most insidious of all weapons used by insurgents and terrorists. IEDs come in an infinite number of designs and types, from command-wire-triggered land mines, to massive radio-controlled "daisy chained" artillery shells (multiple artillery shells, each with a detonator, electrically interconnected to one another). While the Marines of 2/3 utilized a number of techniques to mitigate the threat of IEDs, they ultimately found that the most effective and enduring came from establishing relationships with locals, who would point the Marines in the direction of caches of materials used to make IEDs—as well as identifying those responsible for building, emplacing, and triggering them.

INTERVIEWEES

All are members of the 2nd Battalion of the 3rd Marine Regiment, unless otherwise noted

Allan, Nigel J.R. (Afghanistan Historical Expert)
Anes, Mario Corporal
Bambey, John 1st Lieutenant
Bartels, Matthew 1st Lieutenant
Bradley, Justin Corporal
Brown, Richard Lance Corporal
Burgos, Chris Corporal
Capuzzi, Peter Captain
Chizmadia, Jesse 1st Lieutenant
Cirencione, Salvatore Corporal
Cooling, Norman Lieutenant Colonel (Battalion Commander, 3/3)
Corcoral, Kyle 1st Lieutenant
Crisp III, Lee Staff Sergeant
Diss, Corey Lance Corporal
Donnellan, James Lieutenant Colonel
Eggers, Keith Sergeant

Fisher, Cody Corporal
Geise, Steward 1st Lieutenant
Grissom, Kelly Captain
Guyton, Nick 1st Lieutenant
Hagan, Christopher 1st Lieutenant
Kinser, Patrick 1st Lieutenant
Konstant, J.J. 1st Lieutenant
Lemons, Roe 1st Lieutenant
Long, Robert 1st Lieutenant
MacMannis, Andrew Lieutenant Colonel
Middendorf, Ben 1st Lieutenant
Perna, Mark Lance Corporal
Pigman, Jamie HM3 (Navy Hospital Corpsman)
Plunk, Joshua Corporal
Priddy, Andrew Major (operations officer, 3/3)
Rashman, Zach Captain

Ratkowiak, Casmer Captain
Rock (The Rock) (Interpreter)
Roy, Joe Corporal
Sandvick-Monroe, Jeremy Lance
    Corporal
Scholl, Mike Lance Corporal
Scott, Robert Major
Seiffert, Lance 1st Lieutenant
Strand, Richard (Afghan Historical
    Expert)

Sultan (Interpreter)
Tracy, Matt Captain
Turner, Regan 1st Lieutenant
Waters, Perry Captain
Westerfield, Scott Major
Wood, Tom Major
Others, undisclosed
After Action Reports, undisclosed

REFERENCES

BOOKS

Afghanistan (Map). 1:1,500,000. Nelles Verlag, Germany.

Afghanistan (Map). International Travel Maps, 1:1,000,000. Vancouver, B.C. 2002.

Afghanistan Country Handbook: A Field Ready Reference Publication, DOD-2630-AFG-018-03, October 2003.

Basic Pashto: Language Survival Guide, Monterey, CA: Defense Language Institute Foreign Language Center, October 2002.

Borovik, Artyom. *The Hidden War: A Russian Journalist's Account of the Soviet War in Afghanistan*. New York: Grove Press, 1990.

Bowden: Mark. *Black Hawk Down*. New York: Atlantic Monthly Press, 1999.

Campaigning (MCDP 1-2) U.S. Marine Corps Headquarters, United States Marine Corps, Washington, D.C., 1997.

Coll, Steve. *Ghost Wars*. New York: Penguin Press, 2004.

Edwards, David B. *Before Taliban: Genealogies of the Afghan Jihad*. Berkeley: University of California Press, 2002.

Ewans, Martin. *Afghanistan: A Short History of Its People and Politics*. New York: HarperCollins, 2002.

Giraldo, Jeanne K. and Harild A. Trinkunas. *Terrorism Financing and State Responses: A Comparative Perspective*. Stanford: Stanford University Press, 2007.

Grau, Lester W. *The Bear Went over the Mountain: Soviet Combat Tactics in Afghanistan.* London: Frank Cass Publishers, 1998.

Gunaratna, Rohan. *Inside Al Qaeda: Global Network of Terror.* New York: Berkley Books, 2002.

Jalali Ali Ahmad and Lester W. Grau. *The Other Side of the Mountain: Mujahideen Tactics in the Soviet-Afghan War.* Quantico, VA: The United States Marine Corps. Studies and Analysis Division, 1995.

Joint Tactics, Techniques, and Procedures for Close Air Support (CAS). Joint Chiefs of Staff. Washington, D.C., 2003.

Jones, Schuyler. *An Annotated Bibliographyof Nuristan (Kafiristan) and the Kalash Kafirs of Chitral,* Part One. Hisorisk-filofiske Meddeleslser udviget af Det Kongelige Danske Videnskabernes Selskab, vol. 41, no. 3. Copenhagen: Munksgaard, 1966.

Kaplan, Robert D. *Imperial Grunts: On the Ground with the American Military.* New York: Random House, 2005.

Krulak, Victor H. *First to Fight: An Inside View of the U.S. Marine Corps.* Annapolis: Naval Institute Press, 1984.

McMichael, Scott R. *Stumbling Bear: Soviet Military Performance in Afghanistan.* Brassey's Inc., 1991.

Naylor, Sean. *Not a Good Day to Die.* New York: Berkley Caliber, 2005.

O'Neill, Bard E. *Insurgency and Terrorism.* Brassey's Inc., 1990.

Pakistan (Map). 1:1,500,000. Nelles Verlag. Germany

Palka, Eugene J. *Afghanistan: Geographic Perspectives.* New York: McGraw-Hill / Duskin, 2004.

Rashid, Ahmed. *Taliban.* New Haven: Yale University Press, 2001.

Rubin, Barnett R. *The Fragmentation of Afghanistan: State Formation and Collapse in the International System,* Second Edition. New Haven: Yale University Press, 2002.

Small Wars Manual (Reprint of 1940 edition). NAVMC 2890. U.S. Marine Corps. HQMC, Washington, D.C.

Sun-Tzu. *The Art of War.* Translation by Samuel B. Griffith. Oxford University Press, 1963.

Tactics (MCDP 1-3). U.S. Marine Corps. Headquarters, United States Marine Corps, Washington, D.C., 1997.

Tanner, Stephen. *Afghanistan: A Military History from Alexander the Great to the Fall of the Taliban.* Cambridge: Da Capo Press, 2002.

USASETAF/OEF VI Insurgency / Counterinsurgency—Historical Perspectives. Leader Preparation Monograph #1. 2004.

Warfighting (MCDP 1). U.S. Marine Corps. Headquarters, United States Marine Corps, Washington, D.C., 1997.

Yousaf, Mohammad and Mark Adkin. *Afghanistan: The Bear Trap—the Defeat of a Superpower.* Casemate, 2001.

MAGAZINE, NEWSPAPER, AND SPECIALTY / SCHOLARLY ARTICLES

Ali, Imtiaz. "Spotlight on Terror: The Father of the Taliban: An Interview with Maulana Sami ul-Haq. *TerrorismMonitor.* Volume IV, Issue 2. May 23, 2007.

Brown, Bryan D. "U.S. Special Operations Command: Meeting the Challenges of the 21st Century." *Joint Forces Quarterly,* Issue 40, May, 2006.

"Cotton: World Markets and Trade." U.S. Department of Agriculture Foreign Agricultural Service Tobacco, Cotton, and Seeds Division, Washington, D.C. 1996.

Donahue, Colonel Patrick, and Colonel Michael Fenzel, U.S. Army. "Combating a Modern Insurgency: Combined Task Force Devil in Afghanistan." *Military Review.* March–April 2008.

Jiskani, Mithal M. "Cotton Diseases." *Industry and Economy.* Issue No. 27, 2001.

Magruder, Major J. H. III. "The Marine Corps Officers' Mameluke Sword." USMCR (Reproduced from the November 1954 issue of the *Marine Corps Gazette,* chapter 2).

Marzban, Omid. "Shamshatoo Refugee Camp: A Base of Support for Gulbuddin Hekmatyar." *TerrorismMonitor.* In-Depth Analysis of the War on Terror. Volume V, Issue 10. May 24, 2007.

Rahmani, Waliullah. "Afghanistan's Veteran Jihadi Leader: An Interview with Qazi Mohammad Amin Waqad." *TerrorismMonitor.* Volume IV, Issue 1. May 3, 2007.

Raman, B. "The Curious Case of Amjad Farooqi." *Asia Times,* September 30, 2004.

Shahzad, Saleem Syed. "At War with the Taliban." *Asia Times,* May 23, 2008.

MILITARY PAPERS

Cannon, Jim. "A Brief History of the 2nd Battalion, 3rd Marines." Historical Division, Headquarters, U.S. Marine Corps. Washington, DC. 20380. March 1972.

Cooling, Colonel Norman L. "To Integrate or to Deconflict, That Is the Question: An Examination of Contemporary Challenges in Conventional and Special Operations Forces Command and Control." U.S. Marine Corps. Naval War College. November, 2007.

"Finally, a Talkative Talib: Origins and Membership of the Religious Students' Movement. Confidential—Entire Text. 1995. Islamabad, Pakistan. Document Number: 1995ISLAMA01792. Unclassified 21 May 2003 by the United States Department of State Review Authority.

Hill, Lieutenant Colonel David E. Jr. "The Shaft of the Spear: US Special Operations Command, Funding Authority, and the Global War on Terrorism." United States Army. USAWC Strategy Research Project. U.S. Army WarCollege. Carlisle Barracks, Pennsylvania. March 15, 2006.

Scott, Lieutenant Colonel Robert R. and Major Scott Westerfield. "The Island Warriors in OEF VI."

INDEX

Page numbers in *Italics* indicate map references.